Captives and Countrymen

Captives
and Countrymen

Barbary Slavery and the American Public, 1785–1816

LAWRENCE A. PESKIN

The Johns Hopkins University Press
Baltimore

The Johns Hopkins University Press
2715 North Charles Street
Baltimore, Maryland 21218-4363
www.press.jhu.edu

Library of Congress Cataloging-in-Publication Data
Peskin, Lawrence A., 1966–
Captives and countrymen : Barbary slavery and the American public, 1785–1816 /
Lawrence A. Peskin.
p. cm.
Includes bibliographical references and index.
ISBN-13: 978-0-8018-9139-7 (hardcover : alk. paper)
ISBN-10: 0-8018-9139-6 (hardcover : alk. paper)
1. Slavery—Africa, North—History. 2. Slave trade—Africa, North—History.
3. Captivity narratives—Africa, North. 4. Public opinion—United States. I. Title.
HT1345.P47 2009
306.3'620961—dc22   2008024725

A catalog record for this book is available from the British Library.

Special discounts are available for bulk purchases of this book. For more information,
please contact Special Sales at 410-516-6936 or specialsales@press.jhu.edu.

The Johns Hopkins University Press uses environmentally friendly book
materials, including recycled text paper that is composed of at least 30 percent
post-consumer waste, whenever possible. All of our book papers are acid-free,
and our jackets and covers are printed on paper with recycled content.

CONTENTS

This book is divided into three parts, each of which contains three analytical narratives—chapters, organized around analytical themes, that narrate an aspect of the story of the influence of North Africa upon America. The first part offers a study of how the early national public sphere functioned to spread the news of the Algerian crisis and of how events in North Africa may, in turn, have shaped the American public sphere. In recent years scholars have evinced great interest in the Revolutionary and early national public sphere, yet we still do not understand exactly how it worked.[1] Specifically, what sort of media "content" engaged the public? How did this content get to the public? How did mass media influence the public, and how did the public influence the media? These are big questions that cannot be easily answered, but part 1 attempts to offer some preliminary answers based on the Algerian crisis. Chapter 1 discusses the nuts and bolts of how Algerian news arrived in the United States via a sort of late-eighteenth-century worldwide web of information. Chapter 2 investigates the role of the captives themselves, who spent a surprising amount of time writing to friends, relations, and officials in the United States in a valiant effort to gain their freedom. Although their effort failed in the short term, it was remarkably successful in creating public interest in their plight, and the extent of their success suggests the influence that non-elites could have upon the early public sphere. In chapter 3, the story moves back and forth across the Atlantic as the captives and their diplomatic ally, David Humphreys, attempt to publicize their fate while the public at large and governmental officials react to these efforts, sometimes making their own attempts to relieve the captives' suffering.

Part 2 assesses the effects of Algerian captivity on Americans at home. The Algerian captives were often described, by themselves and others, as "slaves," and their fate played a fascinating part in efforts to remove the issue of race from the burgeoning debate over slavery in the 1790s and beyond. Chapter 4 focuses on the words of the captives, literary authors, and abolitionist societies who brought Algerian "slavery" into the larger debate over abolition. Algerian captivity also played an important role in national self-definition during a crucial time in the new republic's young history, when it was undergoing the process of creating an "imagined community."[2] During this period, the new nation's political system was taking form, and Algerian captivity influenced this process, too—first in making a new, more energetic Constitution seem more desirable and then in the process of party formation in the 1790s. Chapter 5 assesses the generally negative influence of Algerian captivity on national identity. Finally, the encounter with Algiers, depressing as it was, suggested to many Americans the need to make their country stronger. Chapter 6 examines the connection between Algerian captivity, the development of the navy, and, eventually, America's enlarged role abroad.

By extending the story to the capture of the USS *Philadelphia* and its crew during the Tripolitan Crisis of 1803–1805 and to the second Algerian crisis of 1812–1815, part 3 explores how Barbary captivity affected Americans' conception of their nation as a world power as they pushed the new republic away from postcolonial dependence to the brink of empire. Chapter 7 examines the importance of American conceptions of masculinity and honor in driving the new nation toward a more muscular response to the *Philadelphia* crisis. It focuses on the diplomats and naval officers who were involved in formulating American policy and action in Tripoli, including Captain Richard O'Brien and James Cathcart, who earlier suffered nearly twelve years of captivity in Algiers, and also discusses partisan political debate at home. Chapter 8 analyzes the development of American orientalism during the Barbary crisis, how it was influenced by changing attitudes toward Indian "savages" at home, and how it began, by the early nineteenth century, to suggest a possible American empire of trade. Finally, chapter 9 examines the second Algerian crisis, the other War of 1812. The plight of the captured American ship *Edwin* and its crew resonated with Americans, who saw themselves fighting for independence against a British empire that impressed American sailors at sea and, they alleged, persuaded Native Americans to capture American citizens on land. With the end of the War of 1812, the Madison administration, under fire from Federalists for weakness in North Africa, immediately sent the navy to Algiers to liberate the prisoners and punctuate the end to what was becoming known as the second war for American Independence. In doing so, the U.S. Navy also put a period to America's sense of colonial dependence and weakness and marked the start of a more confident, expansionist era.

This book benefited from advice, criticism, and citations provided by numerous friends and colleagues, including Brett Berliner, Hester Blum, David Grimsted, Mary Jeske, Clare Lyons, Matthew Mulcahy, Annette Palmer, Allan Peskin, Richard M. Price, Marta Rojas, Jean Russo, Anna M. Somers, and Edmund F. Wehrle. Robert Allison, James Henretta, Gillian Weiss, members of the Washington Area Early American Seminar, and the anonymous reader for the Johns Hopkins University Press read and provided extensive and useful criticism of portions of earlier drafts. Gary Backhaus, Robert Schulzinger, and the anonymous readers for *Diplomatic History* provided useful advice and the opportunity to publish earlier versions of two chapters. Lawrence Kaplan provided support and encouragement throughout. Robert Brugger of the Johns Hopkins University Press was extremely supportive and encouraging.

Librarians and archivists at Morgan State University, the University of Maryland, Milton S. Eisenhower Library and the William H. Welch Medical Library at the Johns Hopkins University, the National Archives, the Historical Society of Pennsylvania, the University of Michigan Clements Library, and the Library Company of Philadelphia were helpful and remarkably patient. I owe a great intellectual debt to the many scholars of U.S.-Barbary relations whose books and articles emerged over the decade during which I was working on this project, providing much useful information as well as reassurance about the viability of my own subject matter. A sabbatical from Morgan State University and the Stuart Bernath family's endowment of the Stuart Bernath Prize helped to expedite the later stages of research and writing.

Finally, I could not have completed this book without the support of my family.

Captives and Countrymen

Introduction

This is a narrative about captivity, but it is not really a captivity narrative. Captivity narratives—stories of capture by Indians, pirates, slave merchants, terrorists, or other sinister outsiders—have been popular in America from the time of English colonization up to the present.[1] In the early modern world they ranked among the most popular books of their day, inspiring literary masterpieces from *Don Quixote* to *Gulliver's Travels* to *Candide*. Generally, they told the story of the capture by vicious savages of unsuspecting innocents, their subsequent enslavement, and their estrangement from family, friends, and all aspects of their native civilization while they were tortured, starved, imprisoned, or otherwise forced to suffer. In the end, captivity narratives usually recounted a rescue or redemption of sorts and the victims' triumphal return to their own civilization. In so doing, they simultaneously titillated readers with descriptions of sadistic captors and helpless captives, touched their sensibilities with descriptions of despair and sorrow, and stimulated their curiosity with long descriptions of alien, allegedly savage cultures.

The particular examples of captivity with which this book is concerned occurred during the United States' extended Barbary crisis. It began in the summer of 1785, when Algerian seamen cruising the Mediterranean captured two American merchant ships, the *Maria* of Boston and the *Dauphin* of Philadelphia. They took hostage twenty-one Americans, including Captain Richard O'Brien of the *Dauphin* and James L. Cathcart, a sailor aboard the *Maria*, both of whom would play important roles in later negotiations. All the captives were held as "slaves" in Algiers, performing a range of tasks from menial labor to, in Cathcart's case, eventually acting as chief Christian secretary to the dey, or governor, of Algiers.

With few exceptions, these captives either died of the plague or remained in Algiers for more than a decade. The dey expected the United States to pay him well for their return, but the new republic refused. In 1793, when a brief British-Portuguese truce temporarily prohibited Portugal from performing its usual role of Mediterranean policeman, the Algerians captured eleven more American ships, bringing the number of captives to nearly 120. Still America refused to pay, and consequently most of the captives remained in Algiers until 1796, when a treaty eventually bought their freedom. In subsequent years American seamen were twice held as captives en masse in North Africa: first, in the relatively well-known capture of the 307-man crew of the USS *Philadelphia* during the Tripolitan war and, second, in yet another episode in Algiers during the War of 1812. This series of events finally ended with the new nation's military success in the American-Algerian war of 1815, after which Barbary captivity was no longer an important concern for the United States.

Rather than narrating the sorrows, suffering, and triumph of these unfortunate captives, this book considers the influence of events in Barbary upon the captives' countrymen and women, living in relative ignorance of the seemingly alien, barbaric world of North Africa located nearly four thousand miles away, or approximately a two-month journey by sea. That blissful ignorance and sense of distance abruptly ended several months after the first captures occurred, when news of the disaster reached the United States. Americans were simultaneously forced to consider two new truths. First, because of the relatively recent inventions of print journalism and the public sphere, events in distant and exotic locales could have a real and relatively immediate effect on their lives. Second, the new nation, no longer a colony, would have to find its own means of navigating the shrinking, increasingly interconnected world of which it was a part. While perhaps not quite so swashbuckling or bloody as the events in a traditional captivity narrative, this book describes shock, despair, and humiliation, as well as remarkable ingenuity, perseverance, and even bravery. Rather than a tale of a few hundred unfortunate souls in captivity, it is the story of millions of Americans who, in what is sometimes known as an age of sensibility, felt their hearts ache and tears well up as they read or listened to the stories told by their captive countrymen. Finally, it is the story of the action taken by thousands of Americans, from paupers to presidents, whose efforts to assist the captives ranged from attending public meetings, to participating in well-publicized fund-raising drives, to passing laws in Congress to create a navy. It is a central contention of this book that these reactions, and many others, had as profound an effect on early America as they did on the captives themselves.

This book is as much about globalization and America's place in the world as it is about captivity. Globalization has been an issue since ancient times and certainly since Columbus's arrival in America, but the cultural interaction that it creates has become a particularly important issue to historians in the twenty-first century because of international terrorism, environmental concerns, the World Bank, the internet, and all sorts of other manifestations of a shrinking, frequently scary world. Those concerns, the increasingly central position of the modern United States within this shrinking globe, and the rising influence of the discipline of world history have prompted American historians to call for more attention to the history of American interaction with the world rather than more traditional approaches that highlight either domestic developments or diplomatic relations.[2] Captivity is a form of cultural interaction, and ever since Columbus captured his first shipload of Native Americans to bring back to Spain, it has allowed for intensive, if frequently unwanted, contact between the New World and the old. In essence, this book examines Barbary captivity within the perspective of early globalization, providing the first systematic study of the influence of North Africa upon events within the United States and on the new nation's evolving conception of its place within the larger world. It both draws on and offers a new departure from the extensive literature on the Barbary crisis produced within the last decade or so by a talented group of historians and literary scholars interested in particular aspects of America's first interaction with the Islamic world.[3] To examine these issues, I rely on a wide variety of cultural artifacts, ranging from relatively high-culture novels, plays, and histories to cheaply produced pamphlets, popular songs, and extensive discussions of Barbary found in the daily newspapers, which have rarely, if ever, been examined by cultural historians.

The Barbary crisis gained significance because it occurred simultaneously with the development of the late-Enlightenment public sphere. Arguably no nation was more influenced by and influential in this phenomenon than the United States. The new nation was a product of the very Enlightenment-era liberalism that Jürgen Habermas found so necessary for the development of what he termed the "bourgeois," or liberal, public sphere, an arena of political discussion (whether in print or in face-to-face contact) that was novel because it was not controlled by the state and therefore stimulated more and freer communications. The new republic was also, along with the French republic, the prime example of a new type of nation-state that was defined not by traditional notions of lineage, ethnicity, or group history but rather through the mass media—the process described by Benedict Anderson as the creation of "imagined communities."

Finally, in tandem with these other developments, print culture, primarily news-papers, began to emerge in this era into recognizable form. The emergence of the United States (as opposed to the thirteen colonies) defined a new public sphere just as that intensely politicized public sphere defined the new nation through the various Revolutionary-era mass protests, the dissemination of the Declaration of Independence, and the enormous print debate over the Constitution. The events of the Algerian captivity crisis were among the first foreign happenings to be discussed within this developing public sphere, and consequently they both shaped and were shaped by it.

PART ONE

CAPTIVITY AND
THE PUBLIC SPHERE

CHAPTER ONE

Captivity and Communications

How much did Americans know about what occurred in North Africa and how did they learn about it? These questions get to the heart of the story of the reception and influence of Barbary captivity in America. After all, if a ship were captured in the Mediterranean and no one heard (or read) about it, it could have no effect on the new nation. The early national public sphere is sometimes termed the "Republic of Letters" by contemporaries and subsequent intellectual historians, but it was, of course, more than that. Newspapers, oral communications, and diplomatic reports were frequently as important as letters, sometimes more so. Yet letters, which often served as the building blocks for print media, always played a central role. Examining how these media provided information about the Barbary captives suggests that the early national public sphere was more efficient and less removed from the modern world than smug proponents of today's World Wide Web might suspect. It also was more democratic and accessible than the term "Republic of Letters" might indicate. Many plebeian characters, some of them illiterate, played important parts in moving information to and from North Africa during the early national period.

News of the Algerian crisis was not entirely unexpected. In 1785, the United States was in the midst of negotiating with the Barbary powers so as to maintain a presence in the Mediterranean. Although the new nation had some success with Morocco, Algiers remained a problem.[1] By mid-July, ports from the Iberian Peninsula up to the French Atlantic buzzed with sailors' rumors that Algerian pirates were passing through the Straits of Gibraltar and cruising the Atlantic for victims. The warnings came too late for the *Maria* of Boston, under Captain Isaac Stephens, captured July 24 near Cape Saint Vincent, Portugal and the *Dauphin* of Philadelphia, under Captain Richard O'Brien, taken July 30 near St. Ubes (Setubal) about one hundred miles further north. The Algerians stripped both crews naked and brought them back to Algiers, where those who survived the plague and other contagious outbreaks would be held as slaves for nearly twelve years before being ransomed by their countrymen. Word of their capture made its way back to Iberia a month later. A Cadiz merchant with American connections heard the news and hurriedly wrote to an acquaintance in Beverly, Massachusetts, reporting that "a brig from Boston to this place, has . . . been carried into Algiers."[2]

The merchant chose to write to this particular correspondent because at that very moment a Beverly ship, the *Rambler,* commanded by Captain McComb, was docked in Cadiz harbor. Captain McComb had already experienced the threat firsthand. On his way into the port, two Algerian galliots had blocked the *Rambler*'s path and the Algerians began to quiz McComb on his ship's origins and cargo. The well-prepared captain lied that the *Rambler* hailed from Cork and was laden with Newfoundland fish. To prove his non-American origins, he displayed an English flag that he kept on board for such emergencies. His act convinced the Algerians to let him alone. Whether or not he completely fooled them, they knew they did not want to risk the wrath of the English navy by capturing a British merchant ship.

After this close call, McComb agreed to risk another encounter with the Algerians in order to get word of the captures to America. This time, however, the danger would be reduced. Portuguese authorities ordered two ships—a man of war and a frigate—to escort the *Rambler* and several others on the early part of their voyage. As McComb prepared to depart, no doubt scanning the horizon for signs of Algerian xebecs, he carried with him the merchant's letter informing his Beverly acquaintance of the fate of the Boston ship and of the apparent capture of a New York ship. That was not the only news McComb carried. As he finished preparations he happened to meet the captain of an English ship, which, like the *Rambler,* had been detained by Algerians on the suspicion it might be American. Ironically, the Englishman had not fared so well as McComb. The "pirates" seized the ship and hauled it all the way to Algiers before they could be convinced that it really was what the captain claimed. After this ordeal, the English ship made its way back to Cadiz just in time for the captain to inform McComb that "a schooner, Captain Smith, from Boston, and a brig from some other port on the [American] continent, were carried into Algiers, and the crews sold at auction."[3]

Thus supplied with written information from the merchant and oral news from the Englishman, McComb left Cadiz with the Portuguese convoy and sailed as quickly as he could to America. He arrived at Beverly in a respectable fifty-four days. Finally, three months and a day after the *Maria* was captured, McComb's news first appeared in print in the *Salem Gazette*. Later that week it would also be published in nearby Boston. Making its way along the coast, the news arrived in Annapolis about two and a half weeks later and in Charleston by November 24, a month after McComb's arrival and four months after the actual captures. In this way, McComb's original mix of oral reports and letters was translated into print throughout the United States and permanently fixed within the cramped newspaper columns where it can still be read to this day.[4]

McComb's information was just a tiny portion of the news that readers in American cities scanned in the course of a typical day. Due to this large volume of information, then as now, the difficulty for anyone reading the print media lay not so much in finding relevant information as in evaluating it. Readers were bombarded with information from around the world, of course, but even those focusing only on Algiers would have had much to consider. The *Gazette*, one of more than a half-dozen daily and weekly newspapers in Boston, frequently printed warnings and rumors of ship captures by Algerians throughout late 1785. The day that McComb's news appeared in its pages, the *Gazette* also published a false rumor that Algerians had captured another Boston ship. That at least two newspaper editors, one in Boston and one in New York, doubted the reliability of McComb's news because it had not been reported in London newspapers suggests America's continuing postcolonial reliance on British news. New Yorkers were probably skeptical of McComb's report because it arrived at the same time as word from an American captain in France who claimed that the report of a captured ship was a fraud. Perhaps this captain actually referred to the false report of the other Boston ship's capture. If so, that falsehood made McComb's truthful account less believable.[5]

Initially, the United States' small diplomatic corps did not know much more about the captures than did the seamen, merchants, and the public. Nor did they learn the news more quickly. William Carmichael, America's chargé d'affaires in Spain was the American diplomat closest to the action. By September 2, a week after the news first reached Spain, he wrote Thomas Jefferson in Paris that he had seen letters from Cadiz and Algiers indicating that five American ships had been captured and two taken into Algiers, where ships, cargo, and crew were sold. It is not clear exactly when Jefferson received this letter, but by September 11 he indicated he was aware of "as yet" unconfirmed "rumors" that Algerian "pirates" had captured an American ship. It was not until he received an actual letter from Captain O'Brien in Algiers on September 22 (forwarded to him by James Wilkie, an American in Marseilles) that Jefferson became truly alarmed, forwarding one copy of the letter to John Adams in London and another to a correspondent in Boston. On September 16, the same day he forwarded a copy of O'Brien's letter to Jefferson, Wilkie also sent a copy to the Continental Congress in Philadelphia. This letter was apparently the first official news sent to Congress, and it could not have arrived in Philadelphia much before mid-November, when McComb's letter was published in the Philadelphia press.[6] Thus the diplomatic network was not much quicker than other channels; however, O'Brien's letter did provide diplomats with more details than were available to the public at large.

News of the second round of captures, in 1793, reached America much more quickly, largely because of U.S. diplomats' increased involvement. The key player was David Humphreys, minister to Portugal, who happened to be in Gibraltar on October 6, 1793, when a dispatch from the English consul to Algiers arrived with news of a twelve-month truce between Algiers and Portugal.[7] This news was troubling because Americans and others depended on Portuguese hostility to the Algerians to act as a check, keeping the "pirates" bottled up inside the Mediterranean. Without the Portuguese as a counterbalance, Algerians could enter the Atlantic with impunity and capture scores of unsuspecting vessels. Thus it was imperative that American ships be warned of the truce before they were taken unaware by Algerian cruisers.

Humphreys undertook heroic measures to spread the word. He immediately wrote warning letters "to all governors, magistrates, officers civil, military, and others concerned in the United States of America," urging them "as speedily as possible, to give an universal alarm to all citizens of the United States concerned in navigation, particularly to the Southern parts of Europe, of the danger of being captured by the Algerines, in prosecuting their voyages to that destination."[8] These he sent to American consuls in Cadiz, Lisbon, and Malaga in the hope that they would pass the word on to other Americans in the region. All three letters arrived at their destinations by October 8, two days after the first word of the truce. The American consuls quickly warned captains in these ports of the danger. In Malaga, Consul Michael Murphy met with mixed success. While he was able to speak to the captains of both American vessels then in port, the news did not much worry Captain Samuel Calder of the schooner *Jay* of Gloucester, Massachusetts. According to Murphy, "He, having his cargo on board homeward bound, and the wind being fair, he very unwarrantedly put to sea."[9] Unfortunately, Calder's ship would never make it to Gloucester. Algerians captured the

Jay and its ten-man crew off Cape Saint Vincent just three days later. In Lisbon, U.S. consul Edward Church warned Americans all along the Portuguese coast. He sent a cautionary letter to Oporto, nearly two hundred miles up the shore from Lisbon. There, consul Dominick Brown quickly spread the news to the two American vessels in port, a Massachusetts snow and a Connecticut ship. Brown regretted that the news came too late for the schooner *Fayette* and brig *Rozanna*, which had sailed for Boston October 11. Luckily, both avoided capture.[10]

At the same time, Humphreys took further measures to warn American ships that were not yet in port. He hired a Spanish bark to cruise the Straits of Gibraltar for fifteen days and gave an American aboard the small vessel the job of warning any passing U.S. ships of the truce. As all American ships bound for the Mediterranean had to pass through the straits, Humphreys hoped this method of spreading the news would be effective. He also ordered the captains of three U.S. ships anchored at Gibraltar to keep a mate on board at all times in order to get word immediately to any incoming American ships. Unfortunately, the American aboard the Spanish bark had little success. He saw no American vessels whatsoever, although he did speak to several non-American masters who agreed to pass on the information to anyone they might encounter. To make matters worse, after spotting an Algerian xebec in the straits, the terrified Spanish captain refused to continue the mission, despite his contract with Humphreys.[11]

Humphreys made repeated efforts to speed the news of the truce home to America. He sent at least five separate copies of his letter to Secretary of State Jefferson in Philadelphia in the hope that one might get through. In addition, he sent word to the American consuls in Lisbon and Cadiz to charter neutral vessels in an effort to move the news even more rapidly and safely.[12] These orders arrived at the same time as even more disturbing news. On or about October 12, Algerian cruisers stopped and searched a Swedish vessel sailing off southwestern Portugal. Luckily the Algerians respected Sweden's neutrality and allowed the ship to proceed. But others were less fortunate. The Swedes noticed that the Algerians had four American vessels and one Genoese ship in tow, and they appeared to be in the process of capturing two more American vessels. The Swedes rushed back to Lisbon, bringing their news into that port by October 15, just as Consul Church was attempting to comply with Humphreys's order to charter an express to America. On that same day, Captain Roberteau of the bark *Henry* arrived from Falmouth with puzzling news. English merchants, he said, had suddenly begun to eschew U.S. ships as carriers.[13] These two pieces of information led Church to an unsettling conclusion: the English were aware of the truce, and they suspected that American ships were no longer safe due to the Algerian threat. Church and the American merchants in Lisbon were near panic, afraid that many more of their countrymen and their cargoes would soon be captured.

Meanwhile, the consuls continued making arrangements to get the news to the United States. In Lisbon, Church and New York merchant Schuyler Livingston negotiated to charter a Swedish ship, the *Mary*, which they hoped could cross the Atlantic undisturbed, protected by Sweden's neutrality. As they made final arrangements, the news of the captures arrived. Perhaps this information made the Swedes nervous, for they charged Church the hefty sum of £800 sterling to carry the dispatches and Livingston to New York.[14] In Cadiz, Consul Peter Walsh, unable to secure a neutral vessel, negotiated with the captain of a New York ship, the *Two Sisters*. After arguing over whether the United States should pay the now enormous marine insurance premiums, Walsh was able to convince the captain that he would be reimbursed for any loss and to secure a second ship, the *Fair Hebe* of Philadelphia, to carry duplicate dispatches. In the midst of these negotiations, word arrived in Cadiz of American captures, and Walsh supplemented the truce warning with this new information. A little more than a week after Humphreys sent out his first warning, all three ships were ready to sail for America. About one week later, Church chartered a second neutral carrier, the Danish *Statdt Altona*, to carry duplicates of his dispatches.[15]

The *Mary* reached her destination first. Livingston began to spread the warning in New York on December 9, just two months and a day after Humphreys's warning had first arrived in Lisbon. The news spread rapidly, arriving in Philadelphia by December 11, Annapolis by December 19, and Charleston by December 21. In Boston, the news came on December 16 by another source, a letter sent by Lisbon merchants on their own initiative. Rather anticlimactically, the *Twin Sisters* arrived in New York on December 17 and the *Stadt Altona* six days later, both carrying what had become yesterday's (or last week's) news.[16]

One obvious difference between this news and reports of the 1785 captures was the rapidity with which it arrived in the United States. In 1785 McComb's letter first arrived roughly three months after the captures of the *Maria* and the *Dauphin*. It took another month for it to work its way down the coast to Charleston. By contrast, word of the 1794 captures arrived just shy of two months after the events occurred, reaching Charleston in less than two weeks so that the vast majority of the country was aware of the captures two-and-a-half months after they occurred. This improvement was due partly to coincidence. In 1793 a Swedish ship saw the captures as they occurred off the Iberian coast, while in 1785 first word came from Algiers, meaning not only that the news had farther to travel but that it got a slower start. Coincidence was not the whole story, however; the emergence of a centralized national government was also a key factor in making the news move more quickly. Between 1785 and 1793 the United States began to develop a diplomatic corps. It was still small and not particularly professional in 1793, but it clearly made a real difference in expediting the transfer of information. At almost every step in the process of moving the news of the captures from Gibraltar to the United States, David Humphreys and the U.S. consuls played a vital role. Additionally, their participation gave the news an official imprimatur, making it far more believable to the American public than McComb's letter, which many had doubted. Finally, the development of a national postal service intent on encouraging rapid and inexpensive distribution of newspapers no doubt made a difference once the news crossed the Atlantic.[17]

The two Algerian episodes offer an excellent way to begin considering the underlying structure of the late-eighteenth century worldwide web of information.[18] In 1785 and 1793, oral communications, letters, official dispatches, and newspapers were the four components of this web. Other sorts of printed materials such as pamphlets and books eventually played a role in the public consideration of events in Algiers, but they were not produced quickly enough to influence the initial discussion. To inhabitants of a world of daily newspapers, wire services, television, radio, and Web casts, this information system can seem hopelessly primitive. But from another perspective it can seem quite modern. Based primarily on unmediated, unfiltered bits of information from a multitude of sources, it resembles the twenty-first-century World Wide Web more than the twentieth century newspaper. Information carried by ship rather than fiber optics flowed in from all directions as quickly as possible and was frequently unregulated by authorities, unshaped by professional reporters, and unrefined by editors.

Historians' reliance on written sources can easily blind us to the importance of oral communications. But, as the Algerian captures show, oral reports were crucially important in a world of low literacy and limited print media. Consider, for example, McComb's report of his encounter with Algerians, which made a sensation when he told it in Beverly. Or consider Humphreys' efforts to hire the Spanish bark to spread the word—*orally*—of the Algerian-Portuguese truce. This sort of oral communication may seem trivial when compared to the modern mass media of radio and television, which, despite frequently working from scripts, are essentially oral media. This mass circulation/face-to-face dichotomy may, however, be overemphasized. Through the process of frequent repetition, reports such as McComb's could move quickly through large seaport cities. So efficient was word-of-mouth communication that many, if not most, urbanites learned the local news first through oral networks. Editors could assume that by the time a newspaper had been composed, printed, and circulated, virtually everyone in town would know everything that had happened there. Thus, newspapers rarely carried local news.[19]

The division between oral and written communications was far from absolute. McComb's 1785 report also included a written component, the letter he carried with him. Eventually, both the letter and McComb's oral news were printed in newspapers. While oral reports could find their way into writing, written materials often spread by word of mouth. Newspapers were the prime example. Although few people—rarely more than three to five thousand—actually bought a given newspaper, many thousands more would hear somebody read from it, whether in the relative privacy of an urban household or in a busy public coffee house. This connection between the printed word and the spoken word allowed oral communications such as McComb's to circulate even further and more rapidly than they might otherwise. The common habit of reading newspapers aloud bridged the gap between literacy and illiteracy, and even sophisticated urban merchants relied as much on oral information as written reports in learning the news.[20]

In general, oral communications from Algiers fit into two broad categories: the vast majority came from ship captains such as McComb and their crews reporting on possible "barbarian" captures of American vessels, while a second, smaller group consisted of reports from visiting strangers claiming to have been held in captivity themselves. The reports of ship captures were of vital importance to mercantile towns, where a large proportion of the population would be directly affected by such events. Merchants stood to lose their fortunes. Seafarers' wives and children could lose not only their loved ones but also their primary means of support. All of the shipping-related artisanal trades—shipbuilders, riggers, caulkers, chandlers, sailmakers, blacksmiths, and many others—stood to lose a portion of their livelihoods. And should the Algerians become too active, they could potentially shut down America's Mediterranean trade, thereby impairing the entire economy.

To provide this vital information to an anxious public, the seafaring world created a long-distance version of the children's game of telephone. Consequently, there was an element of randomness to oral reports, for they depended on the timely arrival of somebody who happened to have new information. Like McComb, this news bearer might have witnessed events himself or herself. For example, a Captain Farmer arrived in Boston after a sixty-two-day voyage from Portugal to report that three days before he sailed, the Portuguese had begun to put together a large fleet to keep the Algerians at bay. Similarly, a Captain Brogham, arriving in Philadelphia from Cadiz, reported having seen three Algerian ships there readying themselves for an Atlantic cruise, presumably to capture more ships and sailors.[21] More frequently, however, reports came second-, third-, or even fourth-hand. As in the game of telephone, the reports furthest removed from the original source tended to be more distorted and more sensational than firsthand reports. For example, Captain Harding of Liverpool met the ship *Mary*, of Marblehead, at sea. Captain Aris of the *Mary* reportedly told Harding that he had just learned in Bilbao that Algerians had captured fifty (!) American ships. Similarly, a Captain Gage arrived in Boston after a ninety-day journey from Lisbon to report that he had encountered a Captain Cunningham of Petersburg, who reported that an American brig bound from Petersburg to Lisbon had been captured by Algerians.[22] Aris and Cunningham brought information about as rapidly as possible, that is, in roughly the time it took a ship to move from the site of the event to the port city waiting for news. However, both reports appear to have been false.

The sensational information carried by Captain Charles Pelly to Charleston came by a still more circuitous path. Pelly arrived in Charleston on April 3, 1786, after a twenty-two-day voyage from the West Indies. He reported that four days before departing for Charleston he had run into an old acquaintance serving as a mate on an English ship. This acquaintance, Mr. Montgomery, informed Pelly that ten days earlier his vessel had been harassed near Barbados by three Algerian ships looking for American property. After Montgomery's captain convinced the Algerians that his ship was indeed British, the North Africans allowed him to pass, but not before allegedly informing him that they were "on a cruise for American vessels." Pelly thought this information so important that he brought it to the governor of South Carolina and had a justice of the peace witness his oath that "said relation is as near as he can recollect the substance he received from . . . Montgomery."[23] This was indeed timely and important information, for Algerians in the West Indies looking for American ships posed a far greater hazard than they did in the distant Mediterranean, where they were usually kept in check by the Portuguese. However, once again the seafarers' network appears to have got the story wrong; no American ships were ever stopped or captured by Algerians in the West Indies.

The second category of oral reports, accounts of captivity and escape from the Algerians, was even less reliable than those from the seafarers' news network. These reports reveal a group of traveling grifters fashioning the news of the day into confidence scams, the ancestors of the sort of Mark Twain characters whom Huck Finn called "low down humbugs and frauds." Thomas Jefferson encountered one of these men in Paris. He claimed to be Thomas Smith, an American captured by Algerians near Lisbon and held hostage aboard an Algerian ship for more than two years. He said he escaped in Cartagena, but "being entirely destitute of money, and likewise of clothing, too, in some measure," he begged the American minister for money. Jefferson was skeptical. For one thing, Smith "could not speak English but very broken." The "captive" tried to finesse this issue first by claiming to be from Charleston, and, when Jefferson remained skeptical, by claiming that he was actually a French Canadian. After Jefferson observed that Smith was hardly a French name, the "captive" decided that he was instead of German extraction. He tried to recover from this line of questioning by displaying a pass, allegedly from the English consul at Cartagena. This document, Jefferson noticed, was "in broken English" and in the same handwriting as the note Smith had earlier written to gain an audience with Jefferson.[24]

A second case had sadder consequences. A man named James Joshua Reynolds who claimed to have been master of a Philadelphia vessel said that Algerians had captured his ship near Lisbon in 1784 and carried him off to Algiers. There, he claimed, he was held in slavery for two years. In the spring of 1788 he told this story to a group of gentlemen in Greenock, Scotland, providing them with the names of many other men he had supposedly seen in Algiers to give the story verisimilitude. Local newspapers learned of his account, and eventually the news spread to the United States.[25] Two of the people Reynolds claimed to have heard of in Algiers were a Doctor and Mrs. Spence. Spence's mother and stepfather in Virginia read of the account and immediately regained hope that their son, long assumed dead, might still be alive. The stepfather sent a copy of the account to George Washington, asking if it might possibly be true. Washington feared that "the story . . . [was] only calculated to sport with the feelings of the unhappy," but he dutifully made inquiries. Sadly, he discovered that Reynolds's account was entirely false, and he regretted that he was forced to "destroy the hopes of a distressed family" in his response to Spence's parents. Before telling his story at Greenock, Reynolds and a friend had also contacted New York governor Robert Livingston, claiming to have seen his son, midshipman John L. Livingston, alive and in captivity in Algiers.[26] Perhaps Reynolds had heard of these men through the seafarers' network or read reports that they were lost at sea and claimed to have seen them in the hopes of gaining some type of reward from their bereaved families. In these two instances, at least, Reynolds's scam backfired, bringing him no gain and only adding to the pain of two already bereaved families. That he could even make the attempt reveals the extent of news literally floating around the world and the uncertainties that remained due to the difficulties in verifying this large volume of information.

After oral communications, more people probably got their news from letters than from any other medium. As shipowners, merchants had the means and the motive to keep their overseas correspondents well informed. Merchants generally believed the news exchanged in letters to be more trustworthy than either oral information or newspapers.[27] In the case of the 1785 captures, Captain McComb's mission was to carry to Beverly a Cadiz merchant's letter bearing the news. That McComb learned additional news himself and transmitted it orally was a lucky accident. In 1793, despite the efforts of the diplomatic corps, the first word of American captures to reach Boston once again came from a merchant house, this one in Lisbon. Merchants in Iberia, particularly those belonging to American firms or with close ties to the United States, were motivated by fear to share such news as rapidly as possible. Waiting even a day to send word to their partners across the Atlantic could mean the loss of valuable cargo and enormously expensive ships, which might not have sailed had they received warnings. But the merchants' concern was not only for their partners. They expected that letters with such disturbing news would be widely circulated. The Lisbon merchant warning his Boston correspondent of the 1793 captures wrote, "We seize in haste the opportunity, to give you this intelligence, which you will of course make as public as possible to deter vessels from coming out."[28] Thus what might have been a private correspondence was quite willingly made public. The merchant may have been influenced to do so by patriotism or altruism, but he no doubt also operated from a mercantilistic sense that what was good for American shipping was good for him.

Written reports probably offered a bit more reliability than word of mouth. Nonetheless, letters flowed through the same seafarers' network that carried oral reports back and forth across the Atlantic. The seaports were so hungry for any and all news about shipping and possible impediments to trade that recipients probably did not bother to make fine distinctions between written news and word of mouth. For example, seafarers might orally report the contents of letters they had read earlier when landing at a new port, where others might rewrite the news into letters sent to interested correspondents.[29] But, unlike oral reports, writing suggested a fairly simple method of verification; after all, one of the tests that tripped up Twain's grifters in *Huckleberry Finn* was their inability to match their handwriting with that of the men they pretended to be.[30] Once the source, usually American merchants in the Mediterranean, was verified, it was fairly easy for a reader familiar with the mercantile world to gauge its reliability. The firm of John Bulkeley and son, of Lisbon, which had long been crucial to the Philadelphia-Mediterranean trade, frequently sent reports of news and warnings of potential danger to their many mercantile connections throughout the United States. For example, in the spring of 1794, when some Americans were nearly hysterical over the Algerian threat, the Bulkeleys accurately informed their Philadelphia correspondents that the danger had passed.[31] They knew what they were talking about. They maintained an active correspondence with the Algerian captive Captain Richard O'Brien. Furthermore, when not warning ships' captains of truces, Ambassador David Humphreys courted Ann Frances Bulkeley, finally becoming engaged to her in late 1796. A Philadelphia merchant no doubt would have put far more trust in a letter from the Bulkeleys than in an unverified report from a sailor or even a ship's captain. With letters, too, there was less room for the distortions that plagued oral news. Letters were frequently copied word for word and forwarded on to multiple recipients in much the same way that identical e-mail messages are rapidly and widely distributed today (sometimes to the dismay of their modern recipients).

Of course, letters could also mislead. Recall that McComb's true report arrived almost simultaneously with a London merchant's false report that "a large American ship from Boston . . . was captured by an Algerine cruiser . . . and the Captain and crew sent into slavery." This letter could not have referred to the actual capture of the *Maria*, since it was written two days *before* that unfortunate event occurred.[32] Letters were only as accurate as the reports on which they were based, and it is possible that the London merchant heard of the American capture from a confused seaman. At this time, a number of American crews just barely escaped capture by Algerians, sometimes abandoning their ships to the "pirates."[33] Perhaps the London merchant's informant heard of one of these incidents or saw a captured American ship and assumed that the crew had been sold into slavery. It is also possible that he was practicing a clever deception. Aware that letters about ship captures were widely read by the public, he might have placed this piece of false information in the hope that it would steer worried merchants away from hiring American ships and cause them to rely more heavily on supposedly safer English vessels. Such devious manipulation of the news would not have surprised Thomas Jefferson, who in 1785 assured a New York correspondent that the Algerians had captured only two American vessels. "I mention this," he wrote, "because the English papers would make the world believe we have lost an infinite number."[34] The London merchant's letter, and others like it, were at the root of those newspaper reports.

While first word of events in Algiers generally came from third parties, Americans also received numerous letters from the unfortunate captives themselves. Captives began writing home as soon as possible after landing in Algiers. Captain Richard O'Brien began sending letters to American officials by August 24, 1785, roughly three weeks after his capture, and certainly not more than a week or two after arriving in Algiers and being sold into slavery. In 1793, Captain Samuel Calder notified his ship's owner "on my first arrival here" that he had been captured.[35] The most prolific writer in Algiers was certainly Captain O'Brien, a shrewd and articulate man who, after his release, would become a leading American diplomat in North Africa. While O'Brien took the lead, other prisoners, too, were able to send off letters to friends, family, and government officials. These letters served an important news function not only for their recipients but also for the many others who read them as they were passed from hand to hand and even, in some cases, reprinted in newspapers. The prisoners could provide details that virtually no one else could know, and their reports could generally be trusted. Despite the captives' knowledge and moral authority, readers of their letters could not necessarily trust every word. After all, the captives had good reason to bend the truth; their ultimate goal was not to be reliable reporters but rather to be ransomed by their government. As subjects of a republic, they believed that reaching that goal depended in large part on gaining public sympathy. Their letters are examined in more detail in the next chapter.

In theory, a nation's diplomatic service can act as a clearinghouse for news and information about world affairs. A well-run diplomatic corps can gather information more effectively than most merchants or even private news services because of the breadth of its contacts and the power and prestige of the state. However, in the case of the United States, the reality fell far short of this ideal, particularly in the 1780s. In 1785, at the time of the first captures, there were only two U.S. consuls permanently stationed in Mediterranean ports near Algiers—Robert Montgomery in Alicante and Richard Harrison in Cadiz. In addition, a merchant, Thomas Barclay, had been sent from Cadiz as a special agent to negotiate with the emperor of Morocco. Three other American diplomats—William Carmichael in Madrid, Thomas Jefferson in Paris, and John Adams in London—would be involved in Algerian affairs despite their greater distance from the scene.

Thus the early diplomatic network was not in a position to offer much that was new to the public or to the government in Philadelphia. In fact, newspapers may have put more stock in British diplomatic reports in these days. For example, Bostonians could read in their local paper that "some dispatches were received at the Secretary of State's office from Gibralter . . . [that] contain an account of the safe arrival there of upwards of twenty sail of ships from America, and two of which had been stopped and plundered by the Algerines."[36] The "Secretary of State" to which the item referred was at London rather than Philadelphia. One of the major tasks of American diplomats was to pass on information from European newspapers to the capital at Philadelphia, and frequently they seem not to have known much more than they read in these journals. For example, Jefferson wrote to John Adams in 1785, "I observe in the Leyden Gazette . . . the extract of a letter dated Algiers April 15 which says that on the tenth of April an American vessel, the *Clementina,* Captain Palmer from Philadelphia, was carried in there by a cruiser." Jefferson had no way to verify the report, but he concluded that it was probably true because other details in the letter pertaining to American affairs were accurate. Similarly, Thomas Barclay passed on to Jefferson a report from a correspondent in Mogadore that Algerians planned to attack the coast of America. Barclay was skeptical but unsure. He wrote, "I cannot give entire credit to the account as the season of the year is far advanced, and we have not heard that any of the Algerine cruisers have passed the Streights of Gibraltar."[37] These officials were doing their best to gather intelligence, but they simply lacked the manpower to do an effective job.

Even in this early period, the diplomatic network could serve a useful purpose by confirming or denying other reports. When wild rumors of Algerian ships in the West Indies were spreading through the United States, someone published a portion of a report made by P. R. Randall, secretary to the American agent sent to negotiate with Algiers. Randall asserted that the Algerians sailed "very rarely to the Western islands, as many in America have imagined."[38] In January 1796, the first semiofficial word of peace with Algiers, sent by the American consul at Malaga to a private citizen, became public in Boston, almost four months after it had been sent and at least nine months after the first treaty rumors reached Massachusetts. However, the treaty itself was not officially made public in the United States until the Senate ratified it five months after the news first appeared in the newspapers.[39] Clearly, the public could not rely upon official announcements for its news.

By the second round of captures, the diplomatic network was far more active and better developed. In 1793 there were American consuls in the five Iberian ports of Alicante, Cadiz, Gibraltar, Lisbon, and Malaga. Additionally, Humphreys, the minister to Portugal, was also posted in Lisbon. The five consuls were in frequent contact with local merchants and diplomats, and they regularly reported what news they had learned to Humphreys and to the State Department in Philadelphia. For example, on January 20, 1794, Consul James Simpson in Gibraltar informed the Secretary of State that he had received a letter from Algiers one week earlier indicating that the Algerians were fitting out cruisers to attack European ships. He also reported that the English consul Logie was in town asserting that Algiers and Portugal would soon be at peace. In addition, a recently redeemed American captive had just arrived from Algiers with detailed information on the state of the Algerian navy, which Simpson summarized in his report. He also related news from Toulon that on December 18 the French and their allies had been forced to abandon that city, which they had only recently captured, and enclosed a "list of the French stores, ships, etc. burned and taken at Toulon December 1793."[40]

Although America's Mediterranean diplomatic network grew and became more sophisticated between 1785 and 1793, it remained fairly amateurish. The consuls were mostly merchants who spent only a portion of their time on diplomatic affairs. Not all were American. Simpson was an English merchant who served as Russian and American consul in Gibraltar. Montgomery was an American merchant who claimed to have established in 1776 "the first American house of commerce that ever appeared in Spain." Montgomery and Simpson were volunteers who became consuls simply by deciding to write reports to the United States in an unofficial capacity. Having earlier taken it on himself to represent the United States in negotiations with Morocco, in 1787 Montgomery began to report to Jefferson from Alicante in the hope that he would gain an official appointment. Although Simpson began writing reports to the United States in 1790, he does not appear to have been officially appointed consul to Gibraltar until 1794.[41] Naturally, these part-time diplomats gained much of their information from other merchants, and, due to the fact that the United States had no navy, their reports sailed on the same ships that carried other merchants' letters. Thus the diplomatic network remained a nonprofessional but useful source of information that was often not far removed from the merchants' and seafarers' networks.

Oral reports, merchants' letters, and communications in the diplomatic network frequently found their way into newspapers. These newspapers acted quite differently from modern ones, which are staffed by reporters who collect, collate, and analyze information before presenting it to the reader in highly refined form. Eighteenth-century papers more closely resembled moderated listservs, electronic bulletin boards in which information from all sorts of sources from throughout the world is cut and pasted into a printed site by an individual who chooses what to print but does little to modify (or verify) the content. Because newspaper reporters did not exist to filter through these various sources, the readers were usually left to make what sense of them they could.

When considered solely from the perspective of numbers printed, newspapers appear to have been a tiny portion of the early national public sphere. But, as is well known, although few newspapers were printed, each copy could pass through many hands, particularly in coffee shops, which served as reading rooms where customers could read these newspapers aloud to their less-literate comrades.

Beyond this secondary and tertiary circulation, newspapers reflected all aspects of the public sphere by setting into print letters, oral reports, and official documents circulating throughout the cities and across the Atlantic. The illiterate waterman might hear firsthand the exact report that the merchant sitting in his coffeehouse read in the day's newspaper. Neither needed to purchase the newspaper to be exposed to the information printed in its pages. In this way the newspaper served not only to record the day's news but also to echo what people were discussing in the public sphere.

During the early captures, in 1785–87, the largest single source for these reports was the London press, an indication of the new nation's lingering relationship to England. By the second round of captures any residual colonialism had pretty much disappeared from the newspapers. Only 4 percent of reports regarding the Algerian situation in 1794–97 had English datelines, while 95 percent came from the United States.[42] The Post Office Act of 1792 had greatly eased U.S. publishers' practice of exchanging newspapers with each other and, perhaps because of the efforts of the new Department of State, facilitated the distribution of timely information. Yet the overwhelming tilt toward domestic newspaper reports should not be overemphasized. Many, perhaps most, items appearing under domestic datelines must have originally appeared in foreign newspapers. For example, a notice of a foiled Algerian attempt to capture a Lisbon-bound American ship which appeared under a London dateline in the Boston press assumed a Charleston dateline when it arrived in South Carolina three weeks later.[43]

All of these newspaper reports give some indication of the extraordinary size of the late-nineteenth-century worldwide web and the impressive quantity of information available to the public. At least 285 items relating to the Algerian crisis appeared in a sample of four newspapers from the years 1785–97. These items are without a doubt only a small portion of information relating to Algiers that passed through the public sphere of the day. Because newspaper publishers so frequently stole from each other, one would expect frequent repetition of the same items from newspaper to newspaper. In fact, less than a third of the items in the sample were repeated in two newspapers, and virtually none appeared in three. This lack of repetition suggests that publishers had a broad number of Algerian items from which to choose, and combing through the hundreds of newspapers published during this period would probably reveal many other reports on Algiers that were not included in this sample.

Overall, then, the late-eighteenth-century worldwide web appears to have been surprisingly vast and inclusive. The variety of media—oral reports, letters, official documents, and newspapers—allowed a wide swath of the population some exposure to the latest news. Most importantly, in a world where print and oral culture merged, literacy was not a barrier to receiving information. A large proportion of the population was exposed to these media, and many nonelites had an opportunity to influence them to some extent. Most important was the role played by the often-plebeian and frequently illiterate seamen described by one historian as "bearers of culture and information among far-flung groups and places."[44] Within urban centers, there can be little doubt that all sorts of people—male, female, rich, poor, black, white, literate, and illiterate—served as news bearers, reciting what they read or heard to their friends and family every day.

Of course, merely hearing or reciting news did not necessarily make them full participants in what Habermas termed the "public sphere" and contemporaries called the Republic of Letters. It is generally understood that this term implies a *critical* discourse, that is, reasoned analysis as well as repetition of tidbits of information.[45] In this sense many of the individuals who helped spread the news of the Algerian captures might be considered second-class citizens of the Republic of Letters. They were aware of what went on in public discourse and could even contribute to the spread of news and information, but due to illiteracy, race, gender, or social status, they may not have been able to participate fully in the critical analysis that was primarily the domain of the literate, white, male, bourgeoisie. Yet this level of analysis could not occur without access to simple facts, and the initial nature of news reports inevitably influenced subsequent critical analysis. By transmitting basic information, these second-class citizens played an important role in shaping the public sphere in the Republic of Letters, and, as subsequent chapters will show, they took center stage in the Barbary captivity crises.

CHAPTER TWO

The Captives Write Home

The American captives in Algiers were unlikely participants in the Republic of Letters. Most were common seamen with little literary ability, and none had any experience in public affairs. Furthermore, they were held in what they described as slavery, far from their homeland, and deprived of freedom of movement, let alone freedom of speech. Yet, despite confinement, distance, and lack of education, the Algerian captives managed to become active and, in some cases, shrewd manipulators of public opinion. They wrote many letters home. More than ninety arrived in the United States or were delivered into the hands of Americans abroad, and probably hundreds more were sent but subsequently lost. A substantial number appeared in newspapers and other widely read publications.[1] Still others were addressed to influential political figures, who sometimes appear to have read them carefully and followed their advice. These letters and their authors did much to shape the way the American public thought about Algiers and their country's place in the world.

Several factors account for the captives' ability to connect with the American public. First, despite the harshness of the dey, the Algerians must have realized that it was in their interest for the captives to communicate with their countrymen. The purpose of capturing Christian slaves was to gain revenue from the victimized nations through ransom and tribute, payments that, if made promptly, were supposed to prevent further captures. In order for this protection scheme to succeed, the victim nations needed to be made aware that their compatriots had been captured and that there was imminent danger of further captures. Many of the existing letters were intended to inform friends, relatives, and officials back home of the captives' plight and the need for redemption.

Communication between the captives and the United States was also facilitated by Algiers' location. Although considered by Americans a remote land peopled by barbarians, Algiers was nonetheless an important Mediterranean port located within a few days' journey of several Spanish ports and reasonably well connected to the ship-based communications web of the day. Captives could contact the outside world via ships belonging to European countries that had already made peace with Algiers. Mediterranean merchants with American ties, such as the Dohrmans of Philadelphia and Lisbon, as well as friendly European diplomats obligingly carried the captives' messages away from Algiers and brought back letters and news from across the Mediterranean or Atlantic. After 1793 or so, as the American diplomatic corps in the Mediterranean expanded, U.S. diplomats more frequently played letter carriers to the captives.

These extraordinary documents offer firsthand accounts of dramatic events while providing rare glimpses into the minds of merchant mariners. The captives wrote strategically with a clear goal: redemption from an increasingly desperate plight. Relying on the written word as their primary mode of communication, they were forced to confront the problem of how to convey their predicament to their correspondents. Some models were readily available. Many seamen were voracious readers. Relatively high literacy rates, cosmopolitan exposure to a wide range of cultures, and long stretches of idle time at sea drove them to entertain themselves with books.[2] These tars, always on the lookout for an exciting adventure, were no doubt familiar with the captivity narrative, a genre that had fascinated Americans since the late seventeenth century and remained popular throughout the nineteenth. While many of these productions, particularly early ones by Puritans such as Mary Rowlandson and John Williams, were ostensibly written to inculcate religious wonder, tales of Indian brutality and the helplessness of the usually female captives no doubt provided a degree of titillation for many readers.[3]

By the late eighteenth century, these narratives were becoming less didactic and more lurid, "the eighteenth century equivalent of the dime novel," according to one scholar.[4] Captivity narratives thus began to merge with another genre no doubt familiar to many sailors: the literature of sensibility. Based on theories of David Hume and Adam Smith, authors such as Samuel Richardson, Laurence Sterne, and Henry Mackenzie hoped to establish "a code of ethics based on sensibility to compensate for the erosion of traditional notions of social responsibility." In a society increasingly atomized by expanding markets, they believed that strong emotional connections would have to replace more traditional, hierarchical, authoritarian modes of social control. Thus, these authors emphasized the human connections created in "scenes of tearful communion" and "evocations of a feeling too full for expression in language."[5] Authors of captivity narratives who shared such sensibilities increasingly emphasized the victims' suffering. Late eighteenth-century narratives written by John Corbly, Massy Herbeson, Peter Williamson, and Jackson Johonnot and anthologized by Frederic Manheim in 1793 all incorporated the word *suffering* in their titles. This emphasis reached a pinnacle of sorts in *A True Narrative of the Sufferings of Mary Kinnan . . .* (1795), which begins: "Whilst the tear of sensibility so often flows at the unreal tale of woe, which glows under the pen of the poet and the novelist, shall our hearts refuse to be melted with sorrow at the unaffected and unvarnished tale of a female, who has surmounted difficulties and dangers, which on a review appear romantic, even to herself?"[6] The Algerian captives, too, often emphasized their sufferings, frequently employing the language of sensibility, and some eventually wrote captivity narratives that shared elements of Mary Kinnan's story or the Manheim anthology.[7] Such language was often present in their letters home, too.

Captives' letters, however, were less suffused with graphic descriptions and tears of sensibility than one might expect, given the models provided by captivity narratives and the sensibility literature. Most notably, the captives' de facto leader, Richard O'Brien, typically mixed the language of sensibility with what can best be described as the language of expertise. His letters usually overflowed with information about Algiers and the Mediterranean that he hoped might assist his correspondents in negotiating an end to the crisis. These letters were based on yet another model, the official reports written by diplomatic and consular officials that circulated throughout the maritime world providing information and warnings of dangers to merchant and naval officers. Instead of the florid, emotional language of sensibility, they employed a terse but informative language. Many of Captain O'Brien's letters resemble nothing so much as the reports written by American consuls in Gibraltar, Malaga, Lisbon, and other Mediterranean ports. The National Archives has categorized them as part of the consular dispatches from Algiers despite that there was no American consul there until 1798.[8]

One can only speculate on the reasons for O'Brien's preference for the language of expertise over the language of sensibility. Perhaps it had to do with gender. Most of the authors of Indian captivity narratives were women. Novels of sensibility were generally written for women, and their heroes would be considered rather effeminate. Another common genre employing sensibility was the so-called "wife ads," notices frequently placed in newspapers by women condemning their estranged husbands' behavior and creating sympathy for abused wives.[9] In most readers' minds, the language of sensibility was no doubt con-

Numbers of Letters Received from Algerian Captives, 1785–1796

Period	From O'Brien	From Others	Total Number	Letters/Year[a]
1785–1787	17	3	20	10
1788–1793[b]	25	5	30	5
1794–1796	20	20	40	13
Total (11 years)	62	28	90	8

Note: This table does not include letters recorded as sent by Richard O'Brien in his diary for which there is no evidence of delivery to their intended recipients. Several of the letters included have subsequently been lost but are referred to in archival collections. For details see the appendix.

[a] Rounded to the nearest integer.

[b] This period covers 1788 to the arrival of news of the eleven newly captured ships in November 1793.

nected to dependent, powerless people. Men who had recently been free and independent might be reluctant to associate themselves with such a characterization, even if (and perhaps because) it accurately described their captive position. In O'Brien's case, rank, too probably played a part. As captain of his ship, he no doubt viewed himself as responsible for his crew's safety. When he asked for assistance, it was not merely as an unfortunate captive or a dependent person but as the leader of a group of merchant mariners. As a quasi-military official negotiating for the release of his men, the language of expertise seemed more appropriate to his position. Whether they emphasized expertise or sensibility, however, all the captives' letters reveal the power and importance of the written word to men whose freedom depended on the efficacy of the eighteenth-century communications web.

It did not take long for the captives to begin their letter-writing campaign. Two to three weeks after the *Maria* and the *Dauphin* were captured, their crews arrived in Algiers uncertain of their fate and stripped of their clothing, wearing vermin-infested rags supplied by the Algerians. They were then paraded around the strange city and put on sale as Christian slaves. Some were enlisted as palace slaves working in the dey's garden, while others were relegated to the bagnios, or slave prisons.[10] Despite the disorientation, anxiety, and terror that must have accompanied this process, Captains O'Brien and Stephens rather quickly met the major players in Algerian politics—most importantly, the dey and British consul Charles Logie—and they began to appeal to their countrymen to redeem them from captivity. By August 24, roughly a month after their capture, the captains had sent their first letter to Thomas Jefferson.[11] Their next letters went to contacts in Lisbon and Cadiz and to the confederation Congress in Philadelphia. Consul Logie appears to have sent this mail with his own, probably on a British ship sailing out of Algiers. Logie, despite his government's rivalry with the former colonies, had no reason to wish ill fortune on the captives themselves, particularly as many of them were born in Britain and could claim British nationality.[12]

The Going into Slavery at Algiers, engraving, c. 1700. Courtesy National Maritime Museum, Greenwich, London.

The recipients of the Cadiz and Lisbon letters remain unknown, but most likely they were merchants with whom the captains had had earlier contacts in the course of their journeys. It was clearly the captains' intention that these letters be widely circulated. They asked their Lisbon correspondent to "write to Congress and all the states," as well as to the Dohrmans, Philadelphia merchants with a branch in Lisbon, with whom O'Brien, captain of a Philadelphia ship, appears to have been acquainted. O'Brien also asked the correspondent to contact the *Dauphin*'s owners, the Irwin brothers, to whom he also wrote several letters directly, informing them of their ship's unfortunate fate. These letters effectively publicized the captives' plight; the first two were circulated in newspapers, and the letter to Congress as well as one of O'Brien's letters to the Irwins came to the attention of government officials in Philadelphia.[13] This letter writing campaign was probably encouraged by the Algerians, who desired ransom money from America.

These first letters, written at what must have been a very emotional time for the captives, employ a good deal of sensibility. The Cadiz letter, for example, begins as follows: "We, the subjects of the United States of America, having the misfortune to be taken by the Algerines and brought into this port, and made slaves of, being stripped of every one of our cloths, and left in a state of slavery and misery, the severities of which are beyond your imagination." Two of the other letters are similar, with only minor variations in wording. The emphasis on suffering and misery was no doubt calculated to play on the emotions of American readers and in fact appears to have been something of an exaggeration; by the time the letter was written, the captains were living as guests of Consul Logie, where they suffered some indignities but little privation. Their assertion that the "severities" of their situation were "beyond your imagination" in particular reflects contemporary ideas that some emotions may be so strong that it is impossible to represent them with language. Such feelings can only be conveyed through sentimental expressions, such as tears, or, in this case, the emotional "imagination" of a sensitive reader—the very essence of sensibility.

At least one reader of the letters interpreted the captains' language in this way. The unnamed recipient of the Lisbon letter responded, "It will be unnecessary to tell you what concerns we felt, on receipt of the letter you wrote us." Unnecessary "to tell" because sensibility assumes that receptive people will feel strong emotions without the aid of words. Logie's "humanity," the Lisbon recipient writes, "redounds much to his praise and will be ever admired and acknowledged by every person possessed of feeling and in particular by your countrymen."[14] The implication of a sort of kinship of persons "possessed of feeling" again echoes the emphasis on emotional connection in the work of late eighteenth-century novelists and other sentimental writers.

Despite such examples, the bulk of these letters remain surprisingly unemotional, conveying information in the rather dispassionate tone of expertise. To continue with the example of the Cadiz letter, after warning Americans to "beware" the danger of capture by people who are "worse than you can imagine," the captives describe precisely the times and location of the captures, and the status of their ships and crews. They deliver the news that the Spaniards have made peace with the Algerians, enabling the "heathen" to roam the Atlantic with relative impunity, and they report that the Algerians have mentioned potential ransom for the Americans to be as high as £400 to £600 sterling per man. All of this information would be useful to American mariners hoping to avoid capture, and the ransom information would of course be directed at the government or private individuals who might consider coming to the captives' aid. The captains wrote their letter to Congress almost entirely in the language of expertise, adding a great deal of detail to the diplomatic information in the other letters in order to educate Congress about the nature of Spanish-Algerian relations and potential locations of future ship captures, and to provide other information that might be useful in ransoming the captives. All in all, this document is rather dry, almost peremptory. For example, when the captains petition Congress for immediate assistance, rather than pleading their cause as suppliants, they note, rather blandly that it is the "custom and humanity of all Christian persons whose subjects fall into the hands of these people to make some provision for the unfortunate sufferers until they are redeemed."

There are several reasons why the captains affected this somewhat haughty tone. Although they referred to themselves as "humble servant petitioners," this was a role that they, as commanders of merchants' vessels, were hardly used to playing. In addition, the lead author, Richard O'Brien, served as a naval lieutenant during the Revolution and no doubt viewed himself more as an officer reporting to his superiors than as a "humble petitioner."[15] Considering the recent conclusion of the Revolution, the authors might also have assumed a sort of Republicanism in which the divide between subjects and leaders had been dissolved in favor of a society of relatively equal citizens, thereby making it unnecessary to assume an obsequious position of supplication. Finally, because these letters were written so soon after the initial captures, the authors had not really suffered long and probably expected to be ransomed soon. The deferral of this expectation over more than a decade created much greater pathos in later letters.

The first few months of captivity were a fairly hopeful period. All of the European ambassadors seemed helpful, although O'Brien soon soured on the English. The captains continued to live in relative comfort at the house of a French merchant. The common American sailors faced ten hours of daily labor, but they were the favorites of the Algerian officials, from whom they received preferential treatment. While extremely worried about the fate of his wife and young children, Captain Stephens nonetheless wrote John Adams, "Blessed be God, I am middling well . . . and keep my spirits up as well as can be expected with an iron around my leg and bearing all the insults of the Moors." The captain's "irons" were not so onerous as they might sound; as an outside observer explained, "A small iron ring is fixed on one of their legs to denote that they are held in slavery." In a generally upbeat letter to the Dohrmans dated January 1786, O'Brien wrote, "We . . . have reason to think, that we shall soon see one of our countrymen negotiating the peace here." Unfortunately, that countryman would turn out to be John Lamb, who arrived in Algiers on March 25 and left without effecting any change.[16]

For months after Lamb departed, O'Brien still hoped that the captives might be redeemed, but as the extent of Lamb's failure became clear, all the prisoners sank into despair. As late as July 12, O'Brien repeated his understanding that Lamb had come to an agreement with the dey to release the American captives. "I hope for our sakes, and the honor of his country, that [Lamb] will not deviate from his word with the Dey of Algiers," he wrote Jefferson. But, he was also troubled to learn from a letter written by Lamb that Congress had set the limit to be paid for redemption so low that it badly restricted negotiations. The captives, still apparently trusting in Lamb's supposed agreement with the dey, must have been surprised by this admission, which marked the end of their sanguine period. "Mr. Lamb's letter has struck us with the most poignant grief, so that our gloomy situation affects us beyond our expression or your imagination," O'Brien wrote Jefferson, employing classic expressions of sensibility. In the next few months, it became ever clearer that Lamb had either made no agreement whatsoever with the dey or had made one for a sum far beyond what he had been authorized. By September, O'Brien observed, "Ever since Mr. Lamb made his appearance in Algiers we find our redemption to be further off."[17]

Another development soon added to the captives' mounting despair; by the spring of 1787 the plague had arrived in Algiers. According to O'Brien, two hundred Christian slaves died in Algiers between January and May. He wrote Jefferson, "One of my crew is dead, and another after having the pest 14 days with two large buboes on him it has pleased God that he should recover." O'Brien clearly hoped that his report would play on Jefferson's sensibilities, pushing him to further action. "By considering our present unfortunate situation," he wrote, "we hope it will induce our country and countrymen who are charged with Barbary affairs to adopt some speedy and effectual measure for our release, hoping they will never suffer a remnant of their countrymen to die in slavery in Algiers."[18]

These twin catastrophes—Lamb's failure and the plague—spurred Captains O'Brien and Stephens on to new efforts to get themselves and their crews redeemed. The two captains pursued different courses, however. Stephens's strategy was to write letters begging for pity, employing heavy sensibility and large doses of Christian rhetoric to play on his readers' emotions. This approach was dictated, in part, by Stephens's situation as a husband and a father; he was the only one of the twenty-one captives with a wife and child in the United States. Mrs. Stephens employed a similar strategy, writing to Congress in early 1787 that her husband's capture left her and her "three small helpless children" in poverty, reducing her "to the necessity of asking alms or perishing." She begged Congress "that her most wretched husband may be immediately ransomed, and that, in the mean time, such relief may be given to her and her suffering little ones, as Congress, in their wisdom and knowledge shall see fit to grant."[19]

Such language was typical of dependent women stepping out of the private sphere to plea for assistance from officials or the public at large. Captain Stephens himself, now stripped of his independence (and in this sense, of his manhood, too) employed similar language in a touching letter to Congress. "I am become a skeleton with grief and trouble and sorrow, my wife and children poor and naked," he wrote. Explicitly appealing to congressional sensibilities, he urged the legislators to, "realize my state of slavery to the Barbarians, my starving young family, and I cannot think your hearts so hardened as not to redeem me soon." Unlike the earlier captains' letter to Congress, probably written by O'Brien, there was virtually no reference to geopolitical affairs other than a shot at Lamb (he "came here with his finger in his mouth and went away with his thumb in his [ass]") and a hint that, unlike O'Brien, he continued to trust the British consul ("Consul Logie is exceeding kind to us . . . and I believe some scandalous letters were wrote to our ministers against him"). But the bulk of the letter employed the biblical cadences that Stephens may have learned in his New England childhood. It began with what can only be described as an invocation:

To the Honorable and worthy gentlemen of Congress and Commonwealth of the United States of America—O Lord how long will thou turn a deaf ear to our calamities and make Congress and Commonwealth the instruments of cruelty. O Lord hear our petitions and prayers and cause this body of gentlemen to relieve our state of slavery and redeem us soon . . . O Lord hear the cries and prayers of my wife and children and turn the hearts of those gentlemen towards our redemption as soon as possible.

Stephens intended this plea to go beyond the eyes of state and national officials. He concluded by recommending his letter "to the reading of the charitable of the United States." In so doing, Stephens portrayed the captives as charity cases, much like those unfortunates about whom one might hear at church on Sunday. He hoped the charitable in the United States would contribute their bit to free him and his fellow captives and bring them home.[20] There is no evidence that his petition was ever circulated to the public at large, however, and Congress at this stage still lacked the means and inclination to respond.

By contrast, O'Brien reacted to the crises of 1786–87 by becoming a self-made diplomat. By the fall of 1786, once he had given up hope of a quick settlement, O'Brien sent a long letter to William Carmichael, the American chargé d'affaires in Madrid, in which he lectured him on the shortcomings of the new nation's diplomacy. Referring to the Lamb fiasco, he wrote, "We are losing a very favorable opportunity in Algiers respecting paving the way towards our peace, which is of very great importance to the United States." While Stephens focused only on the captives' redemption, stating that peace with Algiers was no more connected to that goal than "the sun has to do with the moon," O'Brien hoped to help his country achieve both objectives. O'Brien decided that he himself would step in where Lamb had failed and provide the new nation's leaders with the advice and information they so obviously lacked. He sent Carmichael and Jefferson page after page of detailed information on the amounts of ransom paid by other European nations to the dey and on the progress of their peace negotiations with Algiers. He learned all of this diplomatic scuttlebutt while held captive, and he also managed to keep current with America's negotiations with Morocco, probably through contacts with European diplomats in Algiers. Jefferson was impressed enough by one of O'Brien's reports to send it on to Secretary of Foreign Affairs John Jay with the expectation that "it will throw further light on the affairs of Algiers."[21]

There can be little doubt that O'Brien's approach was more effective than Stephens's. By casting himself as an expert with useful information to deliver, O'Brien created for himself an important diplomatic role, winning the respect of Jefferson, Carmichael, and other powerful figures. By resorting to expressing the pathos and sentimentality of a dependent "slave," Stephens had in effect emasculated himself. O'Brien not only managed to maintain his authority through his use of the language of expertise, he also eventually advanced his career. Early on he informed Jefferson of his experience as a lieutenant during the Revolution on the fortuitously named brig *Jefferson*, adding that he hoped again to serve his country if the United States should fit out a fleet to attack the Barbary states. In the same letter, he observed that a "sensible man that is well acquainted with the ways of these people . . . might obtain a peace for one half the sum that would be asked [of] the unpolitical consul."[22] Was O'Brien perhaps suggesting that, with his deep knowledge of the Algerian situation, he was just such a "sensible man"? By 1787 O'Brien had determined that the most effective way to gain his freedom was to ensure that negotiations between Algiers and the United States succeeded, and he would stick to that conviction until the end.

In the half a decade between 1788 and 1793, the captives became invisible men. They remained prisoners in Algiers with ever-diminishing hope of regaining their freedom and rejoining family and friends back home. Relatively few of their letters from these years survive. In the first two years of O'Brien's captivity, at least seventeen of his letters reached their intended recipients. However, for the next five-year period, from 1788 to the autumn of 1793 (when eleven more ships were captured) only twenty-one of his letters appear to have arrived at their intended destinations.[23] Between the fall of 1793 and the captives' release in 1796, a three-year period, there are twenty-one letters. The trend with other captives is similar: three letters from 1785–87, twenty from autumn of 1793 to 1796, and only five from 1788 to the fall of 1793. There are several possible explanations for this paucity, but the simplest—that the captives despaired and stopped writing—is simply not tenable. Quite to the contrary, O'Brien seems to have become a more committed letter writer during this period. By late 1788 he claimed to have written about thirty letters to his ship owner, Matthew Irwin. (Only two survive.) O'Brien, distressed that not a single response from Irwin had arrived by late 1788, still pressed on with his publicity campaign, urging Irwin to print his letters "in the public papers so that the United States may see and know that their countrymen is in slavery and that we consider they are duty bound to extricate us from slavery."[24]

In a diary that he kept for thirteen months from 1790 to 1791, O'Brien records sending out thirty-four letters to American officials and personal contacts. He sent ten letters alone to Carmichael, America's chargé d'affaires at Madrid, six to William Short, Jefferson's aide in Paris, two to Jefferson, two to George Washington, two to his mother, and one to the Marquis de Lafayette.[25] There is also evidence that he wrote to the Bulkeleys' merchant house in Lisbon, and to David Humphreys, the American resident minister at Lisbon during this middle period.[26] Not a single one of these letters survives. O'Brien believed that the Spanish consul at whose house he lived and whom he trusted to convey his letters to the various European ships in Algiers harbor had censored or destroyed many of them because they reflected badly on Spain. Some may also have been lost at sea or pilfered during a period when the international wars sparked by the French Revolution made shipping very dangerous. O'Brien constantly complained about how few letters arrived for him in Algiers at this time, although he somewhat miraculously received two letters from his aged mother in Ireland in March 1791, and Captain Stephens received three letters from his family in Boston in June 1790.[27] Assuming that O'Brien continued to write at the same pace that he did during the period covered by his diary, he would have written well over four hundred letters during his time in Algiers, suggesting that possibly more than three-quarters of the letters he wrote in captivity have been lost.

Despite this poor delivery rate, a number of O'Brien's letters found their way to their recipients during this middle period. Why, then, did they not prompt the level of public interest shown in earlier and later periods? The most likely answer is that too much was going on. By 1788, the public's attention shifted to domestic events of immense significance: first to the aftermath of Shays's Rebellion in western Massachusetts and then to the effort to craft a new federal Constitution. Then, in 1789, just as the Constitution was being implemented, the French Revolution, ensuing chaos, and worldwide warfare captured public attention. These events not only dominated the public prints, they also dominated the attention of American diplomats in the Mediterranean basin who, on the whole, were far more concerned with British and French troop movements and threats to U.S. neutrality than with the fate of the twenty or so American prisoners in Algiers. It was not that the American "slaves" stopped writing, it was that the public stopped paying attention. Newspaper publishers, deluged with other news, no longer printed their letters and thus many were lost to posterity. Diplomats, intent on navigating the perilous path of American neutrality, did not pay much attention to them and perhaps did not even always bother to preserve the captives' letters in their journals.

At first, however, the excitement surrounding the new Constitution gave the captives hope. William Carmichael kept them well informed, writing from Madrid in early September that he had just learned of the ratification from a Spanish packet arriving from New York. Up to this point, he wrote O'Brien, "The situation of America has been such that no decisive measures could be adopted because

none could be adopted until our government acquired more energy." Buoyed
by this news, O'Brien immediately went about petitioning George Washington,
recounting the prisoners' three years of grief, misery, and suffering due to the
plague and the "Turkish severity" of their captors. "But now . . . that the new
Constitution is ratified," he concluded, "We hope that Congress will give such
powers to their ministers in Europe so as finally to extricate your unfortunate
countrymen and petitioners from their wretched state of slavery."[28] Perhaps the
end of their suffering was at hand.

Unfortunately, the new government did little to help the captives, and their
conditions actually deteriorated in the coming years. Almost a year to the day
after O'Brien's petition, Captain Stephens sent yet another petition to Congress,
complaining that the small stipend the prisoners had been receiving from the
United States through Carmichael was no longer arriving, apparently due to the
Spanish envoy's own fiscal crisis. Stephens noted that the whole situation was
injurious to the character of the "grand federal states," that is, the new federal
government. In his typical style, he concluded, "My wife wrote me that she was
obliged to put her children out for their living and herself obliged to work hard
for her bread. That is your liberty in sweet America. I put confidence in General
Washington that he with the help of God may turn your hard heart in America
for our redemption before another year."[29]

While O'Brien always signed his petitions on behalf of himself and his fellow
slaves, Stephens wrote only in his own name. This practice might have reflected
strife with his compatriots. Certainly, James Cathcart, Stephens's former subordinate was hostile toward him during this period, claiming that the captain was a
spy and an informer. He also suggested that Stephens remained too friendly with
the detested Consul Logie and accused him of blocking Cathcart's efforts to move
away from the city of Algiers during a plague epidemic in the spring of 1793.
Perhaps Stephens clung too tightly to his rank of captain and resented Cathcart's
advancement to chief Christian slave in the dey's household. Cathcart suggested
as much when he observed, "I forgive Stephens from my heart but if I die of this
distemper he certainly will have his conduct to answer for relative to me, before
a just God who makes no difference between the captain and the sailors."[30]

Six Americans died in the severe plague epidemic of 1787–88, leaving only fifteen survivors.[31] Sporadic reappearances of the plague and the new government's
apparent inaction caused even O'Brien to lose confidence. While he continued
to pass information along to U.S. officials, his letters contained increasingly desperate appeals to the sentiments of his correspondents. For example, in a 1792
letter to President Washington, he wrote, "We beg of your Excellency to consider

what must have been our suffering during this period twice surrounded by the pest and other constant distempers, far distant from our country, family, friends and connections without any real assurances of ever being restored to liberty." He concluded, apologetically, with the hope that "your Excellency will excuse the liberty I have taken in writing to you, but a sentiment of compassion for the truly unfortunate captives we hope will in some degree plea an excuse."[32] For now, O'Brien no longer wrote as though he were an American official providing information and helping his superiors conclude the necessary diplomatic maneuvers. Rather, he had metaphorically dropped to his knees as a suppliant begging for compassion. His efforts to touch Washington's sensibilities point not only to the captives' desperation but also to O'Brien's growing feelings of helplessness, for as long as he saw himself as an active agent in resolving the Algerian conflict, O'Brien had little need to employ such language. At about this time, O'Brien penned in his personal diary an apostrophe to the "federal states" in which he begged them, "your genuine powers exert / To pity melt the obdurate mind / Teach every Bosom to be kind / and humanize the hearts, / Redeem your subjects from Captivity."[33] Apparently, his desperation and use of sensibility were genuine rather than just a ploy to gain support from the United States.

In 1793 a serious new plague outbreak threatened the surviving captives, bringing them to their lowest point yet. James Harnet had gone insane, and the others were losing faith that their country would ever assist them. In late March, O'Brien wrote of his fellows, "They are on the verge of eternity, and to all appearances are destined to be the victims of American independence." Several men, including Cathcart, suffered from the plague, and O'Brien feared he himself was about to become a victim. In a hurried postscript he scrawled, "Pest encreases—it is my lot—I am happy meeting my fate."[34]

Even at this low point, O'Brien's efforts were having some effect. Jefferson was grateful for the information O'Brien continued to provide, noting that "the zeal which [O'Brien] has displayed under the trying circumstances of his present situation has been very distinguished." Unfortunately for the captives, Jefferson decided that U.S. efforts to redeem them would only encourage the Algerians to capture more American ships. He had tried indirect negotiations, which were complicated by the European war. By 1792 the new government was attempting to send another mission to Algiers, but these efforts met with unusually bad luck, as two agents, John Paul Jones and Thomas Barclay, died before they were even able to begin their missions.[35] Unaware of these developments, the captives only knew that they had suffered in slavery for eight years, that their lives were in danger from disease, that their government stipend no longer arrived, and that their country apparently had no interest in their plight. Three of them managed to get private individuals to ransom them, leaving twelve American captives still in Algiers with little hope of redemption.[36]

When the Algerians captured eleven more American ships as a result of the Anglo-Portuguese truce of 1793, Richard O'Brien's worst fears were realized. He had long urged the United States to make peace with Algiers before such a calamity occurred. Two years earlier, he wrote Congress, "When I consider the fatal consequences that would happen to America, if the Portuguese should make a peace with [Algiers], it makes the greatest impression on me of any thing whatsoever that can possibly occur to a patriotic mind."[37] Beyond the humanitarian tragedy of adding to the rolls of American captives, O'Brien was probably also concerned that new captures would make it even more difficult to ransom the existing victims. After all, if the United States was unwilling or unable to pay the price to ransom twenty-one prisoners, how could it free one hundred or more? In fact, the 1793 captures led to a very different result. The enormous publicity associated with them and the effect of the new captives' plight on American sensibilities led to a relatively rapid resolution of the Algerian crisis, at least by the standards of the previous eight years. Arguably, by publicizing their plight and working with the American diplomatic corps to gain their freedom, O'Brien, Cathcart, Stephens, and the new captives were the most important agents in this resolution.

The roughly 105 new captives' first letters were similar to those written by O'Brien and Stephens eight years earlier.[38] At least six of the eleven captains wrote home or to contacts in the Mediterranean to inform them of their capture. Most mentioned the location and circumstances, often emphasizing the degradation experienced at the hands of the Algerians, who, as usual, stripped their prisoners of their clothing and, according to Captain Moses Morse of the *Jane*, "put [them] to the hardest labor" without "the least distinction." For the captains, at least, this social leveling was among the most disturbing aspects of the capture. The captains also reported on the minimal food rations—black bread and water—presumably to justify their requests for funds to ameliorate the poor living conditions.[39]

Like their predecessors, the new captives drafted a petition to inform the government of their fate. They briefly described their situation, thanked David Humphreys, America's Iberian minister, for providing them with some funds, and prayed to be redeemed before the next plague outbreak could carry them off.

In this campaign they no doubt benefited from their predecessors' experience and contacts; O'Brien personally wrote to Humphreys, George Washington, and other diplomatic officials to get help for the new prisoners.[40] But they also shuddered when they realized that they might share the fate of the earlier captives. "All my hopes are blasted and whether even I shall get away from this is entirely uncertain," Captain Samuel Calder wrote to his ship's owner. "Indeed, if I may judge by the unfortunate Captains O'Brien and Stephens, who have been nine years here and most of their crews are already dead, and if our country could not relieve so small a number what will they do when there is nearly 140 men . . . ?"[41]

Captain O'Brien's reaction to these developments was shock, despair, and reproof. "It is needless in me that has suffered so much to touch on the distress of these unfortunate men," he wrote Humphreys, adding that America's failure to redeem the 1785 captives amounted to "cruelty perhaps unprecedented in the annals of tyranny." The failure of the United States to follow his advice to redeem the captives and make peace was the cause of the present disaster. "I had forewarned them of their misfortune, but men in adversity is [sic] generally paid little or no attention to," he complained to Humphreys.[42]

Despite such palpable personal anger, O'Brien continued to focus on policy issues as he wrote numerous letters in the hope of finding a diplomatic solution to the deteriorating situation. Interestingly, his diagnosis of the problem was similar to that of his countrymen at home, whose opinions had no doubt been influenced by O'Brien's earlier published letters. Like many other Americans, O'Brien viewed the British as the leading agents in an anti-American conspiracy. He informed President Washington, "The British nation, the natural and inveterate enemies of the United States, has brought about this truce . . . in order to alarm our commerce, and prevent the United States from supplying the French in their present glorious contest for liberty." To Humphreys he wrote, "Let us never forgive the British and Portuguese . . . God I hope will severely punish both." No doubt much of this anger grew out of his experiences with Charles Logie. On top of their long history of conflict, O'Brien charged that the British consul had recently refused the dey's request to assist in making peace between Algiers and the United States. Additionally, other recent developments in Algiers heightened O'Brien's sense that many "Benedict Arnolds" were using Algiers as their tool to subvert the United States. He wrote that William Chapman and John Cooper, two shady Americans who recently had become interested in North Africa "would become Algerines [and] cruize against the enemies of Algiers, particularly the Americans." He also was disturbed by an American named Captain Carr and his Irish clerk, Foley, who, according to O'Brien, arrived in Algiers with an anti-

American plan of some sort and financial backing from "the villain Lynch" of Gibraltar. "I would be happy in being hangman for all these dogs, Cooper, Chapman, Lynch and Foley, and many others of their damned dispositions," he wrote Humphreys.[43]

O'Brien's proposed remedy was twofold. First, he continued to urge the United States to negotiate a peace with the Dey. To this end he wrote many letters to diplomatic officials detailing what other countries had paid to obtain peace and lengthily describing how to approach Algerian officials and Jewish banking intermediaries. After the 1793 captures, O'Brien increasingly supported a second solution: a strong American navy. A small fleet of four frigates and two brigs "will keep the Algerines in greater awe than the whole marine of Portugal did," he wrote. To Washington he made the far more grandiose suggestion that "the United States have at present no alternative than to fit out with the greatest expedition thirty frigates and corsairs, in order to stop these sea robbers in capturing American vessels." An American fleet would serve not only to shock and awe the Algerians, but also to show the English, Spanish, and Portuguese "that we are not a dastardly effeminate race [and] maintain the honor and dignity of the United States."[44] Ultimately, O'Brien decided that these letters were not enough and that he must return home in order to help resolve the situation. He wrote Humphreys that his fellow captives agreed and were "very desirous that you would have me redeemed, in order to proceed on to Congress and traverse the United States . . . to explain their deplorable state of captivity [to] facilitate their release, and to explain all particulars relative to Algiers."[45]

Unfortunately, the truth of the matter was that at least some of O'Brien's fellow captives were growing impatient with him, and the feeling was certainly mutual. In April of 1794 the plague once again raged in Algiers, killing ten American captives including Captain McShane. Four others died of smallpox during the same period. In this atmosphere of death and frustration, the more recently captured captains turned on O'Brien. Captain Furnass wrote that they regarded O'Brien as "a man not worthy to bear the name of a citizen of the United States." The problem, according to Captains Furnass and Newman, was that O'Brien refused to share with them the contents of his letters from Humphreys. In his defense, O'Brien wrote Humphreys that he had shared the sense of his letters with the other captains, but the newcomers "are not the set of men in general I should trust anything of importance to their perusal, even if I had your orders." After nine years as the de facto leader of the American prisoners, O'Brien refused to endanger his campaign to free the captives by putting it into the hands of men he labeled a "Jacobin party," whose "conduct . . . drinking [and] wranglesome behaviour," were, he claimed, "a dishonour to the name of Americans" and had become common knowledge to "all the consuls in Algiers." O'Brien believed the best hope for rescue lay in cooperation with these consuls. He felt he simply could not risk allowing the "Jacobins" to hurt the Americans' cause with them.[46]

It is unlikely that O'Brien meant the epitaph "Jacobins" literally, especially as he was clearly sympathetic to the French Revolution and an enemy to Britain. More likely, their disorderly behavior and distrust of O'Brien's authority earned the newcomers that sobriquet. Part of the conflict, too, may have stemmed from their different attitude toward letter writing. Considering his circumstances, O'Brien was an incredibly disciplined and active writer, developing correspondences with American officials ranging from consuls to the president. The newcomers initially followed in his footsteps, sending petitions to Congress and the president at the time of their capture. Subsequently, however, they rarely wrote to officials, only sending a few letters to Humphreys (mostly complaining about O'Brien). Captain Newman of the *Thomas* also claimed to have written to "some particular friends in Congress." By and large when the newcomers wrote letters, they sent them to family members and business associates in America, probably with the expectation that they would then have them published, as Captain Taylor explained, "to influence our nation to redeem a set of . . . the miserablest objects upon Earth."[47] While O'Brien focused first on influencing diplomatic officials and only secondarily on informing the public at large, the newcomers' priorities were just the opposite.

By their own admission, the new captives were not the most diligent writers. "Believe me, sir," Newman apologized to Humphreys, "our situation at hard labour in the marine has come so hard upon us that we have not been able to pay that attention in writing to public characters as was necessary." The newcomers' sense of despair also probably made letter writing seem like a waste of time. Referring to the 1785 captives, Captain McShane wrote, "If their small numbers could not be redeemed, we have no hopes of relief; therefore endeavour to make ourselves as happy as possible."[48] What McShane saw as making the best of a hopeless situation, O'Brien saw as laziness, drunkenness, and "Jacobinism."

As the newcomers reached the end of their first year of captivity, the contents of their letters, too, differed from O'Brien's. While he concentrated primarily on policy issues, their focus was on what might be termed humanitarian issues. This focus was quite compatible with their frequent use of the language of sensibility. Like O'Brien, Captains Newman and Smith included information on Algerian ship movements and negotiations with European powers, but they put much more emphasis on their personal hardships and the difficulties they and their "brother sufferers" faced. "Is it not possible that America will suffer its natives to linger out the remains of a miserable life in chains," Smith wondered. The next year, he and members of his crew wrote that they remained "in a most deplorable situation, and almost despair of any relief until death."[49]

The major statement of the newcomers' suffering was written by Captain John Burnham of the *Hope*, who was ransomed by the British consul to Cadiz in March 1794. His account, which was published in various American newspapers, was clearly designed to direct public attention to the captives' fate in much the same way as modern human interest reporting does for today's victims. Like his predecessors, Burnham described in detail how the captives were paraded and sold as slaves on their arrival in Algiers, but he also reported on the dey's sexual predation. According to Burnham, the dey had "always a particular boy, one of the fairest among the [captives], for attending in his bed chamber, with whom it is said he is guilty of the most horrid of all crimes." Burnham described at length the prisoners' work conditions, emphasizing that the captives were essentially slaves, forced to work long hours with little remuneration and virtually no personal freedom. He himself, despite having just recovered from an illness, "was ordered to take up and carry a burden of at least two hundred and fifty pounds," with the result that "after walking a few steps without being able to raise himself upright, he sunk under it and was carried to the hospital." After describing the squalid conditions of the slave prisons and the onset of the plague, Burnham concluded by urging his countrymen to "leave no reasonable measure unattempted, to relieve as speedily as possible their unhappy brethren from slavery and the prospect of death."[50]

There can be no doubt that this account was written with the intention of using the public's heartstrings to pull open their purse strings. Not only did Burnham conclude with a direct appeal for public assistance, but in at least one newspaper his account was printed as part of a larger "Address to the People of the United States of America" aimed at gaining private donations to ransom the captives.[51] While O'Brien prodded American officials to remain involved and gave them necessary intelligence to negotiate with the Algerians, the newcomers filled the public with horror and indignation at the plight of their "suffering brethren." Despite O'Brien's occasional annoyance, these differing approaches proved complementary. By 1794 it looked as though this two-pronged campaign might finally succeed.

One reason that the situation improved was the arrival of David Humphreys on the scene in the spring of 1793. A Connecticut native, Yale graduate, former aide-de-camp to George Washington, and putative poet, Humphreys had become interested in the Algerian situation eight years earlier as a junior diplomat in Paris, where he served briefly as Thomas Jefferson's secretary. The impressionable young American was badly shaken by the first round of captures, writing shortly thereafter to his mentor, George Washington, that the Algerians would probably prove "insolent and intractable" in negotiations. Humphreys soon departed Paris for London, where his duties (or lack thereof) allowed him time to complete one of his more substantial early poems, "On the Happiness of America." A long section of this work—several hundred lines—addressed the Algerian depredations and fantasized about American revenge.[52]

Humphreys's objective as a poet was to blend emotional poignancy with love of country to create what might be described as a patriotic sensibility. Perhaps the best example is "A Poem on the Love of Country" (1799), in which he wrote:

I feel the patriotic heat
Throb in my bosom, in my pulses beat
And on my visage glow. Though what I feel
No words can tell—unutterable zeal!

Thus poems such as "Elegy on the Burning of Fairfield" (1780); "The Glory of America; or, Peace Triumphant Over War" (1783); "On the Death of Major John Palsgrave Wyllys" (1795–97); and "A Poem on the Death of General Washington" (1800) all touch on sublime or poignant moments Humphreys hoped would strike an emotional chord of patriotism. His goal was patriotism as sensibility rather than as the product of philosophical discourse.[53]

The Algerian captives were perfect subjects for such a project. What could be more poignant than their plight? In "On the Happiness of America" (1786), Humphreys lingered over their fate:

How long shall widows weep their sons in vain,
The prop of years in slav'ry's iron chain?
How long, the love-sick maid, unheeded, rove
The sounding shore and call her absent love;
And seem to see him in each coming sail?
How long the merchant turn his failing eyes,
In desperation, on the seas and skies,

And ask his captin'd ships, his ravish'd goods,
With frantic ravings, of the heav'ns and floods?

Humphreys then asks his complacent countrymen, "How long, Columbians dear! Will ye complain / Of these curst insults on the open main? / In timid sloth, shall injur'd bravery sleep? / Awake! Awake! Avengers of the deep!" After describing a lengthy, and ultimately successful imaginary naval battle with "these savage tribes," Humphreys asks his readers to "see raptur'd nations hail the kindred race / And court the heroes to their fond embrace: / In fond embraces strain'd, the captive clings / And feels and looks unutterable things."[54] The deep, "unutterable" emotions of the freed captives provide just the touch of poignancy that makes this patriotic celebration a definitive moment for Humphreys and, he hopes, for readers who share his sensibility.

Having completed both his mission and "On the Happiness of America," Humphreys returned to New York in May 1786.[55] He arrived just at one of the peak periods of newspaper interest in the Algerian crisis, a time when fears of North African invasions of the West Indies or even mainland America coupled with concern about the Lamb mission worked to keep the crisis in the public eye. Humphreys must have been impressed. Even in London he had read American journals closely, complaining to John Jay that "the newspapers of both parties have co-operated to produce a belief that the United States are on the brink of perdition." Back home in Connecticut, Humphreys continued to follow public reaction, reporting to Jefferson that "the public mind is in anxious expectation respecting the piratical powers."[56] The tenor of that reaction was, of course, influenced partly by O'Brien and other captives who wrote letters and petitions that were widely published by newspapers in the months before Humphreys arrived and throughout his stay in America. Humphreys could hardly have failed to notice and be influenced by these items. In this way the publicity drive that the captives spearheaded worked to pique the interest and patriotic sensibility of the man who would eventually become their most important diplomatic ally.

Humphreys continued to fret about events in Algiers on his return to Europe in 1790 to serve as minister to Lisbon. By 1792 he completed a sizable new work, *A Poem on Industry*, one of his most important patriotic pieces. In the emotional climax of his new poem, Humphreys returned to the poignant situation of the captives:

What! Shall that race (forbid its blushing shame)
Whose earli[e]st deeds, enroll'd by deathless fame,
Fix'd Freedom's flag beyond the western waves,
Consent their Sons and Brothers to be Slaves?

No, Americans must instead commit themselves to a new sensibility of patriotism. Humphreys urged them, "Lift up your heads, ye much enduring men! / In western skies the new Aurora ken! . . . Blow ye the trumpet! Sound—oh sound th' alarms— / to arms—brave Citizens! To arms."[57] Having completed this new work and delivered it to President Washington for his approval, Humphreys asked to be given authority over negotiations with Algiers, a request that was granted by the fall of 1793, when he set out for Gibraltar on what he hoped was the first leg of his journey to Algiers.[58]

Thus, even before he made contact with the captives, Humphreys was well informed of their condition and deeply sympathetic to their plight. While he was in Lisbon, his friends and future in-laws, the Bulkeleys, shared with him letters they received from O'Brien, including the despairing one in which he lamented that the captives were "on the verge of eternity."[59] It was at this juncture, on November 30, 1793, that O'Brien finally made contact with Humphreys in a letter dated November 12. The captive offered his expertise, conveying the important information that the dey did not favor a diplomatic visit from Humphreys. In fact, this refusal would doom Humphreys's mission, forcing him back to Lisbon and eventually to America. O'Brien further suggested a detailed plan for buying peace with the Algerians by working through the Swedish consul and various Algerian Jewish merchants.[60]

Humphreys was initially unimpressed by O'Brien's expertise. He dismissed the captain's lengthy analysis of the need for a bellicose policy, noting that "anything that looks like boasting, threatening or predicting can scarcely ever be of any utility in any political negociations." However, O'Brien's offhanded complaint about what he perceived as the American policy of refusing to ransom the captives before concluding a peace put Humphreys on the defensive. "What a foolish idea," the captive wrote, "that the ransom of a few men concerned the peace. We have suffered on this and many other accounts by our country." The hint that the United States was insensible to the captives' sufferings distressed Humphreys, who responded that O'Brien was simply unaware of what he described as many secret measures taken by the United States to free the captives. "It is not at all surprising that you should, at times, have thought your fellow citizens indifferent to your deplorable fate, and deaf to every call for humanity," he wrote, "But be assured that the truth was directly the reverse." Had O'Brien received an earlier letter, sent by Humphreys but never delivered, the captive would find it "was dictated by a heart not insensible to your sufferings."[61]

That same day, in a flurry of guilt-induced activity, Humphreys wrote two other letters. One, addressed to O'Brien and the other captains in Algiers, apologized profusely for Humphreys's failure to free them in his aborted Algerian mission and informed them that the United States would provide them with a small stipend to be distributed by Richard Montgomery from Alicante. "These arrangements," he wrote, "will leave the body to suffer as little distress as the nature of the circumstances will permit." Even more importantly, Humphreys attempted to alleviate their mental anguish with an outburst of sympathetic emotion: "But in your situation, far from your friends, in the power of your foes, what balm is there to put the mind at ease? Who can administer medicine to a wounded spirit? Would to heaven the feelings of others could in any degree assuage your own! Then, not in vain, would my heart bleed for you." Humphreys's other letter, addressed "to the mariners, citizens of the United States of America now held in Algiers," assured these common sailors that, like the captains, they, too, would receive a small stipend and some clothing from Alicante. Humphreys attempted to comfort them: "there is not a good man in the United States of America who is not your hearty friend, and who would not do every thing in his power for your assistance." He pledged that "wherever I may go, or however I may be employed, I will never cease to think of you or to labour in your behalf" and prayed "that you may yet live to embrace your friends, to see good days, and to be convinced that no country in the world has a greater regard for its suffering sons than your own."[62]

While Humphreys wrote these letters in Alicante, O'Brien stewed over his apparent neglect of the captives. On December 6, before Humphreys's letters arrived in Algiers, O'Brien sent the minister another long report detailing the status of negotiations between various European powers and the dey and warning of the renewed danger of attacks on American shipping from Algerian and Tunisian cruisers. The final paragraphs were no doubt calculated to wound Humphreys. "It is needless in me that has suffered so much to touch on the distress of [the captives]," he wrote. "I have known my country [during] nearly nine years captivity by her cruelty, perhaps unprecedent[ed] in the annals of tyranny." He concluded, "I have sir, taken the liberty of writing you my sentiments on our affairs, but I know that you once declined any such correspondence."[63]

These barbs hit their mark. In his response, dated New Year's Day, 1794, Humphreys vehemently denied ever refusing a correspondence. He reminded O'Brien that he had written to him more than a year earlier but that the letter had apparently been lost, and that he had already responded to O'Brien's letter of November 12, a fact of which O'Brien would already be aware, as that letter finally arrived in Algiers in late December. Responding to O'Brien's implicit charge of callousness, Humphreys insisted, "If I do not feel as I ought for the distresses of yourself and your companions in affliction, I do not know my heart." Clearly exasperated, Humphreys then lectured O'Brien on the limits of his powers as a "public servant in a subordinate executive department." He concluded with the hope that O'Brien would send his greetings to the other captives along with "assurances on my part that what I have before written them was the result of feelings warm from the heart, and that I shall ever retain the same sentiments, whether they may chance to hear of them directly from me or not."[64]

The author of "On the Happiness of America" and "A Poem on Industry," the man who hoped to bind Americans together through a patriotic sensibility, could not bear to be criticized on the grounds of heartlessness toward his suffering countrymen. From this point forward, Humphreys sent regular letters to Algiers, if only to assure the captives that he continued to sympathize. This policy, a diplomacy of sensibility, was quite different from that of O'Brien's previous diplomatic contact, Thomas Jefferson. Although O'Brien sent at least nine letters to Jefferson during the early years of captivity, he apparently received only two terse responses. In the first, Jefferson wrote only to confirm receipt of O'Brien's notification of his capture. He pledged to "exert myself for you" and to write again, but he limited the missive to only three sentences because "the fate of this letter is uncertain." The second letter, only slightly longer, informed O'Brien of Lamb's mission and wished the captive "a speedy deliverance from your distress and happy returns to your family."[65] After that there was silence. In part that was due to Jefferson's strategy of pretended indifference to the captives as a means of keeping the ransoms low. This policy was perhaps easier to follow under Jefferson's watch, when the negotiation involved some twenty prisoners, than it was for Humphreys when the number exceeded one hundred, including a handful who had been prisoners for close to a decade. Nevertheless, the shift from Jefferson's cool, rational approach to Humphreys's more emotional style is notable.

Certainly, it brought improvement for O'Brien and his fellow captives. Prompted by patriotic sensibility and O'Brien's monthly letters, Humphreys devoted a great deal of time to the details of the Algerian situation. He saw to it that the captives received clothing and small personal allowances. When the plague threatened to strike Algiers again, he attempted to find them a safe haven in the countryside. He supported O'Brien's request to be ransomed so that he could return to America as a lobbyist for the remaining captives. Humphreys urged the Secretary of State to sponsor a lottery to raise funds to redeem the captives and reopened Jefferson's old idea of creating an antipiratical alliance of neutral European powers. When O'Brien and the "Jacobin" newcomers began to feud, Humphreys personally interceded, explaining to Secretary Randolph, "It gives me great pain to observe that those who are equally smarting under the chains of slavery should be so little friendly to each other."[66]

Despite Humphreys's efforts, conditions worsened for the captives. Fourteen died in the first nine months of 1794, ten from a plague outbreak in late spring and summer and the rest from smallpox.[67] In an angry and despairing letter, O'Brien informed Humphreys that only he, his mate, and one sailor remained of the original fifteen members of his crew. "They have paid the debt of nature," he wrote. "Their redemption concerned the peace—they are extricated or redeemed from bondage by the annual ambassador Death whom [*sic*] is determined to save money for the United States." In other words, he blamed American parsimony and misguided policy for his fellows' sad fates. Aware of Humphreys's sensibility, he assured the diplomat that his anger was not aimed toward him personally and that he was "fully sensible of your humane and tender feelings for your unfortunate countrymen."[68] This letter and the news of the plague deaths prompted Humphreys to make additional efforts to free the remaining captives regardless of the prospects for a more permanent peace. He was in a difficult position. Because of the turmoil in Europe, it was unclear where the United States could find funds for this purpose. Treasury secretary Alexander Hamilton had negotiated a loan from Holland, but with French forces swarming over the Low Countries it was now unlikely that the Dutch bankers could make good on this promise.[69]

Humphreys's uneasiness upon learning of these developments was exacerbated further by a lack of information and instructions from the State Department. As a result, he embarked on a highly irregular course—deserting his post and returning to the United States. He justified this action on several grounds. It would allow him to receive clear and specific instructions. He could attempt to raise money from Americans to redeem the captives, thereby averting the problems with the Dutch bankers. His precipitous departure might lull the British and Spanish into believing that the United States had given up on efforts to negotiate with Algiers. This last justification probably stemmed in part from correspondence with O'Brien suggesting that Logie and the Spanish were trying to undermine American efforts. That concern also led Humphreys to push the government to cultivate France as an intermediary with the Algerians.[70]

Humphreys's decision was a controversial one. According to his biographer, "His motives were by some impugned and sharply censored." Certainly, James Cathcart was critical. Humphreys's abandonment of his post led the dey to conclude "that the United States were trifling with him," an inference that Cathcart finally, with much difficulty, convinced the dey was unfounded. As late as 1802 Humphreys remained defensive about his decision, recalling in "Remarks on the War Between the United States and Tripoli" the hardship of his "winter passage across the western ocean" in that earlier attempt to "hasten the release of our brave countrymen."[71] The Atlantic voyage certainly was terrifying; the ship was tossed and turned, one sailor was thrown overboard, another was badly injured, and Humphreys reported landing in Virginia in "a very bad condition." Nevertheless, the trip did the captives little good. The plan of working with the French was never implemented, the fund-raising efforts proved a dead end, and had Humphreys remained in Lisbon he would soon have received a clarifying letter from Secretary Randolph that would most likely have made the voyage to America unnecessary.[72] Humphreys's offense was not self-interest; far from it, he had erred out of sincere concern for the captives. With his poetic, patriotic sensibilities heightened by the news from Algiers, he had lost patience with his superiors and taken matters into his own hands. O'Brien knew just how to play Humphreys, and although himself a captive, the captain manipulated the diplomat by appealing to his sensibility. Ironically, O'Brien had succeeded all too well in his efforts. The poet's guilt-induced voyage to America led to several months' delay while Humphreys and his assistant completed the long return trip across the Atlantic and back to the Mediterranean.

CHAPTER THREE

Publicity and Secrecy

In the fall of 1794 diplomatic events in Algiers took a worrisome turn. While David Humphreys was temporarily back in the United States, Richard O'Brien and James Cathcart came to believe that Portugal, with the assistance of Spain, was negotiating another rapprochement with Algiers. If successful, this effort would doom the Algerian-American negotiations before Humphreys even arrived and quite possibly lead to further American captives. For the time being, the dey insisted he wished to negotiate with the Americans first. But as days passed without word from Humphreys, O'Brien, already worried about the dey's exorbitant demands on the United States, decided to take matters into his own hands. If the American diplomats were unable or unwilling to handle the dey properly, the inveterate letter writer decided that he could do so himself. So, in late October, he composed a missive purportedly written in Philadelphia July 11, 1794 by "Cunningham and Nisbitt, Members of the Committee of Commerce, State of Pennsylvania" and addressed to "Captains McShane and O'Brien, captives in Algiers." Both Cunningham and Nisbitt as well as the Pennsylvania Committee of Commerce were fictitious characters created in O'Brien's imagination. In the letter they explained to O'Brien that the United States believed the Dey to be a "great, good and generous prince" and were prepared to pay a reasonable price for peace. However, at the same time the government had "established an armie of 100 thousand good troops and orders is given for building upwards of fifty frigates," many of which were now in readiness. Furthermore, they suggested the United States was negotiating an alliance with Britain, a possibility that would make it impossible for the Algerians to attack American shipping or to obtain much ransom money from them in the future. O'Brien's plan was to have Cathcart, now the dey's chief Christian secretary, read the letter to his master. However, Cathcart found the letter so "slight a device" that he refused to read it all, preferring only to read portions to the Dey at appropriate moments.[1]

By the time Humphreys returned, the crisis had eased a bit and O'Brien's plan was forgotten. Although the fictitious letter had little or no influence in the outcome of events, it delineates the limits of O'Brien's ability to control events. After nine years of assiduous letter writing to anyone who might possibly be able to assist the captives, with little ultimate success, O'Brien had finally moved from factual reporting to creating fictional characters, much as novelists like Samuel Richardson moved from writing letters to writing epistolary fiction such as *Pamela*. When real people refused to act according to his script, O'Brien used his now well-honed skills at letter writing to create fictional characters who were more obliging.

Reality was far messier and more difficult for O'Brien or anybody who wished to manipulate public opinion. The very idea of an American public was a novel concept in the 1780s and 1790s. First, the idea of a public sphere and the related concept of publicity were new. In earlier centuries there had been only a fuzzy distinction between the state (or the king) and private households. With the rise of bourgeois republics in the eighteenth century, the public sphere emerged as a mediating force between the nation and private individuals. Second, the notion of the United States of America as a nation was still new, let alone any conception of just how that new nation should react to such a crisis. O'Brien's effort to create Cunningham and Nisbitt and the Pennsylvania Committee of Commerce reflects the thin organizational infrastructure of the new nation's public sphere. While chambers of commerce did exist in Europe—for example, the Marseilles Chamber of Commerce played an important part in negotiating to free French prisoners from Algiers—they were rare in America, and those organizations that did exist had no experience or interest in negotiating with the Algerians.[2] Thus, O'Brien's device begged the question of exactly who should be responsible for redeeming the American prisoners. Of course, the national government must play a leading role, but what about the quasi-governmental bodies, religious organizations, or other associations that constituted the public sphere?

European nations had addressed this question through centuries of experience with Barbary captivity. In the early years the chief agent had been the Church, which was still tightly tied to governmental authority. Money was raised for disaster victims, including Barbary captives, through briefs issued by church officials, often at the prompting of noblemen or other influential figures. These church briefs, which stated the details of the sufferers' plight and their need for assistance, were read in parish churches, where congregants were urged to give free will offerings to a fund to assist the captives. Aristocrats apparently were sometimes required to give specified contributions. In England the bulk of these briefs were issued for fire victims and to rebuild damaged churches, but from the thirteenth century through the eighteenth there was also a steady stream of briefs issued to redeem "Christian captives" in Barbary and the Middle East.[3]

On the continent, responsibility for redeeming captives was often delegated to the brothers of the Order of the Most Holy Trinity (Mathurins), who received papal sanction to ransom captives in 1198. The order raised money from the public by holding "alms-quests," at which they staged theatrical depictions of the prisoners' plight, often starring actual prisoners who had been recently ransomed. Some members of these orders also gained extensive diplomatic experience through participation in vexing and often harrowing face-to-face negotiations with the various Barbary authorities as they attempted to redeem as many prisoners as possible with their hard-won funds. Miguel de Cervantes was perhaps the most famous Algerian captive to benefit from the Mathurins' good works.[4] In England, due to the Reformation and the expansion of the state under the Tudors, charity briefs increasingly became the province of secular state authority. By the early seventeenth century, the king had sole authority for issuing these documents, now referred to as "King's briefs." Sheriffs and constables were charged with distributing them to parish church authorities, who spearheaded collections and then forwarded the money to county receivers-general. Over the course of the eighteenth century, Parliament and colonial legislatures increasingly took the lead in raising funds for disaster relief throughout the empire.[5]

With the advent of new communications technologies and the concomitant growth of the public sphere in the eighteenth century, a much wider swath of the population could easily become involved in this process. By 1787 some writers in an influential English periodical, the *Gentleman's Magazine,* were proposing that charity drives bypass the churches altogether in favor of printed journals. Complaining that collections in church were generally "very small," the editor of the *Gentleman's Magazine* suggested that "the distress of the indigent would be at least as amply relieved if the Government would permit the briefs to be advertized gratis in the Gazette . . . [where] many would *read* them, who very seldom now attend to *hear them read.*"[6] Also in the eighteenth century, private subscriptions set up by local committees increasingly supplanted the more formal and cumbersome charity briefs. Such drives were also facilitated by the growth of newspapers. Hannah More, one of the century's great publicists, once observed,

"There is scarcely a newspaper but records some meeting of men for the most salutary purpose."[7]

Such developments were particularly important in the United States, with its weak central government and lack of an established church. Although church and state would play their part in redeeming the American captives, publicity would be crucial. Consequently, the words of Richard O'Brien and other captives and the efforts of their supporters, particularly David Humphreys, would take on great importance. Such publicity drives were not, however, always viewed as an unmitigated good. Particularly in the area of foreign affairs, publicity was a double-edged sword: While it could mobilize the population, it could also compromise state secrets. Public efforts to redeem the captives forced the new nation to deal with this dilemma and to negotiate between contending needs for publicity and secrecy.

Despite widespread horror and the pleas of the captured ship captains, the American public initially took no action to redeem the captives. This inactivity stemmed from several causes. First, the sense of powerlessness revealed by the captures made any potential action seem futile. If the United States was as weak and poor as it seemed, what could the public possibly do? Beyond that, the public's attention was more focused on resolving the deeper roots of this weakness—the economic and political crises. Furthermore, the new nation had virtually no experience with Barbary captivity and the intricate process of prisoner redemptions. There was no infrastructure in place—no Mathurins, no Marseilles Chamber of Commerce, no Kings' Briefs, hardly even a functioning diplomatic corps. Additionally, in the early stages of captivity, the crisis for the seamen did not seem so dire as it would become; in such situations public sympathy surely correlates to length of captivity. Finally, despite the best efforts of the captains, that so many of the sailors were not American born meant that there were fewer family members and friends to pressure officials and whip their countrymen into action.

Beyond these situational factors, government officials, led by Thomas Jefferson, made it their policy to minimize publicity and to favor secrecy. Jefferson advocated this approach in the wake of the Lamb mission, which had failed because the United States was unable to pay the ransom demanded by the dey. Jefferson had reason to suspect the dey's exorbitant demands were calculated partly on the basis of the generous allowance provided the prisoners by the United States through the offices of Count d'Expilly, the Spanish envoy to Algiers. Consequently, the Virginian recommended that Congress end this policy and make it appear as though the United States had no interest in the captives whatsoever. The hope was that this apparent disinterest would lead the Algerians to lower the ransom.[8]

Jefferson believed his somewhat cold-hearted policy was necessary for the long-term well-being of the captives and the new nation. It "is cruelty to the individuals now in captivity, but kindness to the hundreds that would soon be so, were we to make it worth the while of these pyrates to go out of the streights in quest of us," he explained to John Jay. To John Adams he insisted that Algerian orders "be kept secret even from the captives themselves, lest knowledge of the interference of government should excite [the Algerians] to extravagant demands." While agreeing in general with this policy, Jay hoped to temper it with humanity. He noted that Jefferson's strategic hints that Congress would not redeem the captives had "greatly added to their distress." To alleviate the captives' suffering, he urged that the unused money from the Lamb appropriation be used to provide them with "little supplies . . . conveyed in so indirect a manner as not to be traced by them or by the Algerians."[9]

Meanwhile, Jefferson entered into secret negotiations with the Mathurin order. Because he was situated in Paris he was familiar with this order's work in freeing French captives. He met with the Mathurin general, who pledged "with all the benevolence and cordiality possible" to attempt to redeem the American captives at as low a price as he had redeemed French prisoners. Jefferson was charmed by the prospect of this interfaith cooperation. "The difference of religion was not once mentioned," he wrote, "nor did it appear to me to be thought of." The general also impressed on Jefferson the importance of secrecy. He insisted that Jefferson destroy "at Algiers all idea of our intending to redeem the prisoners" and that "it must not on any account transpire that the public would interest themselves for their redemption." These directions prompted Jefferson to go still further. "Hard as it may seem," he wrote Jay, "I should think it necessary not to let it be known even to the relations of the captives that we mean to redeem them." He later explained that this misdirection was intended to prevent the captives' families from writing letters that might inadvertently alert the dey to the Mathurins' role in the negotiations, a disclosure which he feared might raise the price of the captives to an unacceptable level. These concerns also prevented Jefferson from making a report to the House of Representatives in 1790, when that body referred one of the captives' petitions to the State Department. "No report could have then been made without risking the object, of which some hopes were still entertained," he explained.[10]

Eventually, the Mathurin project proved a dead end. Despite some promising early negotiations, the new nation's financial difficulties prompted long delays as Jefferson attempted to raise money for the brothers. Finally, the French Revolution rendered all these efforts moot, as the Mathurins were dissolved, their property confiscated by the state, and their long career as intermediaries for Christian captives terminated. Their insistence on secrecy, however, continued to influence American officials for years to come. It is a remarkably revealing comment on the efficiency of the late-eighteenth-century communications network that the brothers and Jefferson entertained such fears that prisoners in Algiers might learn of high-level operations in the United States and France and spill the beans to their captors.

The emphasis on secrecy was also apparent when, in the spring of 1788, a few Philadelphians finally undertook a public drive to relieve the prisoners, now in their third year of captivity. This effort was spearheaded by members of the Pennsylvania Abolition Society, who placed an advertisement in various newspapers announcing their intent to "devise some practicable means of affording relief to their distressed brethren in Algiers." At the same time, Tench Coxe, one of the group's influential merchant members, wrote to Secretary of Foreign Affairs Jay requesting information on the Algerian situation and sounding him out as to whether the government was still actively attempting to redeem the captives. Jay quickly responded that Congress and Jefferson were doing all they could, and he urged the society to abandon its publicity drive. "There is reason to fear that every measure that may now be taken *publicly* for their redemption will enhance the price of it, and increase the difficulties which at present exist," he explained to Coxe. Therefore, Jay advised, "Nothing better can be done than to leave the matter entirely to Mr. Jefferson, and *privately* to remit to him whatever monies may be raised for the purpose of their relief or redemption."[11] In other words, the danger that news of the Pennsylvania society's work might reach the Algerians through newspaper publicity, word of mouth, letters to the captives, or a combination of all these factors outweighed the potential good to be done by such publicity.

After the second round of captures, the public became far more involved in efforts to aid and redeem the captives. This development resulted from multiple factors, including the large number of new captives, the appalling length of time during which the new nation had failed to ransom the veterans, and the activities of the captives themselves and their friend David Humphreys. At home, the politicization of the American public sphere in the 1790s also had important implications. With the advent of the first parties, any public action potentially took on partisan overtones, and the effort to redeem the Algerian captives was certainly no exception. This aspect of partisanship worried some Americans, particularly Federalists, making publicity problematic in a different way than it had been earlier.

At the heart of this process was a series of heated meetings during the political crisis of 1794.[12] The majority of these gatherings were politically motivated rallies sponsored by Democratic-Republicans critical of Federalist policies. Participants were angry about a wide range of issues, including English depredation of American shipping, attacks by Native Americans on the western frontier, as well as the Algerian captures, all of which they linked to the Federalists' alleged friends, the English. This Republican movement tied itself most explicitly to efforts to redeem the Algerian captives at the Philadelphia meeting of March 18, held in the State House yard. After condemning the Federalist administration's supposed partiality to Britain and asking "indulgence" toward the French republic, participants called for commercial prohibitions on British shipping and manufacturing and "measures to prevent more of our property from falling into the hands of Algiers, or of Great Britain." In addition, they formed a committee of five citizens "to prepare a plan for soliciting donations from all benevolent and patriotic freemen, for the purposes of establishing a fund to relieve and redeem our unfortunate fellow citizens, who sailing on board of vessels belonging to the port of Philadelphia, have been captured and enslaved by the Algerines or any other piratical states."[13]

Taken at face value, this committee might appear to have been purely charitable, but given the context of the meeting at which it was created, it was clearly a political animal. Whatever benevolent impulses lay behind it, it also served as a device for the opposition party to dramatize the perceived failures of the Washington administration. By taking matters into their own hands, the committee members realized they ran the risk of appearing treasonous by impeding government efforts to resolve the Algerian crisis. They confronted this problem at a subsequent meeting in April when they resolved to pose two questions to Secretary of State Edmund Randolph. The first was "whether any provision is made by government to alleviate the situation of the captives while in bondage." The second was whether the Philadelphia fundraising efforts would "impede the progress of any negociation which may hereafter be entered into."[14] These questions suggest some of the tensions between publicity and secrecy. While publicly critical of the administration, the Philadelphians nonetheless had no desire to impede any efforts already under way to free the captives. Unfortunately, the policy of secrecy (ironically, established by their fellow Republican, Jefferson) made it well nigh impossible for them to know what sort of activities the administration was engaged in, if any. The president's response furthered secrecy: He refused to disclose what steps the government was taking, and he asserted that he had no power to tell individuals what to do with their own money.[15]

All of this was part of a larger issue, what George Washington termed the problem of "self-created societies." The prime examples were the Democratic-Republican societies, which the president and most Federalists would soon blame for the Whiskey Rebellion of 1794. Such organizations, one Federalist explained, were troublesome because if they "set themselves up as umpires between the people and the government," or, as another put it, as an "intermediate power or body . . . between the people and their representatives," they would "defeat the intentions of both."[16] These descriptions accord perfectly with Jurgen Habermas's modern description of a "public sphere" of coffee houses, salons, voluntary associations, and newspaper readers that emerged in the eighteenth century to serve as an intermediary between the private world of the household and the state-controlled "sphere of public authority."[17] In essence, Federalists and Democratic-Republicans were engaged in a contest to define this emerging public sphere. Federalists viewed it as a dangerous development spawning self-created societies that might band together to politicize public opinion, twisting it into a weapon against the state. Whatever its intellectual origins, this was a natural stance for a party that controlled the administration. Democratic-Republicans, on the other hand, were more comfortable with a politicized public sphere, an unsurprising position for an opposition party.

The observer to recognize most explicitly this connection between the efforts of committees like the one in Philadelphia and the contest over the public sphere was an anonymous New Yorker, almost certainly a Federalist. Writing in May of 1794, he warned of the "attempts of certain violent men and popular associations to dictate, direct, or in some measure to influence, the proceedings of government." These violent men were behind the effort to raise funds for the Algerian captives, he alleged. "Instead of confiding in their representatives, who have the best means of information," he explained, "they themselves in private clubs, transient associations, formed and acting on partial or inaccurate statements of facts, undertake to direct and control the measures of government." If these individuals had merely let the administration do its job, the captives would now be free, the critic insisted. Shortly after the Americans were captured "government took the most effectual measures, and the most liberal means were provided, to redeem these unfortunate men," he wrote, claiming vaguely that this assertion was based on "unquestionable authority." But, he continued, when the dey learned of the public interference it derailed the negotiations: "Learning that money was raising by private donations, he has hitherto held [the captives'] redemptions at such an unconscionable price, that no agreement can be concluded with him." In short, the fundraising efforts represented a "hasty popular zeal, inflamed by private passions," and such "efforts to disorganize government and govern by private clubs" foretold "mischief and calamity to America."[18]

The New Yorker's observations reveal much, probably more than he intended, about the problem of secrecy versus publicity in a democracy. Secrecy, he explained, was imperative: "It was for the interest of America that the people should not know what measures were taking, until the business was closed." Secrecy, therefore, was the only means to succeed, because the nature of modern communications insured that publicity would reach the dey one way or another and undermine negotiations. He claimed his assertions were based on "unquestionable authority," yet the readers of his essay had no means of determining whether any of it was true, precisely because of the secrecy he so valued. In retrospect, it is clear that the author was either deliberately deceiving his readers or was, at best, sincere but misinformed; there is absolutely no reason to believe that negotiations with the dey were ever succeeding before 1794 or that American public involvement had any impact whatsoever on the dey's actions.

The New Yorker assigned the individuals whose publicity efforts were "thwarting the operations of government" into two camps: those who acted from "sinister views" and others whose actions stemmed from "misguided zeal." While he would certainly have assigned the Philadelphia committee and the Democratic clubs to the first group, throughout 1794 there were also many efforts—led by church officials, theaters, and others—which he no doubt would have categorized as less-malicious products of misguided zeal. These efforts were probably most numerous in New England, where, in early April, an observer reported to President Washington that the "general topick" was "principally the sufferings of our citizens among the Algerines." Apparently, many ordinary people were willing to donate a dollar or more to ease this suffering. Unlike the "sinister" individuals in the self-created societies, these contributors hoped the call would come from above; according to Washington's correspondent "the general wish was that the President would issue his proclamation for a general contribution," perhaps to be read in church on Sunday where "a prodigious sum would be raised voluntarily."[19]

Despite these sentiments, the impetus would come not from the president but from David Humphreys, acting, he insisted, as a private individual rather than a government official.[20] In Lisbon that February he oversaw what was probably the first organized European celebration of President Washington's birthday. After-dinner toasts included calls for "effectual protection to American citizens by sea and land" and to "our fellow citizens in captivity at Algiers—and a speedy release to them." Afterward, the celebrants contributed liberally to a fund "for the use and comfort of the citizens of the United States, in captivity at Algiers." The fund soon totaled $1,000 before it was distributed to the captives. Somebody, almost certainly Humphreys, saw to it that the entire affair was written up and the description sent to a Boston newspaper. It is probably no coincidence that at just the time this account arrived in New England, the managers of the Boston Theater held a benefit for the captives at which patrons donated more than $800.[21] Similar fundraisers in Philadelphia and Charleston theaters raised $941 and £256, respectively.

In Humphreys the captives had found, and to some extent molded, the ideal publicist.[22] Eminently literate and well connected, he doggedly persisted in putting their case before the public. By the early summer of 1794, he had hatched a new plan: The various states should establish lotteries to raise money to redeem the captives. Tickets could be sold in the United States and Europe, with proceeds gong to ransom the prisoners in the order of their capture. This plan, according to Humphreys, "would not have any unfavorable influence on the general policy, or existing state of affairs, between the United States and the Regency of Algiers" because it was a common practice for victimized nations to "take effectual measures . . . for the liberation of their subjects or citizens from their captivity."[23]

Humphreys did a good job of spreading word of his plan throughout the summer and fall, but some Americans wondered if the project might be better conducted by the government than by private individuals. Humphreys sent an advertisement describing his plan to various printers. A copy reached Philadelphia by September, when a printer there decided to clear it with President Washington before publishing it. That same week, Benjamin Lincoln, Collector of the Port of Boston and former Revolutionary-era Secretary of War, wrote Randolph, "I received a few days since from Col. Humphreys, signed in his official character, an address to the Citizens of the United States representing in very strong terms the distress of our prisoners in Algiers, and in language equally forcible call[ing] on them to make provisions for their redemption." Lincoln wondered whether such an appeal was proper, presumably because it might interfere with government efforts to redeem the captives. "Had I received such an address from any person abroad, other than one of our public officers, I would have considered the appeal an improper one" and ignored it, he explained, but because it came from Humphreys he had determined to ask Randolph to rule on the propriety of publishing it.[24] Randolph's response to this particular inquiry is not known, but when faced with similar inquiries from Boston and Norfolk, he took a laissez-faire approach. Treasury secretary Alexander Hamilton agreed that government should not repress such subscriptions, provided they were not "set on foot by any *political* societies," that is, by Washington's "self-created" societies.[25]

As 1794 came to a close, Humphreys launched a second media blitz. This one was probably prompted by the return of Captain John Burnham, who reached home in November after being privately ransomed in the spring.[26] He brought with him a long firsthand account of his and the other captives' sufferings, which, considering its style, may well have been ghostwritten by Humphreys. A large portion of the December 1 issue of the *Boston Gazette* was dedicated to the Algerian problem. Burnham's narrative graced the front page, along with a signed appeal from Humphreys, no doubt hand delivered by Burnham. In this appeal, Humphreys argued that the need for secrecy and pretended disinterest was over. "However wise or proper the policy might formerly have been to decline ransoming our citizens from slavery at Algiers, until a peace could be negociated with the Regency; at present it appears to me, the principal political reasons on which that policy was founded have ceased to exist," he wrote. With the new captives the crisis had apparently reached a head, and the United States would either have to negotiate a peace or fight Algiers. Either option would minimize the danger of future captures, and as a result the people of the United States no longer had to worry that their efforts to redeem the current captives would lead to future captures or set a bad precedent for later efforts at redemption. Furthermore, the old policy of secrecy had been formulated in large part to keep down the expenses of redemption, but now with the number of captives quintuple what it had been in 1785, expenses were bound to be high whether or not there were subsequent captures.[27]

The editor of the *Boston Gazette* continued to address this subject in the newspaper's next edition, printing two more plans for redeeming the captives. The first, conceived by John M. Pintard, the U.S. consul to Madrid, had already received publicity in New York and Philadelphia. Pintard, a prominent New York merchant, proposed to pay four dollars toward the captives' ransom for every pipe of Madeira wine purchased from him by citizens of the United States. In the second plan, three upstate New York land proprietors pledged to donate any profit in excess of fifty cents per acre from their land sales to the "relief of the Americans in captivity at Algiers." They estimated that ten thousand dollars could possibly be raised in this manner.[28] Of course, both plans were somewhat self-serving, but that merchants believed they might profit from the public's desire to assist the captives only underscores how successfully their plight had been publicized.

All of these earlier efforts were merely the prelude to the publicity drive of 1795, which would prove to be David Humphreys's greatest undertaking yet. The ambassador most likely planned it out on his hasty winter trip to America, which he hoped would allow him to cut through the various delays that had stalled his mission while he remained in Lisbon.[29] After a difficult voyage, Humphreys arrived in Virginia waters on January 28 and landed in Newport, Rhode Island, on February 3.[30] Within a day or two, a long, solemn, pathetic entreaty ostensibly written by Richard O'Brien appeared in the local papers. This item was undoubtedly a forgery, and it was almost certainly written by Humphreys.

In his letter "O'Brien" urged Christians to use an upcoming thanksgiving day to pray for the captives and to contribute money to assist them.[31] Nearly a year earlier Humphreys had suggested that Washington proclaim a fast day to ask God to assist the new nation in freeing the captives.[32] Less than a month before O'Brien's letter was printed, on January 1, President Washington had proclaimed February 19 a day of public thanksgiving to celebrate the nation's domestic tranquility and its avoidance of foreign wars. It seems most likely that when Humphreys read of Washington's thanksgiving proclamation, he penned the "O'Brien" letters as a means to reframe the upcoming holiday along the lines of his earlier plan. The real O'Brien could not possibly have known of the president's proclamation in time to write the letter and get it published; at best, news of the proclamation would not have reached Algiers before mid-February, and O'Brien's response, even if written and delivered onto an outward-bound ship immediately, could not have arrived in New England much before mid-April. Therefore, the "O'Brien" piece, which quoted or paraphrased the presidential proclamation several times, could not possibly have been written by O'Brien.

In style and content, too, this petition reads differently from O'Brien's usual work. It is far more polished and emotional and far less informative than his letters. After summarizing the terms of Washington's proclamation, it emphasizes the prisoners' religious fervor (a topic never mentioned before or after by O'Brien) and notes that, "Although our harps are hung upon the weeping willows of slavery," America remains "our chiefest joy" and "the last wish of our departing souls shall be her peace, her prosperity, her liberty, forever!" Therefore, Americans are urged to, "Pray, earnestly pray, that our grievous calamities may have a gracious end," and to "Entreat the CHRIST, whom you adore, to let the miserable captives go free." Finally, the petition appeals to the clergy of New England: "Your most zealous exertions, your unremitting assiduities, are pathetically invoked! . . . Arise ye ministers of the Most High! Christians of every denomination, awake unto charity!" This sounds like nothing O'Brien ever wrote, but it is remarkably similar to Humphreys's style of apostrophe and exclamation.

In ghostwriting such a petition, Humphreys astutely avoided some of the criticism directed at earlier publicity efforts. The idea was allegedly formulated by the captives rather than any politically influenced self-created societies. Furthermore, the day of thanksgiving was proclaimed by the president, even if raising charity for the captives had not been his intention. Finally, by involving the churches and the clergy, Humphreys signaled his determination to work within the existing power structure rather than to challenge authority. New England's Congregational churches were the closest thing to an established church the United States has seen, and during this period they were closely aligned with the Federalist power structure.[33] They could hardly be accused of using the Algerian crisis as a means of undermining Washington's administration. Additionally, the petition was worded in the traditional form of a charity brief. After calling on Christians to "awake to charity," "O'Brien" writes, "Let a brief, setting forth our hapless situation, be published throughout the continent." This brief was to be "read in every house of worship on February 8th." The following Sunday, ministers were to preach a sermon on the subject so that on the actual Day of Thanksgiving, February 19th, the churches could "complete the god-like work" of emancipating the captives through their benevolence. In short, Humphreys had crafted a charity brief based on the moral authority of the captives themselves. What could be less threatening to Washington's administration?

Word spread quickly throughout northern New England. Congregants in the neat little hillside hamlet of Francestown, New Hampshire, raised a "handsome collection," as did their brothers and sisters in meetinghouses throughout Maine, Massachusetts, and upstate New York. All told, they probably raised well over $1,000.[34] Churchgoers further publicized the captives' plight by reporting on their charity in the local press. The Francistowners expressed their wish that other towns would follow suit in publicizing their collections so that "others encouraged thereby would 'go and do likewise.'" This activity, in turn, inspired the Episcopal bishop of Connecticut and Rhode Island to urge southern New England clergy to hold collections "for the relief of our Brethren in captivity in Algiers" on March 3.[35] Newspaper publicity spurred a second round of collections in southern Maine in early March, and Federalist newspapers in Philadelphia and Baltimore also began to publicize the drive.[36] Humphreys's one-man media blitz was well on its way to becoming a national phenomenon.

Word reached Baltimore by Monday, February 16. On that day, the *Federal Intelligencer* announced, "The sufferings of our countrymen at Algiers have, at length, roused our feelings." On the following Thursday, the day of thanksgiving, the clergy planned to ask their congregants to contribute to the fund and to form committees to consider further measures. The plan, however, was subject to cancellation "in case Congress have taken up the business or are likely to do so." In other words, the Federalists were still being careful not to step on the administration's toes. Public committees must not hinder official action. Two days later, in anticipation of the thanksgiving, the *Intelligencer* reprinted an exceedingly enthusiastic prediction from Boston's *Federal Orrery* that inhabitants of that city would contribute $20,000 to the cause, that towns throughout the nation would follow in their footsteps, that Congress would immediately make up the difference between the public contributions and the remainder needed to free the captives, and that Humphreys would quickly "receive orders to negotiate the full liberation of our prisoners." However, shortly after the type for the paper was set, information arrived in Baltimore "which entirely superceded the necessity of carrying into execution the proposed plan for the redemption of our brothers in chains at Algiers."[37] The whole publicity drive now came to a sudden halt.

What had happened? First, the administration learned of Humphreys's plan. This realization appears not to have occurred until February 11. On that day, fully a week after the "O'Brien" letter began to appear in the New England papers, Humphreys met in Philadelphia with his boss, Secretary of State Edmund Randolph, and newly appointed Treasury Secretary Oliver Wolcott. Randolph, still no doubt rather nonplused to see his minister to Madrid and Lisbon so unexpectedly on American soil, was skeptical about Humphreys's publicity drive. After the meeting he conveyed to the president a document, subsequently lost, that was presumably a copy of the O'Brien letter. "I submit sir, to your consideration whether something like the enclosed is not proper for the public ear," he wrote Washington, adding that Wolcott was looking into the financial details of ransoming the captives.[38]

It was not the first time Humphreys had sprung such a fait accompli upon the administration. The year before, word of his state lottery plan had reached American newspaper publishers at roughly the same time it reached the administration. Humphreys may not have felt any compulsion to clear his activities with the government; in writing to the captives, he often emphasized that he took such measures in his capacity as a private individual rather than in his role as a government official.[39] At best, this argument was the result of a somewhat specious logic. At least the newspaper publishers seem to have thought so. In 1794 they had been reluctant to accept his lottery plan precisely because they viewed him as a public figure quite possibly acting on his own initiative rather than on the direction of his superiors.[40]

Perhaps it was to get around such concerns that Humphreys kept his name off this new appeal, attributing it solely to Captain O'Brien. Randolph and Washington could not have been happy with Humphreys's ruse. The administration had recently condemned the Republicans for their "self-created societies," which had mobilized the public to raise money for the Algerian captives without administration approval. Now, through the pages of the Federalist press, Humphreys was doing essentially the same thing. Even though he was working through the established churches rather than "self-created societies," Republicans would not have appreciated this fine distinction and might well have had a field day had they realized what was afoot. Additionally, many Federalists themselves would probably not have approved of such a blatant effort to enlist publicity by a member of the administration. Such concerns lay behind the resolve of Baltimore's Federalist editor to seek further information from the administration before collecting donations for the captives. This request would have arrived in Philadelphia just a few days after Randolph and Humphreys's meeting. It was now too late to stop the plan from reaching fruition in New England, but the administration quickly quashed it in Baltimore and Philadelphia. Or, at least, it was apparently the administration that did so. Three days after reporting that the fundraiser had been killed due to new information that came from the government, the Baltimoreans ran an unusual correction stating that, "those words 'came from the government' were inserted through misapprehension."[41] Probably one of two things had happened. The administration, afraid that by killing the publicity drive they would appear to be connected to it and that such a connection would be seen as untoward, may have ordered the correction as a clumsy way of covering their tracks. Or, Humphreys may have ordered the Baltimoreans to kill the fundraiser and run the correction himself in an attempt to continue his sophistic effort to insist that he acted merely as a private citizen rather than as a government official in this affair. In either case, the Federalists continued to act under the assumption that politicians should not appear to enlist public pressure in such matters.

Whatever the philosophical and political objections, Humphreys's plan was also impractical. He may have raised a thousand, or perhaps even several thousand dollars, in small-town New England churches. But freeing the captives would cost many hundreds of thousands of dollars, a sum that seems likely to have been completely unrealizable from church meetings, even if the drive had spread through the mid-Atlantic and southern states. Furthermore, as Humphreys well knew, the government had already determined to borrow $800,000 in Europe to pay the captives' ransom and sue for peace with Algiers. The problem, as Humphreys also knew, was that, due to the French Revolution and consequent European turmoil, the United States was having trouble securing this loan from its Dutch bankers. It is probable that the people who contributed to the fundraising drive were unaware of these developments. Congress passed the enabling act without open debate, and the actual act made no mention of Algiers, instead blandly ordering that up to one million dollars be appropriated "to defray any expenses which may be incurred, in relation to the intercourse between the United States and Foreign Nations."[42]

What Humphreys did not know was that just as he arrived in America, Congress was considering legislation that had the potential to assist the government in obtaining the loan. Hamilton's so-called "valedictory" funding bill sought to put the national debt on better footing, in part by converting foreign debt into domestic debt. One portion of this bill would dedicate imposts on sugar and other goods to pay for the Algerian loan—although, like the enabling legislation, the bill never mentioned Algiers by name, specifying only a loan for "defraying the expenses of foreign intercourse." By mid-February this legislation looked almost certain to pass. Therefore, ultimate funding for the captives' release was far more likely to come from funds raised through domestic taxation than from $50 collections in New England churches. It may well be that the promise of these dedicated funds ultimately assisted Humphreys in gaining key loans from Leghorn and Lisbon to pay the ransom on his return to Europe.[43]

In retrospect, the Federalists' unease with Humphreys's publicity schemes can be seen as part of a larger effort to retain what has been described as the "federal monopoly of international negotiation." Federalists feared that public involvement in the details of foreign affairs could provide a means for America's enemies to use domestic faction to further their cause. For an example, they needed to look no further than the Genet affair of 1793, when the French envoy allegedly threatened to appeal to the Francophile public over the objections of the administration. They were also concerned about the Democratic-Republican Societies, which in 1794 openly demonstrated support for the French Revolution despite Washington's official policy of neutrality.[44] Humphreys's fundraising drive was not a direct threat to administration policy, but it was troubling nonetheless. The Democratic societies' and the Republicans' use of the Algerian issue in 1794 to embarrass the administration made Humphreys's revivification of the issue less than welcome. Furthermore, Humphreys's activity violated the administration's consistent wish for minimal public involvement in the details of foreign negotiations. It is not difficult to view Humphreys's actions as a public official's rogue effort to harness public opinion to influence the administration to take action in North Africa.

From the Federalist administration's perspective, it was far better to allow Congress to handle the matter quietly than to encourage public involvement, no matter how decorous the public. This concern would be further articulated with the passage of the Sedition Act of 1798 and the Logan Act of 1799, both actuated by fear that members of the public would ally themselves with the enemy (then France), either through domestic publications or foreign travel. The Logan Act, in particular, demonized citizens who negotiated with foreign powers on their own initiative.[45] In short, Federalists perceived public participation in foreign affairs beyond the level of general policy as a potential threat to national security.[46] Earlier concerns about secrecy merged with Federalists' fear of Democratic-Republican treason, prompting the federal government to guard jealously its foreign policy role from public participation—an attitude that subsequent administrations down to the present have also adopted without, for the most part, much public protest.[47]

In the case of the Algerian prisoners, public fundraising efforts were now at an end, and the administration was firmly in control. Humphreys's assistant Joseph Donaldson would successfully negotiate for the captives' release and for a peace with the dey in good time. Procuring the actual funds from European bankers to secure the captives' release would prove trickier, but neither the administration nor private individuals would ever look to the public again for contributions. Eventually, after a year's wait for the funds, the prisoners happily departed from Algiers—a few after nearly a dozen years captivity. They would follow a circuitous and dangerous route home, in the course of which they were nearly recaptured by other North African pirates and were quarantined in Marseilles for the plague. Finally, in February of 1797, they returned to the United States.[48]

Upon their arrival on American soil, the former captives once again became proper objects for public charity. They arrived in Philadelphia with a letter from Joel Barlow, the new American consul in Algiers, urging his countrymen to contribute to their well-being. "Several of them are probably rendered incapable of gaining their living," he wrote. Others, Barlow explained, were blind, physically hobbled by hard labor, or permanently weakened by the plague. "Some of them are doubtless objects of the charity of their countrymen," he concluded, "but whether this charity should flow to them through the channel of the federal government is a question on which it would be impertinent for me to offer an opinion." Without waiting for the federal government, Philadelphia's citizens began to raise funds on their own initiative. Now that the survivors were back on American soil, there was no question that such publicity would interfere with foreign policy. Might the hostages now also receive the thousands of dollars pledged for their relief two years earlier in those many New England meetinghouses? Or had Humphreys already found a way to get it to them in Algiers? What happened to that money, or even whether it was ever all collected, remains a mystery. However, at least one promise was fulfilled. The $887.28 raised in a benefit at the Boston Theater in May of 1794 was at last distributed to the captives upon their return, allowing each of the former "slaves" to return home with from thirty to sixty-five dollars in his pockets, depending on his rank.[49] With that, most of them slipped out of the public view and resumed anonymous private lives.

PART TWO

THE IMPACT OF
CAPTIVITY AT HOME

CHAPTER FOUR

Slavery at Home and Abroad

While Captains O'Brien and Stephens and their crews suffered in Algiers, another man began to write the story of his own captivity on the other side of the Atlantic. Olaudah Equiano, an African, was sold into slavery and shipped to the Americas but eventually gained his freedom and an education that enabled him to write one of the most famous captivity narratives of his age. *The Interesting Narrative of the Life of Olaudah Equiano* was first published in England in 1789 and New York in 1791. By the time the second group of Americans was captured by Algerians in 1793, English and Dutch editions had sold widely throughout the Atlantic world.[1]

Superficially, Equiano's story was the mirror image of most captivity narratives, which portrayed the sufferings of Europeans among dark complexioned "savages." A carefree and well-born young African, Equiano was suddenly kidnapped by slave traders who forced him on board a European ship, which took him to an American port, where he was sold into slavery. Equiano, who had become a devout Christian before writing his narrative, portrays his European captors as satanic demons and their ship as a hellish nightmare. At first sight of the ship, young Olaudah believed he had "gotten into a world of bad spirits." On board, he saw "a large furnace of copper boiling and a multitude of black people of every description chained together." After a fainting spell, he asked some fellow Africans if they "were not to be eaten by those white men with horrible looks, red faces, and long hair."[2] Many European accounts of capture by Algerians, or by Indians for that matter, likewise portrayed the captors as devilish heathen. The difference, of course, is that in Equiano's tale the heathen were European Christians and the peaceful victims were non-Christian Africans. Equiano reinforces the racial reversal throughout the narrative as he adopts Christianity while his tormentors continually violate central Christian tenets through their involvement in slavery and the slave trade.

Although the racial and religious dynamic of Algerian captivity was indeed the opposite of Equiano's narrative, American authors writing about Algiers often employed the same trope of European savagery that was so evident in Equiano's account. In a literal sense, Christians were the victims rather than the aggressors in these narratives, but their authors also stressed Christians' broader culpability in the slave trade. In his history of Algiers, Mathew Carey commented, "For this practice of buying and selling slaves, we are not entitled to charge the Algerines with any exclusive degree of barbarity. The Christians of Europe and America carry on this commerce an hundred times more extensively than the Algerines." Similarly, in a fictional argument between a mullah and an American slave in Algiers, novelist Royall Tyler had the mullah remark that, unlike American masters, Algerians immediately freed any slave who converted to Islam: "We leave it to the Christians of the West Indies, and Christians of your southern plantations, to baptise the unfortunate African into your faith, and then use your brother Christians as brutes of the desert."[3]

Equiano wrote his narrative in large part as antislavery propaganda at a time when there was growing abolitionist sentiment throughout the Atlantic world. By pointing out the barbaric un-Christian behavior of the European captors, he hoped to shame them into renouncing their role as slaveholders. Many American authors like Carey and Tyler who wrote about the Algerian captives hoped to make a similar point by comparing the savagery of the Algerians to that of American slaveholders, usually to the detriment of the Americans. Linda Colley has recently posited that British captivity narratives expressed the deep-seated sense of vulnerability shared by a fairly small group of people living on a very small island involved in colonizing large groups of Africans, Asians, and Americans.[4] The United States was not yet a colonizing empire, but it had, in a sense, internally colonized nearly three-quarters of a million Africans. For many American authors writing about Algerian captivity, the fate of their "enslaved" brethren in far away North Africa offered an opportunity to reflect on some of the evils of the institution of slavery closer to home.

Not everyone who wrote about Algiers shared this concern. Most notably, none of the captives who wrote letters from Algiers compared their situation to that of Africans in America. The captives wrote primarily to inform Americans of their plight and to convince their countrymen to free them. Consequently, it is not particularly surprising that they were uninterested in dwelling on the irony of a slaveholding nation protesting when its own citizens were held in slavery in North Africa. Furthermore, given the racial hierarchies of their homeland, it is unlikely that as white Americans they would want to imagine the possibility that they might somehow become equivalent to actual black slaves in a concrete nonmetaphorical way. Nevertheless, the captives did frequently label their situation as "slavery," and they described horrors such as wicked overseers, limited rations, and, most frequently, the way their captors forced them to wear chains. Captain O'Brien's letters were filled with such references. In choosing to describe themselves as "slaves" rather than "captives," O'Brien and his comrades no doubt hoped to coin a metaphor that would prick the public's sentiment. Laurence Sterne, the master of sensibility, famously wrote, "Disguise thyself as thou wilt, still slavery! . . . still thou art a bitter draught."[5] The captives played a difficult hand here, hoping to draw from this well of public sympathy toward victims of slavery without marginalizing themselves or offending slave-owning benefactors by creating an exact equivalency between their own situation and that of African American slaves.

After their release, many former captives produced longer, more formal narratives of their captivity, much as Equiano had done. These, too, made little reference to the paradox of American slavery. A foreigner could easily have read the most ambitious eighteenth-century narrative, *The Journal of the Captivity and Suffering of John Foss*, without finding any hint that slavery existed within the author's home country. Nevertheless, slavery was the central theme of Foss's narrative. The title page featured a poem in Sterne's sentimental style, which began, "O Slavery! Thou friend of hell's recess!"[6] Foss, who was captured by the Algerians in 1793 as he sailed aboard the brig *Polly*, repeatedly and extensively discusses the horrors of Algerian slavery in his lengthy narrative. He includes extended and graphic accounts of the slaves' work routines and grizzly descriptions of their punishment. These are no less disturbing for the fact that they are mostly plagiarized from Mathew Carey's *Short History of Algiers*, but this borrowing does prompt one to wonder whether Foss's treatment was really quite so harsh as his readers might otherwise infer.[7]

An African American named Scipio Jackson makes a memorable appearance in Foss's work. Jackson, described as a "blackman belonging to New-York," was lying near death in an Algerian hospital in 1796. When he recovered enough to be able to get out of bed, an Algerian "taskmaster" named Salamoone ordered him back to work. As Jackson protested, Salamoone "gave him several strokes with his stick, saying, 'if you are not able, I will make you able.'" Jackson managed to drag himself to the marine, where many of the slaves labored, and do a bit of work, but he soon keeled over and was returned to the hospital to die that afternoon. The moral Foss draws from this incident is that "the untimely death of a Christian, is nothing more thought of, by the inhabitants, than the death of one of their domestic animals."[8] What he does not mention, and could not know, is that Scipio Jackson's experience was eerily similar to those later described in narratives written by American ex-slaves in the nineteenth century.[9] One wonders whether Scipio Jackson had ever been enslaved in the United States, and, if so, whether he found it a more "bitter draught" there or in Algiers.[10]

Foss's fate was, of course, ultimately far happier than Scipio Jackson's. In describing his approximately two years of captivity, Foss frequently emphasizes the contrast between freedom and slavery. After recounting David Humphreys's early failed negotiations with the dey, Foss recalls, "We despaired of ever tasting the sweets of liberty again. Here we expected to end our days in the most laborious slavery, pregnant with unutterable distress." When yet another ship is captured, he writes that its crew members "were now add[ed] to our number to participate in our distress and partake with us the horror of unspeakable slavery, and bemoan the loss of the blessing of liberty." Finally, when release appears imminent, the whole mood changes. Foss reflects that "for a long period we had been suffering the most inhuman slavery; loaded with almost an insupportable weight of chains, and were not expecting to enjoy Liberty; the greatest blessing human beings ever possessed."[11] The contrast between slavery and liberty is crucial in creating the pathos of these passages, but like earlier American revolutionaries who described their condition under King George III as slavery, Foss does not acknowledge the irony of making such analogies in a nation of slave owners.

Captain John Burnham, author of the other firsthand eighteenth-century Algerian captivity narrative employed the term *slavery* in similar ways. Burnham was able to get himself ransomed and returned home in 1794. His much shorter narrative was originally published as a long newspaper article in 1794 while the captives were still in Algiers.[12] Clearly, its purpose was to influence the public to free the captives; to achieve that goal Burnham heavily emphasized the misery of their slavery. When it was republished in the *Rural Magazine*, the editor entitled it "The Curses of Slavery."[13] The curses suffered by the Americans included being sold at a slave market, being subjected to their masters' sexual advances, being put in irons, suffering from inadequate clothing and bedding, and being forced to live with domestic and exotic animals—"Christians, monkeys, apes, and asses altogether." Except for the monkeys and apes, the description would have had a familiar ring to American antislavery authors who wrote about conditions in the United States, but, like Foss, Burnham made no reference to American slavery.

The antislavery editors of the *Rural Magazine* could not leave it at that. Instead, they appended to Burnham's account a second, fictional captivity narrative.[14] It was called "Treatment of the African Slaves in America," purportedly written by one Cato Mungo, an African traveler who observed the treatment of slaves in the American South and in Connecticut. Beginning with the requisite quote from Laurence Sterne, this account provides the usual descriptions of suffering slaves, including their capture, sales at the market place, attempts at escape, and, in an echo of Burnham's encounter with domestic animals, the assertion that runaways were treated "the same as stray horses and cattle." Interestingly, Cato Mungo holds out little hope that northern abolitionists will be able to raise the funds to free the slaves by compensating their owners. A Connecticut Yankee tells him that "there were several Americans now in slavery in the kingdom of Algiers . . . And that their countrymen could not find themselves generosity enough to redeem them," implying that Americans therefore could not be expected to raise the funds to emancipate 700,000 African American slaves. In this way, Americans' apparent stinginess toward the Algerian captives is made to reflect a general lack of will to free slaves of any sort.

At least one other American captive made the connection between American and Algerian slavery but in a rather different way. In an angry letter written to Congress in 1788, Captain Isaac Stephens, suffering in his third year of captivity, repeatedly decried his miserable servitude to the "barbarians." He marveled at finding "myself a slave that has lived a freeman thirty eight years in the Bay State." In the margin of the letter he scrawled, "You free your Negroes and won't free us!"[15] This remark no doubt referred to the abolition of slavery in Massachusetts, one of the great achievements of the northern antislavery movement. Stephens seems to be expressing incredulity that the people of Massachusetts would free their African slaves but apparently refused to take action to free white Americans held in slavery in Algiers. Like so many authors who wrote about Algiers, he was appalled by American hypocrisy, but from Stephens's perspective the hypocrisy came not from too much attention to the Algerian captives and too little to the African American slaves but rather from too much northern antislavery rhetoric and too little concern with white captives in Africa. Stephens was understandably consumed with the effort to get himself freed and to return to his struggling wife and children. Yet, despite his suffering and degradation in what he and his comrades described as slavery, this Massachusetts native simply could not bring himself to cross the color barrier and identify with enslaved Africans in any way.

At least a dozen works of literature inspired by the Algerian crisis were published in the decade and a half from 1785 to 1800 by Americans who were not themselves captives. These works represented a broad range of genres from poetry, to novels, drama, and history. The volume of publications, the number of genres, and the popularity of many of the pieces reflects the broad influence of events in Algiers on the public imagination. These works also reflect the widespread impact of the post-Revolutionary antislavery movement. The majority explicitly compare Algerian slavery to American slavery, and, unlike the captives themselves, the bulk of these authors also employed the civilization versus savagery trope used by Equiano.

Perhaps the best example is a poem called "The American in Algiers, or the Patriot of Seventy-Six in Captivity" (1797).[16] This poem was really about the contrast between freedom and slavery in America and Algiers. The first half was a captivity narrative told from the perspective of a Revolutionary war veteran who never "dream'd, I serv'd my country eight long years / To end my days in slavery in Algiers." Nonetheless, he was captured by Algerian pirates, brought to Algiers, exhibited at a market, "and by a Moor at public auction bought / In whose dark bosom all the vices reign / The vilest despot and the worst of men." As a result, "Naked and hungry, days, and months, and years / I've served this thankless tyrant in Algiers."[17]

The second part moves away from Algiers, "that piratic coast where slavery reigns / And freedom's champions wear despotic chains," and returns to America, where patriots enslave Africans. This section of the poem takes the form of a slave narrative that is remarkably similar to Olaudah Equiano's story. The narrator was born in West Africa where he lived in peace and freedom until, like Equiano, he was kidnapped with his sister (and unlike Equiano, also with his new bride) and put aboard a "floating hell" of a ship. Like the American patriot (and Equiano) he is finally taken off the ship to be sold, in this case in Baltimore. As the poem ends, he lives on a plantation: "In leaky hutt, all comfortless I lie / Left there alone in fortitude to die."[18]

Like Equiano, the narrator made note of the savagery of the supposedly civilized Americans. In Maryland, he wrote, "The galling whip unceasing greets my ears / Wielded by savage brutes and overseers." The horrors he encounters are "the murders—such the deeds of blood / Vile Christians perpetrate to serve their God / who ne'er taught me his brother to enslave / But dy'd, they boast, all human kind to save." But the author of this poem, unlike Equiano, more frequently contrasts savagery with the secular ideals of the Declaration of Independence than with the teachings of Christianity. After quoting Jefferson's immortal words, the narrator asks, "What then, and are all men created free, / and Afric's sons continue slaves to be?" He later wonders, "Hath not the African as good a right, / Derived from nature to enslave the white?" Throughout, he repeatedly calls the Americans "tyrants" and excoriates them for their "inconstancy": "They fought for freedom, yet enslave the free."[19] In short, their savagery and hypocritical despotism is just as deplorable as that of the patriot's Algerian slave master.

The two major histories of Algiers published in the United States during this period made similar points, although this irony was not really their focus. Mathew Carey's *A Short History of Algiers* (1794) was quite popular and influential. It went through three printings between 1794 and 1805 and was plagiarized by several other authors, including the captive narrator, John Foss.[20] First published shortly after the capture of the eleven American ships in 1793, it provided basic information about Algiers and its history to Americans still shocked that so many of their countrymen were held in captivity in a strange land. Not surprisingly, Carey made much of the Algerians' backwardness and savagery. He wrote of the bloodthirstiness of the ruling deys and the harsh treatment meted out to Christian slaves. But, as has already been noted, he also castigated Americans for their own brutality in carrying out a slave trade "an hundred times" more extensive than that in Algiers. "Before therefore we reprobate the ferocity of the Algerines," he admonished, "we should enquire whether it is not possible to find, in some other regions of the globe, a systematic brutality still more disgraceful?"[21]

James Wilson Stevens's *An Historical and Geographical Account of Algiers* (1797) was far more comprehensive but less influential than Carey's earlier work.[22] Perhaps fewer readers were willing to slog through more than three hundred pages on Algiers than were willing to read Carey's concise seventy-six page account. Those willing to make the effort would be rewarded with the best contemporary account of the American captives, a history based in part on interviews with at least one of the captives and offering a full account of the Algerian crisis from start to finish. Like so many fictional and factual accounts, it was not complimentary toward the Algerians. In his short preface, Stevens writes that they, and all of Africa, were in "a state of the most deplorable barbarism," and he accuses them of lacking civilization (at least since the fall of Carthage) and of being notable for their "villainy." The text maintains this tone, particularly when discussing the cruelty of Algiers' leaders from Barbarossa to the then current dey, who was supposed to have told the American prisoners "in the tone of savage triumph, 'Go now you dogs and eat stones.' "[23] He particularly singles out the overseers of the American captives, who "in their treatment towards the slaves seemed actuated by a principle of the most savage cruelty." Of one of these individuals, he writes, "The inordinate ferocity of the barbarian had proved the death of many a slave."[24]

Yet Stevens was well aware that savage overseers were not unique to Algiers. For the practice of slavery, "The Divans of Great Britain are equally reprehensible," he wrote in the preface to his chapter on "The Slaves of Algiers." From the British, America learned this "execrable practice," and, "The United States, emphatically called the land of liberty, swarm with those semi-barbarians who enthrall their fellow creatures without the least remorse."[25] With these facts in mind, he asks: "With what countenance then can we reproach a set of barbarians, who have only retorted our own acts upon ourselves in making reprisals upon our own citizens? For it is manifest to the world, that we are equally culpable, and in whatever terms of opprobrium we may excoriate the piratic despotism of the Africans, yet all our recriminations will recoil upon ourselves."[26] While Stevens's history was not intended primarily as ironic criticism of the United States, nevertheless, he was an honest enough observer that he could not entirely shut his eyes to the hypocrisy of the citizens of one of the world's largest slaveholding nations criticizing others for owning slaves who happened to be American.

Several fictional prose accounts also dealt with the issue of savagery in Algiers. A writer pretending to have been an "English slave-driver at Algiers" wrote a fictional letter published in the *New York Magazine* in which he reported overseeing, and frequently whipping, twenty Christian slaves in Algiers. In his defense, he writes that, "For one white slave that we have here, the English have ten black ones in the West-Indies, and they use their slaves much more cruelly than we do ours." Even English seamen, he argues, were probably better off becoming Algerian slaves than remaining as sailors who were tyrannized and flogged by their captains. He concludes, "We just do here to the whites what the whites do to the blacks in the West-Indies; only we use them more mercifully."[27] Without knowing whether the author was really English or American, it is hard to be certain whether this piece was originally directed at slaveholders in the United States. At a minimum, the author was using the topic of Algerian slavery to reflect on European savagery. Presumably, by choosing to print it, the editor of the *New York Magazine* was implicitly criticizing the practice of slavery in the new republic.

Two other accounts avoided the Christian savagery trope while still managing to address issues of liberty and tyranny. The shorter and cruder of these pieces, Robert White's "Curious, Historical, and Entertaining" narrative of Algerian captivity was used to fill space in an almanac. The author, who claimed to have been captured while sailing on the American brig *Squirrel* and used as a slave by the Algerians in 1783, appears to have written his story in order to help raise money for the real American captives in Algiers. From start to finish, and without a trace of irony, he condemns the "black, swarthy" Algerians for their "butchery" and "cruelty." By emphasizing and considerably darkening the Algerians' skin color, he equates blackness with savagery. The swarthy Algerians are, according to the author, "the most savage, brutal, inhuman, and *unmanly* set of wretches I ever met with."[28] In a second piece, "The Narrative of the Captivity of John Van Dike," the real captive is a beautiful young woman named Polly Davis.[29] The protagonist, John Van Dike, is captured by Algerians while at sea but never really held in onerous servitude due to a profitable deal with his putative master. Polly, however, is an English captive on the verge of being ravished by her master and added to his seraglio. Van Dike rescues her, and they escape together on a stolen ship. They arrive in England where they get married and, presumably, live happily ever after. The story is clumsy and lacking in charm, and the setting is minimal beyond occasional references to Algerian cruelty and barbarity. It is essentially a damsel-in-distress romance that could take place virtually anywhere. The only real exception comes early on when Van Dike describes his master as having "a fine plantation and a great many slaves," and he deplores "the bad usage of slaves in that country and their buying and selling women, as we do horses and cattle."[30] This description, with its reference to slave plantations, is far more evocative of chattel slavery in the antebellum South than of Algerian captivity. It offers a tantalizing suggestion that perhaps when the author and his American readers envisioned Algerian slavery they imagined it occurring on a sort of racially inverted southern plantation rather than in its typical urban, multiracial North African setting. If so, part of the horrors of Algerian slavery for the American readers may well have been this racial inversion.

The most important play of this period based on the captives' plight, Susanna Rowson's *Slaves in Algiers*, focuses more on gender issues than on slavery. Like most contemporary captivity literature, *Slaves in Algiers* stressed the contrast between liberty and slavery; however, the slaves in the play are really the women who are held in various stages of thralldom by fathers, husband and suitors, rather than the male American captives. In fact, references to Algiers are so generalized that one might even question whether the play had any relation to events in the 1790s. Mrs. Rowson wrote that it was in part based on a much earlier source, the story of the capture of Don Quixote, which in turn was loosely based on Cervantes' own experiences as an Algerian captive. However, Mrs. Rowson also claimed that the thought of writing the play had been "hastily conceived" only two months before the first performance, a claim that would date its composition back to the period of great agitation over the news that the Algerians had captured eleven American ships.[31] Surely, the play's widespread popularity also reflected continued public interest in Algiers.

Only in the end, when the Christian slaves revolt and the dey is captured, does Mrs. Rowson's play seem to refer to chattel slavery, as opposed to the metaphorical slavery of love and marriage. When a Spanish slave urges the Christians to bastinado their former oppressor, their American leader refuses. "We are freemen, and while we assert the rights of men, we dare not infringe the privileges of a fellow-creature," he explains. When the Spaniard presses the issue, insisting the dey should be made a slave, the American heroine responds, "By the Christian law, no man should be a slave; it is a word so abject that, but to speak it dyes the cheek with crimson." The Americans must free themselves, she adds, "but let us not throw on another's neck, the chains we scorn to wear."[32] Like Van Dike's, Rowson's words are ambiguous enough that readers or theater goers could interpret them in a number of ways. But, considering the context of the times and the more explicit statements made by contemporary authors such as Mathew Carey, it seems entirely likely that these lines—few in number but at a climactic moment in the play—were meant as an ironic comment on the hypocrisy of American slavery.

Another contemporary play, David Everett's *Slaves in Barbary,* was far less subtle in its antislavery sentiments. Unlike Rowson's drama, *Slaves in Barbary* did not achieve renown from theatrical performances. Instead, it has gained lasting fame due to its inclusion in Caleb Bingham's *Columbian Orator.* This influential text included a number of short dramas and orations designed to teach students public speaking and to "inspire the pupil with the ardour of eloquence, and the love of virtue."[33] It is perhaps best known today as the book that Frederick Douglass used to teach himself to read. Douglass frequently mentioned it in his memoirs, describing it as a "gem of a book" containing "eloquent orations and spicy dialogues, denouncing oppression and slavery—telling of what had been dared, done and suffered by men, to obtain the inestimable boon of liberty."[34]

Although Douglass never specifically mentioned *Slaves in Barbary,* that play certainly denounced oppression and slavery through a double usage of Equiano's ironic Christian savage trope. Although it was set in Tunis, *Slaves in Barbary* was no doubt written during the Algerian crisis, and the first publication of the *Co-*

lumbian Orator in 1797 coincided with the freeing of the American captives. It is a good bet, therefore, that the author and his readers thought of Algiers and the Americans held captive there when they considered this play. The suspense of *Slaves in Barbary* hinges on Hamet, the bashaw of Tunis. Early on, there are hints that he might be ready to offer kindnesses to some of the slaves, but most of the characters believe that he remains a cruel tyrant. An Italian slave named Ozro condemns him for his participation in the slave trade, declaring, "That ruler has but an ill title to humanity, who suffers his subjects to traffic in the dearest rights of man, and shares himself the execrated commerce." His brother, Amandar, is not so sure. He suggests that Ozro consider their native Venice. "We have seen the Turks sold there in open market, and exposed to all the indignities which we have borne with in Oran," he reminds him.[35]

As the play continues, two recently captured Americans are involved in a similar but still more ironic situation as they suffer through a slave auction. Kidnap, an American slave owner and slave trader, initially refuses to believe that he is now on the other end of the sale after having been captured by the Tunisians. One of his captors relates that after Kidnap was imprisoned, "he ordered six dozen of port, gave Liberty and Independence for a toast, sung an ode to Freedom; and after fancying he had kicked over the tables, broken the glasses, and lay helpless on the floor, gave orders, attended by a volley of oaths, to have fifty of his slaves whipped thirty stripes each; and six more to be hung up by the heels for petitioning him for a draught of milk and water, while he was revelling with his drunken companions."[36] This despot's fate is inadvertently determined by another American, his slave, Sharp. When the Bashaw asks Sharp whether his master is a kind man and if he would like to remain with him, Sharp replies to the Bashaw, whom he mistakes for a "planter," "He will kill me dead! No! No! Let a poor negur live wid a you, masser planter; live wid a masser officer; wid a dat man; or any udder man, for I go back America again; fore I live wid a masser Kidnap again." As a result, the Bashaw orders Kidnap to be sold to the highest bidder and to "let misery teach him what he could never learn in affluence, the lesson of humanity." Sharp is sold quickly enough after being described by the auctioneer as an "honest negro lad, who has been under the benevolent instruction of a task master, and converted to Christianity by lectures applied to the naked back with a rope's end, or nine-tail whip." Sharp's purchaser also buys the African American's former master and plans to have Sharp use an occasional "whip lecture" to instruct Kidnap how to be a slave.[37] Thus the "civilized" Christian master receives his rightful dues at the hands of the "barbarous" North Africans and his own African American slave.

Finally, at the play's end, it is revealed that the Bashaw himself had once been sold into slavery in Venice, only to have been rescued (coincidentally) by the father of Ozro and Amandar. This kindness is the secret source of his magnanimity toward the Christian slaves. "Had it not been for you," he tells the brothers' father, "I might till now have been a slave in Venice."[38] Thus, the unexpected kindness of the Venetian Christians and the all-too predictable savagery of the slaveholding American are both repaid in kind by the eminently civilized Bashaw. Importantly, after all these twists and turns and all the inversions of captor and captive, the great villain is clearly the American slave owner, while the magnanimous hero is the "savage" Bashaw. It is hard to imagine how this little drama could more unequivocally denounce American slaveholders.

Royall Tyler's *The Algerine Captive* (1797), probably the best-known fictional account of Algiers, was published in the same year as the *Columbian Orator* and "The American in Algiers." Like these works, it has a strong antislavery emphasis. The author was a New England jurist and literary figure who, in later life, displayed antislavery sentiment.[39] The first half of Tyler's picaresque novel takes the New England–born hero, Updike Underhill, on a tour throughout the United States. In the South, he professes his New England conscience to be shocked by a minister who, running late for church, takes out his frustration on his slave by "belabor[ing] the back and head of the faulty slave all the way from the water to the church door, accompanying every stroke with suitable language." Unable to find work as a teacher in the South, the medically trained hero eventually becomes ship's surgeon aboard a slave ship (ironically named *Freedom*), where he is shocked by the casual acceptance of humans as property and distressed by his new complicity in the slave trade. Using Underhill's voice, Tyler provides a fairly graphic portrayal of the middle passage that would not have been out of place in an antislavery tract.[40]

In the closing pages of the first book of *The Algerine Captive*, Underhill's ship is captured by an Algerian corsair. The protagonist accepts his plight as punishment for his participation in the slave trade. He prays that "the miseries, the insults, and cruel woundings, I afterwards received when a slave myself, may expiate for the inhumanity I was necessitated to exercise towards these MY BRETHREN OF THE HUMAN RACE." Once on board the Algerian ship, Underhill is touched when one of the African slaves he had treated on the slave ship charitably provides him with water. "Is this," Underhill exclaims, "one of those men, whom we are taught to vilify as beneath the human species, who brings me sustenance, perhaps at the risk of his life, who shares his morsel with one of those barbarous men who had recently torn him from all he held dear, and whose base companions are now transporting his darling son to a grievous slavery?"[41] Once again the Christians are the barbarians, while the Africans (northern and sub-Saharan) seem extraordinarily civilized.

Finally, Tyler echoes Everett in the conversation between the "Mullah" and Underhill cited earlier in this chapter. Here, as the Mullah attempts to convert Underhill to Islam, our hero objects that, "Our religion was disseminated in peace; yours was promulgated by the sword." It is in response to this assertion that the Mullah reminds him that Muslims "gave civil laws to the conquered, according to the laws of nations; but they never forced the conscience of any man." Christians, on the other hand, he insists, have forced their baptized slaves to continue at hard labor. This point is similar to that made in Everett's *Slaves in Barbary* when the Muslim auctioneer describes the African American slave Sharp as having been converted to Christianity "by lectures applied to the naked back with a rope's end," and it certainly comports well with the Christian savage trope found in so much of this literature.[42]

Tyler, Everett, and most of the authors of these literary works realized that the Algerian crisis offered them an opportunity to discuss American slavery in a context that might appeal to readers who would otherwise have little interest in the subject. They could count on the great public engagement in Algiers to sell copies of their work to individuals who would not normally purchase such fare. By setting their tales in a distant and exotic locale, writers could discuss slavery in a way that would be far less controversial and potentially less offensive than narratives set in the United States. Finally, by focusing on white slaves rather than African Americans, these authors would appeal to the sensibilities of readers who, due to racism or disinterest, might not be moved by stories about black slaves.

These literary works were part of what has been described as "an outburst of discussion" about African Americans beginning in the late 1780s and resulting from the formation or revitalization of abolitionist societies throughout America.[43] Like their more literary friends, many abolitionists used the popular interest in the Algerian crisis as a way to bring antislavery arguments into the public eye in a relatively noncontroversial manner. These early abolitionists have often been criticized as timid and paternalistic, and, looked at from one perspective, their use of the Algerian crisis could be seen as a good example of such timidity and, perhaps, even racism.[44] After all, why waste so much effort on a few white "slaves"—who weren't really chattel slaves at all—thousands of miles away, when hundreds of thousands of African Americans remained legally enslaved for life within the United States? On the other hand, abolitionists may well have viewed the Algerian crisis as an entering wedge, a means of enlisting racist or otherwise indifferent Americans in the battle against slavery.

One of the most influential early antislavery organizations was the Pennsylvania Society for Promoting the Abolition of Slavery, which greatly expanded its membership after it was reorganized and revitalized in 1787.[45] At its quarterly meeting in April 1788, members of this society began to consider the problems of the American slaves in Algiers. Several individuals, including Tench Coxe, a prominent merchant and new member of the society, were appointed to serve as a committee "to consider and report on the case of our fellow citizens now in captivity in Algiers." The committee soon determined that "the affecting situation of the Americans now in slavery in Algiers" called "for the attention of every friend of liberty and humanity and particularly of this society whose declared objects are the mitigations of the rigours of slavery and the total abolition of that unjust and cruel practice." The committee began by contacting abolitionists in other cities to gain more information about the captives and to strategize on how to redeem them. By May they had written to Benjamin Russell of Boston and John Jay of New York, who was U.S. secretary of foreign affairs as well as president of the abolitionist New York Manumission Society.[46]

The society also composed a newspaper advertisement seeking further information about the captives and suggestions on how to redeem them. This ad, signed by members of the Algiers committee, eventually ran in papers in Boston and Philadelphia. In it, the committee justified its involvement in this issue by explaining that the mission of the society was "to extend their attention to every species of slavery."[47] Meanwhile, in the society's letter to John Jay, Tench Coxe suggested that the roots of the Algerian crisis reached back to the European powers and their encouragement, or at least lack of discouragement, of the Algerian "rovers." He suggested that the United States consider instituting a small tariff on goods imported from these nations in order to raise the funds to redeem the captives.[48] In essence, the Pennsylvania Society was acting in a manner analogous to modern lobbying organizations, attempting to influence government policy on their particular issue. In a way, the tariff proposal was consistent with their other major effort in 1788: tightening state legislation against importing slaves. Regulating Atlantic trade could help free the Algerian captives and prevent similar incidents in the future, just as it could impede the trade in African American slaves. In his response, Jay lamented the situation of the Algerian captives and praised the Pennsylvania society for its efforts to improve its state's legislation of the slave trade. But, as discussed in chapter 3, he urged the society to stop publicizing its efforts to free the Algerian captives to insure that such publicity would not hinder the government's ability to free them through secret diplomacy.[49] The Pennsylvania society continued to consider the Algerian issue for several more months, but it does not appear to have taken any further action.[50]

Another new member of the Pennsylvania society revived the issue a little more than a year later. That member was the aged Benjamin Franklin, who became president of the reorganized society in 1787. Although a slave owner, over the course of his long life, Franklin had come to see the inhumanity of slavery. In 1790, at the age of eighty-four he most likely was the author of an antislavery petition sent to Congress by the Pennsylvania Abolition Society urging that the blessings of liberty afforded by the new Constitution be extended to the slaves. "These blessings ought rightfully to be administered without distinction of colour to all descriptions of people," the petition insisted. These sentiments prompted an angry response from Georgia congressman James Jackson, who insisted that slavery was an economic necessity and was sanctioned by the Bible as a means of converting the heathen.[51] Franklin was incensed. No doubt remembering the society's earlier conversations about Algiers, he took pen in hand and wrote a satiric letter to the editor of the *Federal Gazette* in which the fictional Divan of Algiers, Sidi Mehemet Ibrahim, gave a proslavery speech that was remarkably similar to Congressman Jackson's. This would prove to be Franklin's last publication. He was already on his deathbed when he wrote it, with a little less than a month left to live.

Franklin's parody makes ample use of the Christian savage trope. The purported author, Sidi Mehemet Ibrahim, is responding to an antislavery petition supposedly submitted by the "Purist" or "Erika" sect. Sidi Mehemet writes that the Christian slaves' own European governments "hold all their subjects in slavery, without exception" and that "even England treats its sailors as slaves." In short, these Europeans "have only exchanged one slavery for another." And, in fact, Algerian slavery is preferable to European slavery because it is enlightened by "the sun of Islamism." Thus Franklin attempts to level the supposed distinction between Christian benevolence and Islamic savagery, much as many of the authors of the literary works about Algiers had done and would continue to do. Franklin, however, pushed the metaphor one step further in the implicit comparison between Sidi Mehemet and Congressman Jackson. The Algerian essentially makes the same points the Georgian had made in his speech. Like Jackson, he asserts that slaves are economically necessary: "If we forbear to make slaves of their [Christian] people, who in this hot climate are to cultivate our lands?" He pleads that eliminating slavery is too expensive and argues that despite the claims in the petition, slavery most definitely had religious sanction: "How grossly are they mistaken to suppose slavery to be disallowed by the Alcoran! Are not the two precepts, to quote no more, '*Masters treat your slaves with kindness; Slaves, serve your masters with cheerfulness and fidelity,*' clear proofs to the contrary?"[52] By putting the arguments made by Jackson (and other proponents of slavery) in the Algerian despot's mouth, Franklin is, of course, suggesting a moral equivalency. Despite Franklin's point that Algerians were no worse than Europeans, he certainly understood that comparing Jackson to a North African Muslim would be taken as a wicked insult rather than as clever irony by the southerner and his supporters.

The publication of Franklin's letter may have influenced two other local discussions of slavery later in 1790. What is most remarkable about these incidents is that they occurred in the slave-owning states of Maryland and South Carolina, where, particularly in the latter, such discussion was far rarer and less free than in the North. It may well be that references to Algiers and reminders of the universally deplored situation of the American captives made such discussion more palatable to individuals otherwise reluctant to speak about American slavery.

The Maryland incident was prompted by a November 1790 letter to the *Maryland Gazette* signed by "A Freeman;" possibly the Methodist preacher Ezekial Cooper. The author began by asking, "Is not LIBERTY the grand American shrine?" Slavery, he continued, contradicted the republican ideals of liberty and freedom. Some argued, he continued, perhaps with Congressman Jackson in mind, that blacks "were providentially intended to be slaves." That position was groundless. Perhaps in consideration of Franklin's satire, he wrote that if such providential arguments were true, then "The Algiers [*sic*] with equal propriety might argue providence in their capturing *Europeans* and *others*, and condemning *them* to slavery." He concludes bitingly, "I can find neither proof nor reason that a difference in colour, features or hair, should distinguish any man as an unhappy subject of bondage."[53] This letter was probably prompted by the discussion occurring within Maryland's House of Delegates over whether manumissions by will should be legalized in that state. In turn, it prompted a rebuttal by an author who conceded that slavery had been a "curse to the southern states" but maintained that abolishing it could wreak economic havoc and possibly cause physical danger to whites from freed slaves if they were able to remain in Maryland. "A Freeman" then responded to these arguments, prompting yet another rejoinder from his opponent.[54] While the Algerian issue was fairly tangential to much of this debate, the Maryland example demonstrates how the plight of the Algerian captives had become a useful tool in the rhetorical arsenal of the early national antislavery movement.

In Charleston, South Carolina, the *Evening Gazette* in the summer of 1790 ran a story that made heavy use of the Christian savagery trope. Although not actually set in Algiers, it shared many features with Franklin's Algerian letter and other similar satires. The author, "T.D." of King Street, reported having taken part in an after dinner conversation about a Frenchman (M. de Brisson) who had been captured by Arabs in the African desert. The entire party, with the exception of one old gentleman, was deeply touched by the Frenchman's plight. A few days later, T.D. met the contrary gentleman on the street and asked him why he seemed to lack sympathy for Brisson. He replied that he did feel pity but that he had no respect for the slaveholder who told the tale: "What rights has a man to expect that I should believe his pity for M. de Brisson in Africa, who has himself at this moment an African starving in the workhouse?" To explain his position, the gentleman gave T.D. a document entitled "The Sufferings of Yamboo, an African, in South Carolina."[55]

This document, "reprinted" by T.D. in the *Gazette*, was purportedly written by a slave who served as overseer on the gentleman's plantation. Purchased at vendue and badly undernourished, Yamboo was "so experienced in planting and so faithful in every trust reposed" that he became responsible for the great prosperity of the old gentleman's plantation. Yamboo's story was much in the vein of Equiano's. Born into a prominent Gambian family, he was captured, underwent the Middle Passage, and was sold to a succession of masters, some extremely cruel. As he draws his account to a close, he pleads with his readers, "Let us be slaves, but do not let the lowest wretches trifle with our very being—do not leave us to the mercy of overseers, whom you would not trust with a favorite horse—whose delight it is to treat us like brutes." T.D. concludes, in his own narrative voice, that it might be interesting to translate Yamboo's story into Arabic. He imagines that the "Talbe of a savage horde" might then read it to "a large circle." In that case, "let anyone assert, if he dare, that [the Africans] would not have as much cause to pity Yamboo amongst us, as we have to pity M. de Brisson when he fell into their hands."[56]

This story bears many of the hallmarks of the Algerian narratives of its era. It uses the savagery versus civilization trope to imply American savagery and African civilization, and it contrasts the plight of a captured Christian in Africa to that of a captured African in America. However, unlike the other narratives considered, its point of entry is the capture of a Frenchman in the North African desert rather than of Americans in Algiers. Charlestonians were well aware of the plight of the Americans in Algiers; their newspaper gave the matter much coverage in the late 1780s. Perhaps the Frenchman's story was used with an eye to southern sensibilities; comparing an African slave to an American captive might have been far more controversial than comparing Yamboo's plight to that of another foreigner. Furthermore, by including the fiction that the story was submitted by a respectable old gentleman who owned many slaves and a prosperous plantation on the Santee, the author might have hoped to deflect any protestations from local planters that the piece was an attack on slave owners. By blunting some of the sharp edges of the African captive genre, he might have hoped that Charlestonians would consider his criticism of slavery instead of immediately rejecting it. He most likely was disappointed in this aspiration. Shortly after Yamboo's story was published, several readers, presumably angry at the attack on slavery, complained to the editor about it. In his defense, the editor wrote that T.D. was "a gentleman of the first rank and fortune, and possessed of as large a share of negro property as most others in the state." The editor also defended his own prior proslavery record, noting that when reprinting the recent congressional debate on the "Quaker petition" against slavery he had "inserted none of the speeches of those who advocated it, because he thought they might be of dangerous tendency in this state."[57]

Both the South Carolina and Maryland editors seem to have employed comparisons between Africa and America as a means of condemning American slavery in a somewhat indirect fashion. They and the authors of the many contemporary narratives about white Americans in Algiers attempted to criticize slavery without getting bogged down in issues of racial inferiority. Condemning African American slavery outright could open up a Pandora's box of racial concerns. By condemning enslavement of whites rather than of blacks, these authors no doubt hoped that readers might momentarily be able to separate the inherent evils of slavery from the racist justifications underpinning that institution in America. The Charleston newspaper resorted to this same strategy some four years later when it reprinted lengthy antislavery extracts from Mrs. Rowson's play, *Slaves in Algiers*.[58] Such a strategy could backfire, as the reaction to the T.D. piece reveals, and there was no guarantee that even readers who enjoyed tales of white slaves in Africa would take the next step and condemn slavery at home. But in the Deep South particularly, where even in the relatively abolitionist 1780s and 1790s antislavery protestations were rare, it might have been one of the only feasible methods.[59] Surely humorous satires such as those of Franklin and many contemporary fiction writers and playwrights went down more easily than the more explicit petitions drafted by the Pennsylvania Abolition Society and similar organizations.

Ultimately, however, the failure of late eighteenth-century abolitionism, particularly in the South, suggests that American notions of racial inferiority were already so deeply ingrained that the Christian savage trope could have only a limited effect. In order to succeed it would have had to accomplish two difficult tasks. First, it would have had to transcend race at least temporarily in order to create an equivalency between black and white slaves in American minds. Like Captain Stephens, most white Americans probably had neither the imagination nor the desire to see such a moral equivalency. Secondly, it would have had to create an equivalency between "savage" African slaveholders and "savage" American slave holders, which, as the reaction to T.D.'s story shows, was also no easy task. In the end "tawny" skin, savagery, and slavery were simply too tightly connected in too many Americans' minds for this approach to have widespread success. Nevertheless, American antislavery activists such as Frederick Douglass, Charles Sumner, and Abraham Lincoln continued to be influenced by and to employ the metaphors of Barbary slavery to fight slavery at home throughout the antebellum period.[60]

CHAPTER FIVE

Captive Nation

Algiers and Independence

When James Cathcart began to write his memoirs, he described himself and his fellow Algerian captives as "victims of independence." In 1785 this would have been an apt description for the United States as a whole. The independence achieved in 1783 created new problems abroad and led to a severe economic crisis, which would in turn lead to internal violence in places like western Massachusetts. Rather than celebrating triumph over the world's greatest superpower, post-Revolutionary Americans wondered whether they could long survive as an independent nation. Ordinarily, the capture of twenty-one seamen in a remote corner of the world might not seem all that important. America wondered, however, whether the capture foretold an inability to pursue commerce as an independent nation without the aid of the British empire and whether it would be forced to slip into postcolonial dependence on the former mother country. Thus the misfortune of the *Dauphin* and the *Maria* became a national tragedy.

Before the Revolution, Algiers had not been an issue precisely because of the colonies' position within the British empire. Blessed with superior naval power, Britain was able to negotiate alliances with Algiers on favorable terms. So long as they were protected by the British flag, American colonists had little trouble with the Barbary "pirates." After the Revolution, when they could no longer depend on this protection, Americans were confronted with the truth that all adolescents must one day learn: independence comes with new responsibilities as well as new freedom. At least one report from the mother country chortled at the new nation's hard lesson. "How different is the case now from what it was," observed one London newspaper, recalling that before independence "the American vessels could sail secure, and had no other enemy to dread but the wind and waves!"[1]

Far from being organic and timeless entities, modern nation-states have been constructed to some extent by their inhabitants. The United States is a prime example. In 1775 it was a collection of colonies with widely varying histories, settled by peoples from throughout the Atlantic world following different religions, speaking different tongues, and practicing different forms of government. By July 1776, with the stroke of a pen this motley assortment had become "one people" ready to "dissolve the political bands which have connected them with another." Strictly speaking, it was the ensuing Revolution that separated the putative United States from Great Britain. But, historians emphasize that it was the Declaration and other writings, celebrations, and newly contrived rituals that constructed a new nation.[2] This notion of constructedness implies a group of people securely in control of the process of creating nationhood. That certainly was not the case in the United States. Nations, whether ancient or newly declared, are rarely left alone for long, and their relations with the outside world are just as likely to affect their sense of identity as are carefully constructed domestic rituals and celebrations. The most obvious example is the newly declared French *état*, the nature of which after 1791 was influenced as much by its ongoing warfare with European monarchies as by domestic rituals celebrating *liberté, egalité,* and *fraternité*. America's Algerian crisis was hardly as dramatic, but because it occurred when it did, it had an inordinate influence on the new nation's sense of identity. Unlike the Declaration and the popular fêtes of the early republic, its influence was largely a negative one, leading Americans to see their nation as weak and generally incompetent in its relations with the outside world.

The initial impact of the Algerian captures was enormous. As the new nation digested the first reports, Louis Guillaume Otto, the French chargé d'affaires in New York wrote, "The hostilities of the Barbarian corsairs have made a great sensation in America."[3] In Paris, Thomas Jefferson publicly discounted the danger, claiming it was exaggerated by the British press. But privately he was terrified that his daughter Polly might be captured during the 1785 crisis. "My mind revolts at the possibility of a capture," he wrote her uncle, Francis Eppes, "so that unless you hear from myself . . . that peace is made with the Algerines, do not send her but in a vessel of French or English property; for these vessels alone are safe from prizes by the barbarians." He was so concerned that he repeated this advice in two subsequent letters to Eppes.[4] Even the most confirmed landlubbers reacted on a personal level, particularly in the port cities, where the next captured ship might contain one's daughter, husband, father, mother, or wife. In 1790 Virginia's George Mason urged his son John not to sail in the Mediterranean as "the danger of falling into the hands of the Algerines is such a shocking circumstance, as I would have you by all means avoid." Similarly, just after the second round of captures, Hyram Faris of Annapolis pleaded with his brother to cancel his voyage to Amsterdam "on account of the Algerines." His brother, St. John, was less concerned. He "laughed" at the report and continued his preparations. Charles Carroll of Carrollton also hesitated to send his children across the Atlantic in an American ship due to the "piratical" threat.[5]

Other families had moved beyond concern to despair and back to hope. There are three documented cases of predatory grifters claiming to have seen missing Americans in Algiers, and almost certainly there were many more undocumented cases.[6] In the documented cases the families of the missing men were skeptical enough to ask public officials to investigate the grifters' stories. William Livingston of New Jersey, for example, wrote that Charles Blinkhorn "makes such mistakes in his description of [John Livingston] as that he is lame, has a cast in his left eye, and a scar on his forehead, tho' he declares that he has frequently messed with him, and with him been harnessed to the same carriage, as to induce a strong suspicion of his veracity."[7] Yet despite these and even more obvious lies on Blinkhorn's part, Livingston still had some hope that the story of his son's slavery was true, if only because the alternative was even bleaker. Yet this alternative, death at sea, was a commonplace in the eighteenth century, when uncertainty and sudden death were all too prevalent. The prospect of Algerian captivity was perhaps not the most terrifying thing in this world, but the plights of Livingston and others concerned about sea-going relations show that the events of the 1780s had made it a real and pervasive fear.

This fear can also be seen in the many erroneous rumors given credence by American newspapers, which frequently published reports of American ships captured by Algerians. In 1786 alone, there were at least nine such reports, yet the only two American ships captured by Algerians and their crews enslaved during these years were, of course, the *Dauphin* and *Maria* in 1785. A few other American ships seem to have been captured without their crews, so it is possible that some of these newspaper reports had some basis in fact, but most seem to have been wildly erroneous conjecture made believable by pervasive fear after the 1785 captures. Another report that was certainly false was the famous rumor,

*Number of Newspaper Reports of American Ships
Captured by Algerians (excluding the
Maria and Dauphin)*

Year	No. of Reports
1785	2
1786	9
1787	3
1788	1
1789	1

Sources: Boston Gazette, Oct. 31, 1785; Jan. 2, 1786; Mar. 6, 1786;
July 1, 1786; May 7, 1787; July 23, 1787; Nov. 16, 1789; *Charleston
Evening Gazette / Columbian Herald,* Apr. 3, 1786; Apr. 7, 1786; May
17, 1786; July 19, 1786; *Pennsylvania Gazette,* Apr. 23, 1785; May 9,
1787; Oct. 8, 1788; *Maryland Gazette,* Apr. 20, 1786; Nov. 9, 1786.

also in 1786, that Benjamin Franklin was captured by Algerians and borne into slavery on his return from Paris.[8]

Even more hysterical were the reports that Algerians were making their way toward America to terrorize the new nation. These fears lay behind the cold reception received by three Algerian visitors to Virginia in November 1785. The Commonwealth detained the Algerians under lock and key in various locations before interrogating them. The interrogation failed to determine their business in Virginia or even to ascertain that they were indeed Algerian. In the climate of fear, the strangers' North African origins and the mysteriousness of their business led the Virginia legislature to deport them out of the state and to grant the governor power to deport any other suspicious aliens. Two of the group reappeared in Charleston a few months later. There, newspapers reported, an unspecified question asked by a Charlestonian, perhaps pertaining to the threat that they allegedly posed to America, caused one of them to "draw a dirk" and attempt to stab the questioner. The Algerians were once again locked up and, presumably, eventually deported.[9] This incident, no doubt, made Charlestonians more susceptible to reports in 1786 that the Algerians were on their way to the nearby West Indies, allegedly on a "cruise for American vessels."[10]

While fear of personal captures contributed to the hysteria, Americans also worried about more pecuniary matters. Every captured ship contained a cargo as well as a crew, and even if the crew were to escape the cargo would be lost. The *Dauphin,* for example, carried a shipment of salt and nine hundred crowns in cash.[11] Because of timing, the significance of the losses was far greater than just these goods. The year 1785 marked a low ebb for the American economy during the postwar depression. Avenues of trade in the British world that had been open to the colonies were, if not completely shut, at least narrowed, and merchants suffered from a double whammy of inflation and a glut of British goods. In the cities, artisans unable to sell their own products due to this glut called for heavy protective tariffs. One of the few bright spots in this doleful situation was the prospect of increased Mediterranean trade, perhaps with the help of French allies.[12] The Algerian captures threatened to destroy this hope by shutting the United States out of the Mediterranean altogether. Even those captains brave enough to risk capture had to contend with the prospect of exorbitant insurance rates that would capture any profits not stolen by the Algerians. Americans in the port cities were well aware of these concerns. An American in the British West Indies wrote, "As to trade, our commercial gentlemen have made a few paltry attempts to keep it afloat, but without success. The Algerians have put an entire stop to all sort of traffick in American bottoms." In New York a writer reported that "the Mediterranean [was] shut to America by the depredations of the Barbary corsairs [and] the French and British West India Islands [were] refusing admittance to American vessels but in a very limited way." A Philadelphian who contended that the Algerian danger was exaggerated nonetheless conceded that Mediterranean commerce could only improve should American negotiations with the Moroccans and "the detested nest of Algerine plunderers" yield peace and lower insurance rates.[13] Thus, all Americans, not just the captives, seemed "victims of independence" in 1786.

An important aspect of diplomacy is to create a positive image of one's nation in foreign capitals; hence, Benjamin Franklin's famous choice of plain, "rustic" American clothing in France to emphasize the new nation's republican spirit. In the case of the United States, foreign diplomacy also helped to shape the new nation's image at home. American statecraft in the 1780s produced a sense of dismay and helplessness, largely because of the manifest failures in Algiers. Even before the United States took any action, the diplomatic conundrum in Algiers accentuated America's weakness. There were essentially three responses open to the new nation, as Thomas Jefferson himself noted at the start of the crisis.[14] First, the United States could attempt to force the Algerians to free the captives and respect American shipping. Second, the new nation could negotiate a settlement with Algiers that would include some form of ransom or tribute. Finally, Americans could withdraw from the carrying trade, thereby washing their hands of the Mediterranean altogether. Jefferson, John Adams, and other diplomatic leaders discussed all of these options, as did the public at large.

Few Americans took the first option seriously, particularly during the early stages of the crisis. That the new nation had no navy whatsoever made it highly improbable that it could force the Algerians to release the captives. The one possibility was for the United States to ally itself with other powers. This was the course favored by Jefferson, who went so far as to draw up papers for an unusual multinational alliance against the Barbary States. Jefferson hoped this alliance would initially include the United States, Naples, and Portugal, and eventually many other small European states. A few scattered, mildly hopeful references to a potential alliance made their way into the American press. Given the general indifference to Jefferson's pet project at home and abroad, however, most Americans probably agreed with the assessment of a London observer reprinted in the Charleston press that "such a union is difficult to bring about, and almost always ineffectual when brought about."[15] At best then, this option was a long shot, and the need for such an alliance put the United States solidly in the ranks of Europe's weakest powers.

The second option, negotiating a tribute or essentially paying protection money to Algiers, garnered more public approval. In New York, Louis Guillaume Otto wrote Jefferson that "several people support the war, but more would prefer to pay an annual tribute, provided it will not be excessive." Like most supporters of this option, John Adams preferred it because it seemed cheaper and more practical than building a navy. Yale University president Ezra Stiles agreed with Jefferson that "Algiers must be subdued." As this option was not immediately practicable, Stiles explained, "In the meantime we must expend £200,000 and subsidize that piratical state." The subsidy would be beneficial because commerce thereby reopened would likely be worth at least the price of tribute. A New Yorker believed that if the United States were to send a diplomat to Algiers with a frigate, presumably as tribute to the dey, "those unhappy [prisoners] would be relieved, and our trade to Europe rendered safe."[16]

For Adams, this debate rapidly took on an air of futility. After discussing the matter back and forth with Jefferson, he concluded that "neither force nor money will be applied." His logic was depressing but prophetic: "Our states are so backward that they will do nothing for some years. If they get money enough to discharge the demands upon them in Europe, already incurred, I shall be agreeably disappointed. A disposition seems rather to prevail among our citizens to give up all ideas of navigation and naval power, and lay themselves consequently at the mercy of foreigners, even for the price of their produce. It is their concern, and we must submit, for your plan of fighting will no more be adopted than mine of negotiating." While Adams found this prospect "humiliating," others were more optimistic. A Baltimore newspaper correspondent wrote that the situation offered the United States the opportunity to wash its hands of Europe, improve its own manufactures, and render itself "a great, a happy and truly independent people."[17] Perhaps the writer was part of the movement to encourage American manufactures, which became extremely influential in the mid-1780s when urban artisans and merchants pushed the state governments to implement protective tariffs against the European powers.[18] In the long run this approach might lead to a stronger, more self-sufficient United States. That many Americans were willing to support it in 1785 also reflected a great deal of pessimism about the ability of the new nation to succeed in foreign trade. Thus, consideration of all three potential responses to the Algerian crisis—fighting, negotiation, and withdrawal—brought Americans back to the sad certainty of their national weakness.

Even before the first captures, American negotiators had been making their way to Morocco and Algiers in an effort to keep the Mediterranean trade open to the new nation. Unfortunately, the agent to Algiers, Captain John Lamb, did not arrive until after the captures. Thus he was faced with an unexpected double task—negotiating a peace treaty and redeeming the captives. Still, newspaper reports expressed some hope. A correspondent in Madrid reported that Lamb and his secretary, Paul R. Randall, had arrived there in March and had succeeded in gaining strong Spanish backing before making their way across the Mediterranean to Algiers. Similarly, a correspondent from New York conveyed news from Morocco, which, he believed, "gives reason to hope that the negotiations with Morocco and Algiers will issue successfully for the United States."[19]

While negotiations in Morocco did proceed successfully, hopes for Algiers were short lived. The same day that it printed the optimistic New Yorker's report, the *Boston Gazette* also published the disquieting rumor that redemption of the twenty-one Americans in Algiers alone would cost at least $27,528, more than a third of the total money allocated by Congress to ransom the captives and negotiate peace treaties with all three Barbary states.[20] By July, a Newburyport correspondent wrote that, due to the anticipated expenses, "There is not, in my opinion, [much] probability of a peace with the Barbary Powers." By late summer and early fall, the news from Algiers appeared hopeless. The *Gazette* printed a report that Lamb had returned to Alicante, "having been able to do nothing." That same month, the *Maryland Gazette* printed a report from London that Lamb and Randall "have returned without having effected their purpose, and even without any hopes of success."[21]

In diplomatic circles the situation looked even worse. Early successes in Morocco had engendered some enthusiasm. Lamb himself confidently wrote foreign secretary John Jay, "I do not believe that the Algerians will refuse a treaty, but I cannot say at what price until I am their [*sic*]." This sunny prelude made the reality more appalling. On his long-delayed arrival in Algiers, Lamb learned that the dey absolutely refused to discuss a peace treaty. He did consent to discuss ransoming the American captives, but Lamb reported to Adams, "I am assured and by good authority that they will cost upword [*sic*] of thirty five thousand dollars." This figure was far above that reported by the *Boston Gazette* later that spring and nearly ten times the amount of two hundred dollars per captive that Lamb was authorized to spend. To Jefferson, Lamb reported similar figures, noting, "Your Excellency sees how feable [*sic*] we are." Unfortunately, Lamb's negotiations only drove the price higher. After waiting more than a week, he was finally permitted to meet with the dey, who, Lamb reported, set "an exorbitent price, far beyond my limitts [*sic*]" for redeeming the captives. Over the next two weeks he had two more interviews. At the last meeting, the dey relented a bit, setting the price of the captives at $59,496.[22]

Even before this fiasco there had been questions about Lamb's fitness for the job. His qualifications were and are unclear, beyond the fact that this Connecticut Yankee apparently had spent several years in Morocco. It is not clear what he did there, although there is some insinuation that he was a horse and mule trader. According to James Monroe, the committee on foreign affairs had recommended against Lamb's appointment despite support for his candidacy from Foreign Secretary Jay and Samuel Huntington, then president of Congress. Congress ignored the committee's recommendation, much to Monroe's dismay. Lamb was, Monroe wrote Jefferson soon after the appointment, "from his station in life and probable talents, by no means worthy of such a trust." Certainly, Lamb's letters show a tenuous grasp of spelling and punctuation, even for an age when there was little standardization in these matters. Perhaps to keep an eye on Lamb, Congress appointed Randall, a smart young New Yorker, as his secretary. At almost the first opportunity, Lamb dispatched Randall from Algiers to carry messages to Adams and Jefferson warning that the dey was expected to ask very high prices for the captives. Randall must have been afraid that this peremptory action would suggest some malfeasance on his part, for he took the unusual step of securing a letter from Lamb praising his conduct and asserting he had committed no financial irregularities. Randall was less generous to his boss. He implied to Jefferson that Lamb sent him away for no real reason. "I asked Mr. Lamb what I could say to the Minister except that the Dey had refused to treat of peace," Randall wrote, but Lamb "would make me no reply or give me any instructions."[23]

As more news of Lamb's mission seeped out of Algiers, his reputation sunk further among his fellow diplomats. Thomas Barclay, the American agent to Morocco, wrote from Madrid of receiving a letter written in Lamb's typical style. "Mr. Lamb's letter is short and obscure nor do I understand the whole of it," Barclay wrote, adding with some consternation that Lamb apparently planned to return to Spain for further orders without, Barclay believed, ever meeting with the dey. In London, Adams fulminated that Lamb had not written him for months and that Randall was missing in action. He recommended that both be recalled as soon as possible and that the United States cease all negotiations with the Barbary States on the grounds that, "It will be only so much cash thrown away [and] it will only increase our embarrassment, make us and our country ridiculous, and irritate the appetite of these barbarians." In Hartford on a brief respite from his diplomatic duties, David Humphreys reported that many in Lamb's home state shared the diplomatic community's opinion of him. "Lamb's conduct in obtaining his appointment is considered as very extraordinary; his character is perhaps much lower here than we could have conceived," he wrote in the spring of 1786.[24]

The sequel seems to have confirmed some of these concerns. After leaving Algiers, Lamb, citing ill health, refused to return to the United States or to meet Adams and Jefferson in Europe. Jefferson strongly suspected him of stealing much of the money appropriated for his mission. Whatever the fate of those funds, Lamb did not use them to pay the Spanish captain he hired to deliver his report to Congress. Months later, Randall met that unfortunate mariner walking the streets of New York without friends or money, carrying, according to Randall, only empty promises from Lamb. Randall, too, was burned by the episode; as late as 1788 Congress had still failed to pay him the 150 guineas Adams and Jefferson had promised him as Lamb's secretary.[25]

The failure was not entirely Lamb's fault. Jefferson noted, "An Angel sent on this business, and so much limited in his terms, could have done nothing," and other diplomats agreed. Even Sidi Hassan, the dey's heir apparent, put in a good word for the old mule trader.[26] In the end, it did not really matter whether these diplomatic failures were the result of Lamb's ineptitude, his avarice, or the inherent difficulties of his situation. The remarkably negative reports that reached the diplomatic community and the public had damaged the national psyche. America, it seemed, was not only a third-rate power, it was also remarkably incompetent.

The public attributed much of the blame for this disaster to Congress's ineptness. In early 1786 a Charlestonian speculated, "Perhaps Congress have not been as alert in this business as they should: for certain it is, that a long period has now elapsed and nothing been done." In a widely republished newspaper article, a New Yorker complained that problems in the Mediterranean resulted from Congress's feebleness. "The union of the thirteen states is much too weak, even to combat the machinations of any petty Prince, however contemptible, who shall chuse to insult the American flag." Not only was Congress politically weak, it was also fiscally frail. This impecuniousness made a resolution of the Mediterranean issue impossible according to one New Yorker, who wrote, "There is not in my opinion, any possibility of peace with the Barbary powers. Congress are destitute of that which alone can obtain it."[27]

Diplomats, too, linked Congress's weakness to the Algerian crisis. Jefferson, in particular, saw the problem as a lack of national power. "The Algerines will probably do us the favour to produce a sense of the necessity of a public treasury and a public force on that element where it can never be dangerous [i.e., a navy]," he wrote David Humphreys. To Monroe he expressed the hope that enthusiasm for his pet project of an alliance against Algiers might spur the states to find a way to overcome the fiscal weakness that made it so difficult for Congress to raise a navy. While fiscal difficulties inhibited resolution of the Algerian crisis, Jefferson also realized that the continuation of the crisis deepened America's economic woes. He blamed Shays's Rebellion in Massachusetts partially on disruptions in the fish trade so vital to northern New England. "Much of [New England's] fish went up the Mediterranean, now shut to us by the pyratical states," he wrote. Thus, he concluded, the rioters faced mounting debt, while, due to the economic disruption caused by the Algerian crisis, "the means of payment have lessened."[28]

Foreign Secretary Jay strongly believed that Lamb's problems in Algiers reflected structural flaws inherent in the Articles of Confederation. Congress depended on voluntary contributions from the states to raise money for a peace treaty or for any other purpose. Therefore, before any action could be taken, Congress must persuade the states to contribute funds. Jay recommended Congress transmit "a fair and accurate state of the matter" to the states to convince them of the need for money and that it remind the states "that until such time as they furnish Congress with their respective portions of that sum, the depredations of those barbarians will, in all probability, continue and increase." Privately, he was not hopeful. In late 1786 he wrote, "The situation of our captive countrymen at Algiers is much to be lamented, and the more so as their deliverance is difficult to effect." He explained, "Congress cannot command money for that, nor indeed for other very important purposes; their requisitions produce little, and government (if it may be called government) is so inadequate to its objects, that essential alterations or essential evils must take place."[29]

For Jay, then, foreign policy embarrassments, particularly in Algiers, were a crucial reason for writing and ratifying a new Constitution. In his contributions to the *Federalist Papers*, he stressed the importance of the Constitution in insuring national safety, which, he noted could be endangered by "foreign arms and influence" (such as the Algerian cruisers) as well as by "domestic causes" (such as Shays's Rebellion). A strong union, he argued, would be less likely to become embroiled in wars, in part because of its strength. "It is well known," he wrote, "that acknowledgments, explanations, and *compensations* are often accepted as satisfactory from a strong united nation, which would be rejected as unsatisfactory if offered by a state or a confederacy of little consideration or power."[30] In other words, a stronger federal government would be in a better position to negotiate a less expensive treaty with Algiers.

Jay made this point more explicitly in a less famous pro-ratification essay entitled "An Address to the People of New York." Here he complained: "[Congress] may make war, but they are not empowered to raise men or money to carry it on. They may make peace, but without the means to see the terms of it observed. They may form alliances, but without ability to comply with the stipulations on their part. They may enter into treaties of commerce, but without power to enforce them at home or abroad." Thus, even though the Articles of Confederation granted Congress wide responsibilities in issues of foreign affairs, that body's inability to raise funds undercut its power. From this "new and wonderful system of government," Jay continued, "it has come to pass that almost every national object of every kind is at this day unprovided for; and other nations, taking the advantage of its imbecility, are daily multiplying commercial restraints upon us." These constraints, as he enumerated them, included British incursions into the American Northwest, all sorts of European offences in the West Indies, and finally, the fact that "the Algerines exclude us from the Mediterranean and adjacent countries; and we are neither able to purchase nor to command the free use of those seas."[31]

Considering these arguments, it is clear that the debate over the Constitution was not merely a rational Enlightenment discussion of the advantages and disadvantages of a proposed frame of government. It also tied in to deep emotional anxieties about the emerging national identity. Historians have long disputed whether conditions in the mid-1780s were as critical as the supporters of the Constitution described them. In the economic realm, at least, it now appears as though a recovery was under way in many places well *before* the Constitution was ratified. But in this discussion, those sorts of facts were not necessarily paramount. What was crucial was the sense of national weakness that emerged from the various crises of this period, not the least of which was the reaction to the Algerian captures. Ratification, then, was an effort to exorcize this spirit of weakness from the national psyche.

While the first Algerian captures contributed to an inward-looking discourse on national weakness, the second round led many to lash out at an external enemy: England. Strangely, considering the history of relations between the West and the Islamic world, the press in the 1780s did little to vilify Algerians beyond the usual references to "Barbarians" or "pirates." This lack of interest probably reflected equal measures of contempt and self-centeredness. Americans were so concerned with their internal weaknesses and lowly position in the world of European statecraft that they had little time to devote to contemplation of Algiers. Furthermore, those "contemptible banditti," as David Humphreys called them, may have seemed unworthy of consideration. As early as 1785, a few Americans had seen the hand of their former mother country behind the captures. Ralph Izard of South Carolina wrote Jefferson that "it is said that Great Britain has encouraged the piratical states to attack our vessels." Such conjecture may have appealed to Americans who believed, as one Philadelphian did, that in the wake of the Revolution, Britain hoped "to destroy without possibility of redemption, the trade and manufactures of America" or who doubted Algiers was capable of causing so much trouble without assistance.[32] While this sort of anti-British rhetoric was particularly popular with pro-tariff mechanics, it generally did not spread to those concerned with overseas trade. American ship captains continued to fly British flags when approached by Algerians, and newspapers reassuringly reported that Britain condoned such measures.[33] It was almost as though, despite the Revolution, Americans still instinctively turned to their mother country for protection or, conversely, saw it as the cause of all their troubles.

This instinct applied to the first captives, too. Captain O'Brien reported that of all the European consuls in Algiers, only Charles Logie, the British consul, helped them. He took O'Brien and the two other captains into his house, an act of apparent generosity that O'Brien frequently brought to the attention of American diplomats.[34] It was probably this praise that prompted American newspapers to commend Logie for his civility. The *Boston Gazette* reported that "Mr. Logie . . . has behaved with a deal of humanity towards the American captains," while Charleston's *Evening Gazette* wrote that the captains "found in Mr. Logie, the British Consul, an active, valuable friend." In London, John Adams made a point of conveying to Logie through O'Brien "my sincere thanks for his humane attention to you and your fellow sufferers."[35]

This era of good feelings did not last long. O'Brien became disillusioned by early 1786, when he reported that Logie "treated us with indifference" and that the American captains left his house for that of a French merchant. They were glad, he wrote, to be "relieved from a dependence so humiliating to Americans." Thus reenacting their country's revolution, they rejected dependence on their "mother" Britain in favor of a more equal alliance with the French.[36] O'Brien's distrust of Logie grew throughout 1786 despite, or perhaps because of, the fact that the consul and Lamb became "bosom friends." Logie's about face in his behavior toward the Americans, O'Brien speculated, actually masked an effort to torpedo Lamb's peace overtures, which Logie may have feared would allow American ships to carry the new nation's produce throughout the Mediterranean, thereby loosening American merchants' dependence on British ships. O'Brien accused Logie of notifying British authorities when Algerian vessels were cruising for victims in order to prompt English insurers to raise rates on American ships. The American also charged that British officials spread exaggerated reports of the dangers to American commerce in order to keep insurance rates high and squeeze Americans out of the Mediterranean trade. O'Brien was not alone in this supposition; Thomas Jefferson frequently complained that the British press exaggerated the danger from the Algerians.[37]

It is difficult to know whether Logie really was subverting Lamb. Some of O'Brien's logic is plausible. However, all accounts agree that Logie was somewhat erratic and perhaps an alcoholic to boot. Even after 1786, he made several efforts to get the American captives redeemed, which probably indicates some good will, although freeing the existing captives was more a humanitarian measure than a long-term solution to the Algerian threat to American shipping.[38] Whatever motivated Logie and Whitehall, the American press began to follow O'Brien in taking a more suspicious attitude toward British activity in the Mediterranean after 1786. The *Boston Gazette*, previously complimentary to Logie and British efforts to protect Americans, printed a violently anti-British piece in the summer of 1787. The author, apparently from Portsmouth, New Hampshire, wrote that "step dame Britain still considers us her rebellious children and seems disposed to whip us into obedience." Continuing the metaphor, the author described Britain scolding the Americans: "See, you unruly boys, I only 'cry'd havock, and let loose the dogs of war' upon you, my beloved and adopted children, the Algerines." Yet, as late as 1788, the *Maryland Gazette*, which frequently counseled suspicion of

British actions in Algiers, printed a letter praising Logie for aiding the American captives.[39]

During the second round of captures, this incipient Anglophobia dominated the American reaction to the Algerian crisis. That the Algerian-Portuguese truce that made the 1793 captures possible was engineered by Charles Logie himself served as a red flag.[40] Many of the early press reports stressed British involvement in the truce. A correspondent to Charleston's *Columbian Herald* who had just returned from Gibraltar reported, "It is generally thought, in that place [the truce] was put on foot at the instigation of the British ministry, in order to exclude American vessels from participating in the trade of the Mediterranean." A letter from an American in Lisbon presented similar suspicions. He wrote, "The negotiation of peace with the Algerines, was executed by our *old friends the British,* unknown to this court, in order to drag us into this fatal war."[41]

Such suspicions were widely shared by America's diplomatic corps. In Gibraltar, David Humphreys wrote that the truce was "effected by Mr. Logie," although, he added, "there are strong circumstances to induce me to believe, it was without the authority or even the knowledge of his own court." From Lisbon, Edward Church confirmed Logie's role in the truce, which Church viewed as part of a coherent British anti-American strategy. British conduct in the affair, he wrote, "proves that their envy, jealousy, and hatred, will never be appeased, and that they will leave nothing unattempted to effect our ruin."[42] Perhaps the most vituperative response came from Nathaniel Cutting, a junior diplomat who accompanied David Humphreys on his failed 1794 mission to Algiers. While he was writing his report to Secretary of State Jefferson, Cutting happened to notice Logie walking by his window. The sight of the now former consul unleashed a flood of condemnation. Logie had maintained to Humphreys that he was innocent of plotting against the Americans. But Cutting would have none of it. Logie, he wrote, "like many other agents of British perfidy . . . pretends to entertain a great degree of friendship to the United States," while, in effect, stabbing his so-called "friends" in the back.[43]

American diplomats were now skittish about British plots even when Logie and his countrymen seemed cooperative, as in the strange case of William Chapman and John Cooper. Cooper, a resident of Suffolk, Virginia, was an old acquaintance of Peter Walsh, the American consul in Cadiz. In May of 1793 he wrote Walsh that he was tired of living in the United States and planned to move abroad. He sent Chapman, an English associate, ahead to Cadiz with a letter of introduction to Walsh. Chapman continued on, as the Americans later learned, to Algiers. In November, after the new captures, he returned to Gibraltar on his way to England. There he allegedly voiced strong anti-American opinions. This combination of circumstances—his Englishness, the visit to Algiers, and his anti-American attitude—greatly worried America's diplomats in the Mediterranean. A later rumor that Cooper was a "Mahometan" who "most cordially hated all Christians" confirmed their suspicions. Even the "perfidious" Logie would have nothing to do with Chapman and expelled him from Algiers as a "suspicious character."[44]

The exact nature of the alleged plot remained unclear, but the Americans suspected Chapman and Cooper hoped to gain permission from the dey to capture American ships as Algerian privateers. Humphreys recalled that "the British consul for Morocco some time since told me himself that General [Benedict] Arnold once applied to him to use his influence in negotiating with Algiers or some of the Barbary states, for commissions to cruise against nations with which the powers were at war . . . meaning principally the Americans." Was Cooper a new Benedict Arnold scheming in Virginia to betray America to the British via the Algerians? If so, his expectation of British assistance must have come from the widespread belief that Logie and his government were behind the Algerian captures. Even if Cooper was no Benedict Arnold, the episode reflects diplomats' continuing fears of anti-American plots involving the British and their "stepchildren," the Algerians. The danger seemed serious enough at the time that even members of Congress were made aware of it.[45]

If there was ever a time to worry about world events, it was late 1793 when the Terror and Anglo-French hostilities intensified following the execution of Louis XVI. In this context, American fear of international plots becomes more understandable. Many Francophiles suspected that the Algerian captures were part of a British plot to get at France through her American ally. Joel Barlow assumed the whole affair was "a manoeuvre of the English, to prevent our provisions coming to France, and at the same time to injure America." A Bostonian warned that Britain had "covenanced with Spain, Portugal, Russia, and even with the Algerines! to destroy the liberties of France and America."[46] These Anglophobes were on the right track in connecting the Portuguese-Algerian truce to the war with France, but there is no evidence that revenge against America was an important motive. In retrospect it is apparent that Whitehall's primary motivation was the less sinister goal of freeing up Portuguese ships to assist in the allies' struggle with France.[47]

In 1793 and 1794 Americans simply did not have the necessary perspective to realize that the fate of a hundred or so Americans in Algiers was, at best, peripheral to England's foreign policy. Nathaniel Cutting, stewing over Consul Logie's "perfidy" saw the events in the Mediterranean as just one piece in a larger British plot. He observed: "It is evident that the English government has ever been jealous of the growing greatness of the United States of America and on numerous occasions has betrayed a gloomy apprehension that the increasing splendour of their stars would rapidly gain such an ascendancy in the hemisphere of Human Glory as must necessarily eclipse the declining rays of their imaginary omnipotence which English arrogance has so long vaunted." To support these charges Cutting cited "ungenerous restrictions . . . early imposed on our commerce," which meant, primarily, restrictions on the West India trade. Next, he cited "the unjust detention of the Posts on our Western Frontiers, and the consequent war with the savages of America, whose disposition is naturally less savage than that of the British agents who, there is reason to suppose, instigate them to ravage our new settlements." Third, he cited "the unjust capture of so many of our ships on false and frivolous pretences." Finally, he wrote, "I am convinced that the same government, by its malevolent inclinations, has paved the way for, and incited the Algerines to actual hostilities against our nation."[48]

Cutting was not alone in his suppositions. Many other diplomats and writers also saw a British plot behind these developments.[49] Their fear was more paranoid than realistic. True, all of Cutting's allegations other than British complicity in the Algerian captures have some credibility. However, the sum was less than the parts. England may have followed policies obnoxious to America. Probably the English did so out of spite and in order to undermine economic competition. But throughout, these concerns were secondary to the truly catastrophic events in Europe, as the allies and the French republic's forces locked in what was becoming a massive struggle. To paraphrase Richard Hofstadter, Cutting and many others saw the Algerian captives as one part of a grandiose theory of British conspiracy against America.[50] At least Americans had moved beyond the reaction in 1785 when they could only bemoan their own ineptitude. After contemplating a new Constitution and enjoying several years of prosperity, they felt they were at least important enough to become the target of British revenge and jealousy.

All of these strands—paranoia, Anglophobia, and belligerence—came together by early 1794 in the passionate meetings that caused Federalists to worry about public involvement in foreign affairs.[51] News of the Algerian captures reached America in December of 1793, less than two weeks after President Washington delivered a major foreign policy address highly critical of Britain's restrictions on American shipping and her continued occupation of the Northwest posts. These concerns were reinforced by Jefferson's "Report on the Privileges and Restrictions on the Commerce of the United States in Foreign Countries," issued the same week that news of the Algerian captures reached America. In this report, Jefferson argued that Great Britain had created a commercial system designed to subject Americans to commercial dependence and that Americans had no choice other than to retaliate against such economic subjection. At the same time, James Madison initiated a campaign to convert Jefferson's words into action through a system of "commercial discrimination" aimed at forcing Britain to end her economic and maritime depredations against the new nation.[52]

In early 1794 Anglophobic supporters of these measures, mostly Republicans, staged public meetings in most major cities. Boston was among the first. Supporters of commercial discrimination filled the local press with diatribes against Great Britain, her "creatures . . . on the high seas," and "the creatures of that creature residing among us." A correspondent using the pseudonym "Mild" huffed, "Sorry I am that this vile [British] government was not destroyed previous to this time—together with the whole host of combined despots in Europe, who are contending against France." Britain, "Mild" continued rather obliquely, was attempting "to entangle America with her in a war against the French republic."[53]

Despite such vituperation, the vote at the Boston meeting was four hundred to three hundred against commercial discrimination. This defeat only served to make some Anglophobes still more conspiracy minded. "Truth" accused the "friends of the British" of stage managing the meeting so that the vote was taken at a time when the number of supporters of commercial discrimination was at its lowest. Had the vote been taken earlier, he contended, the measures might have passed by a large majority. Another writer accused discrimination opponents of attempting to keep America dependent on Britain. He accused John Adams, one of their number, of arguing that "we are in fact and ought to remain servants of Great Britain." Yet another critic of the meeting's leaders was convinced they were "wholly under British influence, and their chief aim is to set up British tyranny on Columbia's shore."[54]

The story was similar in New York. There, a remarkably paranoid Anglophobe declared that Britain and, to a lesser extent, Spain had decreed "all France to be blockaded, with no other intention than that of ruining our commerce." That same day, New York's Republicans announced a meeting to discuss "the embarrassments and injuries offered to the commerce of our country by Britain and her savage allies," a reference no doubt to the Algerians as well as Native Americans. The meeting, attended by an estimated two thousand citizens, produced some strong anti-British resolutions, including one calling for New York harbor to be fortified in anticipation of war with England. It did not, however, endorse Madison's discrimination plan. Extreme Anglophobes were not satisfied. One revealed that some of the meeting's leaders asserted that Britain had no role in "setting the Algerines on us." He or she stewed, "It is supposed by many I have heard discourse on the subject, these gentlemen must have obtained this piece of extraordinary information by inspiration" as no actual evidence could apparently support any assertion of British innocence.[55]

This Anglophobia ratcheted up after March 7, when news of another British Order in Council reached America. This order appeared to create a complete blockade of the French West Indies. Word soon came back from the islands that the British had seized more than 250 American ships and treated their sailors harshly. From Jamaica, an observer wrote, "The limits of an usual letter is insufficient to describe the mysterious and unjust conduct the English are exercising upon our trade." To this writer it was clear that these depredations were linked to the others. The British "say, 'throw off your French connection, declare against her monsters, and we will protect you—we will silence the Algerines we will dispose the Indians to peace—we will make a treaty of alliance and commerce, and you shall trade unmolested to all the world.' "[56]

Even normally Anglophilic Federalists like Alexander Hamilton now began to prepare for an embargo against England and, perhaps, for eventual warfare. Subsequent meetings in the spring of 1794 mobilized popular support for such measures while stoking the fires of Anglophobia still higher. A Philadelphia meeting called by Republicans charged Britain with, among other things, "insidiously let[ting] loose the barbarians of Africa, to plunder and enslave the citizens of the United States" and called for "measures adapted to prevent more of our property from falling into the hands of Algiers or Great Britain." Bostonians connected the Orders in Council to the Algerian captures when they called for an embargo to insure that "the Algerines of Africa and the Algerines of the Indies be disappointed of getting our ships." In May Boston's Federalists and Republicans joined together to support continuation of the embargo. Soon afterwards, a group of Baltimore seamen echoed their pro-embargo sentiments, resolving not to go to sea until able to sail "without apprehension of insult and robbery." "It is well known to our government," they explained, "that many valuable citizens have been lost to their country by the captures of the Algerines, and it appears to be believed by all, that the same nation which insults us in the West Indies, has been instrumental in letting loose those barbarians."[57]

As the year progressed, New Yorkers continued to fortify their port, but the furor was gradually dying down. In retrospect, it is clear that the Order in Council was aimed primarily at France, not the United States, and it was quickly superseded by a much narrower directive. No major new outrages occurred on the high seas. The British backed down in the West Indies. The Algerians did not capture any more Americans, and rumors floated through the press that the Portuguese-Algerian truce was at an end. Domestically, conflict had given way to consensus that something must be done, prompting the Washington administration to send Jay to negotiate with the British. While Jay's Treaty would ultimately prove quite controversial, in 1794 there was some hope that it could mend the situation. In the fall, a widespread report indicated that his treaty included a clause expressly declaring "that the release of American prisoners in Algiers shall be procured."[58] This rumor would prove false, but for a time resolution of the Algerian situation and the larger Anglo-American crisis seemed imminent, and, consequently, Anglophobic paranoia fell into remission.

Although it did little to resolve U.S. foreign policy concerns, the Anglo-American crisis of 1794 exerted a great deal of influence on the formation of national political culture. This was the period when growing internal policy differences within the second Washington administration catalyzed the rise of pro-French Democratic Republican societies, which eventually shaded into the Democratic-Republican party. Approximately thirty-eight of these societies were founded between 1793 and 1795, and their members no doubt contributed greatly to the Anglophobia. They certainly stoked resentment against Britain and, by proxy, allegedly pro-British Federalists for the Algerian captures. Thus, while toasting the French victory at Toulon, the New York Democratic Republican society offered a toast for "our captive brethren in Algiers," adding the hope that "the insidious and persecuting government of Great Britain feel the shapes of reproach more strong than the sting of an adder."[59] This attitude of extreme hostility toward either France or Britain and fears that other Americans were too friendly to one or the other would, of course, become a central dynamic of the developing first party system.

Partisan conflict would no doubt have emerged even without the Algerian crisis. Because the Algerian captures occurred at such a crucial moment and elicited such genuine horror, however, they played an important part in intensifying Anglophobia, which, in turn, further intensified internal partisanship. This deep partisanship, probably more than any sort of nonpartisan celebratory rhetoric, helped to shape Americans' perceptions of their nation and their place within it from the 1790s down to the present.[60] Ultimately, though, the story must go beyond partisanship. For the events of 1794, domestic and especially foreign, did not merely foster conflict. They also contributed a great deal toward creating a shared national identity. However intense Federalist-Republican, Anglophile-Anglophobe conflict became, in the process both sides also had to realize that they were *not* English, just as they were not French. If they were not always "one people" as they had declared in 1776, they were at least one nation. Their interests were no longer those of England nor were they exactly those of France. In Algiers, as in world affairs generally, they now had to realize that by throwing off their colonial "parent," they had become adults who must mind their own affairs. Perhaps more than any written documents or public celebrations, foreign affairs, beginning with Algiers, taught Americans for better or worse what it meant to be an independent nation. Washington drew on these lessons, reinforced by the anti-French hysteria of the later 1790s, in his Farewell Address, when he warned Americans that "inveterate antipathies against particular nations and passionate attachments toward others should be excluded, and that in place of all of them just and amicable feelings towards all should be cultivated." His exhortation to "steer clear of permanent alliances with any portion of the foreign world" was a second Declaration of Independence of sorts, recognizing that America was truly no longer part of Europe, despite the intrusion of European interests upon domestic politics. It did not, however, mean that the new nation would withdraw from world affairs entirely, as future events in Barbary would demonstrate.

CHAPTER SIX

The Navy and the Call to Arms

The United States had no permanent naval establishment before the Algerian captures. Early in the Revolution the Continental Congress had established a navy, commissioned more than a dozen ships, and established a Board of Admiralty, but in the end it relied primarily on privateers and the French. With the war's end, Congress sold off this small fleet and disbanded the navy, an action in line with republican distrust of permanent standing military establishments.[1] It was roughly a year after this naval disestablishment that the *Maria* and *Dauphin* were captured. Some officials, including Thomas Jefferson, John Adams, and John Jay, then considered the possibility of reestablishing a navy, probably to act in concert with other European powers to subdue the Algerians. But the fiscal and legislative weakness of the confederation government made such a course seem unwise, and instead Congress attempted to negotiate a settlement with the ill-fated John Lamb mission.[2] With the ratification of the new Constitution, the United States finally had the means to establish a navy, and some commentators connected ratification to naval armament. During the ratification debates, Hugh Williamson of North Carolina wrote that, so long as the United States "have not a single sloop of war," Algerian pirates could sail into America's port cities and enslave their residents. Alexander Hamilton commended the Constitution for making possible a federal navy that might allow the new nation to "become the arbiter of Europe in America, and to be able to incline the balance of European competitions in this part of the world as our interests may dictate."[3] Conversely, anti-Federalists condemned such arguments as mere scare tactics. William Grayson of Virginia feared that a navy could prove too expensive and might eventually endanger American liberties. Senator William Maclay of Pennsylvania echoed this argument two years later in response to another proposal to establish a navy. The expense of a standing army and navy would, he said, lead to a "host of revenue officers, [and] farewell freedom in America."[4]

One of the leading naval proponents was the captives' old friend David Humphreys. During the height of the Algerian crisis, he found time to write a belligerent, jingoistic call to arms he called "A Poem on Industry" (1794), Inspired by the captives, Humphreys's poem reflected the attitude of many of his countrymen at a time when political and economic maturation as well as Anglophobia fed a growing desire for aggression:

Victims to Pirates on th' insulted main
Whose lot severe, these soothing lines complain!
Lift up your heads ye much enduring men!
In western skies the new Aurora ken!
(Tho' long the night, and angry lowr'd the sky)
Light up your heads, for your redemption's nigh . . .
Blow YE THE TRUMPET! Sound—oh, sound th' alarms—
To arms—to arms—brave citizens! To arms . . .

Nevertheless, the United States still possessed no navy, no marine corps, and no money in the treasury. Furthermore, many politicians and plain citizens, influenced by republican antipathies to military establishments, were unwilling to respond to Humphreys's call. The Algerian captures of 1793 marked a turning point, however, after which many more Americans were ready to reconsider the possibility of a naval establishment. Subsequently, many naval historians have credited the crisis as the inspiration for the creation of the U.S. Navy and all of the involvement in worldwide commerce and world affairs that naval power implied. While possession of a navy need not necessarily lead to a more active role abroad, it was probably impossible to accumulate much power without one. The new nation need only look to its former mother country to see the crucial role that naval power played in world domination. Beginning to build a navy would certainly mark an important and controversial step for a new nation, particularly one just emerging from colonization by the world's greatest naval power. The issue created conflict in Congress and among the public. While the Algerian crisis was the catalyst, the actual debate reached beyond the immediate problem of North Africa into the vexing question of the nature of the new nation's involvement in world affairs. It offered an opportunity for a large portion of the public to consider what role, if any, the new republic should play on the world stage. In so doing, the crisis helped to crystallize the incipient divisions between the first American political parties.

Americans in the Mediterranean, including the captives, played a role in this debate, along with congressmen and other political leaders. Even before the second crisis in Algiers, the newly declared war between the French republic and the English monarchy and their respective allies threatened the new nation. The United States' 1778 treaty of amity with France in particular could serve as a source of danger if it were to pull the militarily puny United States into a war with Britain. In April, President Washington publicly declared the United States neutral and forbade its citizens from aiding either side in an effort to avoid entanglement in the developing conflict. More quietly, his administration began to consider how to protect the country should the program of neutrality fail, as seemed likely while the European powers interdicted American shipping and as Citizen Genet, the new French minister to the United States, ignored the president's refusal to allow French privateers to use American ports. By the summer of 1793, Secretary of War Henry Knox had already begun to shore up homeland security. In September he reported to the president that he was in the process of implementing a program to procure adequate guns and ammunition and to repair three Hudson River forts "in order in some degree to place the United States in a situation to guard themselves from injury by any of the belligerent powers of Europe."[5]

Meanwhile, a small group of vocal Americans living in the Mediterranean urged the administration to reconsider the idea of establishing a navy. These Americans, all of whom shared a strong interest in stimulating the new nation's Mediterranean trade, were well known to each other. Those who were not merchants were closely connected to American merchants and the Europeans with whom Americans traded in the area. With the onset of the war in Europe, they envisioned vast profits for American merchants acting as neutral carriers in the Mediterranean, particularly if they could secure a monopoly of the potentially lucrative dried codfish trade with Portugal. However, the lack of a navy could hinder trade negotiations were the Portuguese to calculate that American ships would always be vulnerable to the British or the Algerians. Therefore, Edward Church, America's consul in Lisbon, repeatedly urged Secretary of State Thomas Jefferson to commission a small navy to reassure the Portuguese. Similarly, Michael Murphy, the American consul in Malaga, wrote Jefferson of his fears that naval weakness and the continued risk of Algerian captures threatened the lucrative

Mediterranean trade. He urged the administration to move "a small naval force" into the Mediterranean to resolve this problem. Humphreys, U.S. minister to Spain and Portugal and in-law to a partner in a leading Lisbon mercantile firm, could be considered these militants' spokesman; he corresponded with just about every prominent American in the region, and, like the others, he now pushed full tilt for an American navy. Humphreys urged Jefferson to commission one or more of the American merchant vessels in Lisbon to intercept the Algerians or to "arm some large East India or merchant ships" in what would prove to be a futile attempt to prevent the Algerians from capturing more American ships.[6]

Back home, the president began to push Congress to pass a wide-ranging defense package. His annual address, delivered to Congress days before the nation learned of the captured ships, focused almost entirely on the heightened security threat posed by the war in Europe. Perhaps the greatest threat was to American vessels at sea. Consequently, Washington detailed his plans to prevent the warring parties from capturing neutral American ships. He insisted that these efforts must include a defense buildup. "There is a rank due to the United States among nations, which will be withheld, if not absolutely lost, by the reputation of weakness," he wrote. "If we desire to avoid insult, we must be able to repel it; if we desire to secure peace, . . . it must be known, that we are at all times ready for war."[7] To insure peace Washington discussed the need to build militia power, in part to protect against threats from frontier Indian nations who Americans had long suspected acted with British assistance. Additionally, as subsequent actions made clear, the administration also hoped to institute an ambitious plan of fortifications to protect U.S. ports and to establish a navy to protect U.S. ships. The last part of this project would prove to be the most controversial with Congress, where James Madison was pushing a program of commercial discrimination as an alternative to a navy. This plan called for a system of tariffs as a diplomatic method of convincing European powers to open their trade to American ships. Madison hoped the peaceful and inexpensive threat of commercial discrimination rather than the expensive, potentially deadly creation of a powerful navy, would insure that other powers would respect American shipping.[8] By offering such an alternative to establishing a navy at a time when there was little imperative to do so anyway, Madison helped to prevent, for the time being, any potential pro-navy groundswell. He also contributed to the growing rift between congressional factions, which would ultimately develop into the divide between the two first parties.

After the 1793 Algerian captures, Americans in the Mediterranean became still more vociferous in insisting on the need for a navy. From Malaga, Murphy continued to argue that it would help to protect commerce and to resolve the Algerian crisis. Nathaniel Cutting, David Humphreys's assistant, wrote from Lisbon that the captures rendered it "more necessary than ever that the principal preliminary on our part be a respectable *naval armament.*" A navy would "protect our flag from insults and facilitate the conveyance of our superfluities to foreign markets on the best terms in safety."[9] In Algiers, even Captain O'Brien, long a supporter of a negotiated settlement, joined the chorus, insisting that, "It certainly is requisite as long as the United States is at war with the B[arbary] states that we should have a respectable fleet of corsairs in Europe." The idea so appealed to him that when he tried to intimidate the dey into freeing the captives with the fabricated letter supposedly written by the Pennsylvania Committee of Commerce, he included the "news" that "orders is given for building upwards of fifty frigates."[10]

Shortly after the captures, and also after the dey of Algiers refused to negotiate with Humphreys or even allow him into Algiers, the ambassador wrote the president a long letter apprizing him of the situation. Normally, ambassadors would communicate such information with their superior, the Secretary of State, but Humphreys's special position as Washington's personal friend and former aide-de-camp allowed him to go over the heads of his superiors. In this letter, he wrote Washington, "I need not mention to you, my dear and most respected general, that a naval force has now (to a certain degree) become indispensable; or that the future reputation of the United States in Europe and Africa will depend very much, and for a very great length of time, on the success of our fleet at its very first appearance in the ocean." He further urged Washington to declare a fast day in honor of the Algerian captives and desired that the "whole nation" be "roused into exertion" to push for a navy and freedom for the captives.[11] Humphreys and his friends succeeded. Washington eventually (albeit somewhat belatedly) declared a day of thanksgiving and, much more promptly, pushed Congress to support a naval bill in its next session.[12] To convince Congress to begin the naval program, the president provided them with a confidential report, prepared by the Secretary of State, detailing American negotiations with Morocco and Algiers. This report included many of the communications sent to Secretary Jefferson by American diplomats in the Mediterranean such as David Humphreys and Benjamin Church. After viewing these documents, Congress resolved to construct a naval force "adequate to the protection of the commerce of the United States against the Algerine corsairs."[13] This resolution passed by only two votes. It was a narrow victory for Washington and the pro-navy members of Congress, who now faced a potentially long and contentious debate to determine what sort of navy, if any, the new nation should build.

However sincere the Americans in Iberia were in their sympathy with the prisoners, it is hard to escape the conclusion that for many abroad and at home the captives also represented a useful opportunity to satisfy a long-held desire for more naval power to support their commercial aspirations. Virginia Congressman Alexander White wrote to James Madison that the captures offered a way to convince Americans to accept "regulations and burdens to which they would not submit until the danger became imminent," including expenditures for coastal forts and a small naval force.[14] Humphreys suggested the administration deceive the public into supporting a naval buildup when he advised Washington that pretending only to fund defensive convoys while covertly preparing for "offensive war" would "probably be the only way by which we can hope to catch some of the corsairs separate, and perhaps out of the Mediterranean." Furthermore, as Humphreys wrote the Secretary of State, the issue encompassed far more than Algiers and the captives. "If we mean to have commerce, we must have a naval force (to a certain extent) to defend it," he wrote, adding that such a force would be crucial in allowing the United States to maintain neutrality in the developing European wars.[15] In short, the Algerian crisis proved a boon to those who had long hoped to establish some sort of naval presence to protect American commerce in the increasingly dangerous Mediterranean.

The naval question fed the developing partisan conflict of the 1790s. Factional debate initially centered on economic and constitutional issues provoked by Treasury Secretary Alexander Hamilton's activist program to expand the central government's role in the national economy. Critics opposed his plans as unconstitutional in that they gave the federal government powers not explicitly granted by the Constitution. They viewed Hamilton as a dangerous figure attempting to impose on the new nation a corrupt financial system modeled after England's powerful central government. By 1793, these issues were becoming secondary to foreign policy. The French Revolution and the dawning European wars widened the existing schism in Congress, so that Hamiltonians increasingly supported English efforts to defeat the French while their opponents sympathized with France's antimonarchical government. The furor over the Algerian captures and the ensuing naval debate played into the foreign policy and domestic aspects of this dispute. While America's relationship with the former mother country was a crucial concern, congressmen also feared that founding a navy might lead to big government on the English model.

At the outset of the Third Congress, the proposal to establish a force of six relatively small ships (four of forty-four guns and two of twenty) immediately prompted opponents to raise the British specter. Madison suggested that if the Algerian crisis had been prompted by England, a naval armament would likely entangle the United States in war with Britain as well as Algiers, rendering a small navy useless against such a superior power. Therefore, he suggested, it would be far more sensible to follow his program of commercial discrimination against Britain, scrap the idea of a navy, and merely negotiate a cash settlement with Algiers.[16] John Smilie, of Pennsylvania, believed "Britain would assist the Algerines underhandedly, as she did an enemy in another quarter [presumably Native Americans in the Northwest], and would continue to do so." John Nicholas, of Virginia, echoed the widespread belief that Britain and Consul Logie had engineered the Portuguese-Algerian truce in order to allow Algerians to attack American ships. He doubted, however, that Portugal would let the truce continue very long. Therefore, it was foolish to embark on construction of a navy. His fellow Virginian, William Giles, agreed that Britain was behind the truce but was less sanguine about its outcome. He doubted Britain would allow the United States to destroy the Algerian fleet: "May it not rather be inferred that [Britain] will send their aid to their allies, the Algerines, to destroy the force set against them?"[17] Other opponents suggested that, even if Britain did not support Algiers, the very existence of a new American navy might lead to conflict with His Majesty's ships at sea. For Madison, this was another argument for commercial discrimination, since, "there is infinitely more danger of a British war from the fitting out of ships" than from the proposed embargo against England.[18]

Naval proponents generally discounted the insinuation that Great Britain's hand lurked behind the Algerians' actions. They doubted that Britain would use U.S. efforts to build a navy as a pretext to drag the new nation into a larger war, and they believed a small number of ships would be more than sufficient to deter the Algerians from further depredations. Furthermore, a navy would punctuate the new nation's independence and fulfill its right of self-preservation. They rejected Madison's alternative of commercial discrimination, in part because they doubted that Britain lay behind the attacks and in part because it would be too slow. While the United States waited for discrimination to take effect, according to William Smith of South Carolina, "The Algerines would seize our vessels and carry hundreds of our fellow citizens into captivity." Although he suspected that Britain probably was behind Indian depredations in the Northwest, Maryland's

William Vans Murray nevertheless "did not believe the evidence as to Algerian interference strong enough to induce an argument [that] . . . Great Britain had effected the truce, so she would aid Algiers against us." Without British military might behind Algiers, and considering the Algerians' somewhat rickety navy, four frigates and two smaller ships ought to be a sufficient American force, Pennsylvania's Thomas Fitzsimons asserted.[19] In the end, the United States not only had a right to develop a navy, but, according to Smith, it was "the only means in our power of protecting our commerce from ruin, and our fellow citizens from a most dreadful captivity." At the least, creating a navy would stimulate the domestic economy. According to Murray, "If you fit out frigates, you employ your money in nourishing the roots of your own industry; you encourage your own ship building, lumber, and victualing business."[20]

The naval debate also involved the problem of expenses and big government. The congressional committee charged with investigating this issue concluded that a fleet of four forty-four-gun ships and two twenty-four-gun ships would cost $600,000 to construct and fit out initially and that subsequent annual expenses would be $247,960. James Madison calculated that the expense of building a navy would be greater than the total value of America's Mediterranean trade and would not save the government much money compared to merely buying a peace.[21] Other naval opponents suggested that the funds would be wasted because the problem would likely be resolved even before the navy could be completed. Although the British were enemies of America, the Portuguese were not. They had been tricked by the British into the truce with Algiers, and would soon end it, according to this line of argument. Americans would save money by hiring the Portuguese to check the Algerian ships, Abraham Clark of New Jersey suggested, a proposal that Madison later seconded.[22]

Perhaps more importantly, opponents feared that once Congress launched a navy, expenses would continually grow. They suspected that Hamiltonians supported a navy because they wished to emulate corrupt monarchical efforts to concentrate power in the hands of the few who controlled the government. These concerns, of course, echoed earlier criticisms of Hamilton's domestic policy, making them all the more believable to individuals already suspicious of the developing Federalist faction. From Monticello, a worried Thomas Jefferson predicted that the naval armament and the fortification bills would easily pass. It was "not that the monocrats and papermen in Congress want war," he explained, "but they want armies and debts." Similarly, congressman Abraham Clark feared "once [a fleet] had been commenced, there would be no end of it." "We must then have a Secretary of the Navy, and a swarm of other people in office, at a monstrous expense," he predicted. All of this seemed a bit too European, and often too British, for some congressmen. "The greater part of the immense debt of England had been lavished on her navy," John Smilie noted. For William Giles, the example that came to mind was the French ancien régime, which he believed was ruined by its naval expenses. "A navy," he asserted, "is the most expensive of all means of defence, and the tyranny of governments consists in the expensiveness of their machinery."[23]

For their part, supporters of the navy argued that in the long run it would be more expensive *not* to build a navy than it would be to build one and that this navy need not be a permanent establishment. At a minimum, the lack of a navy could lead to oppressively high insurance on America's foreign shipments; Maryland's Samuel Smith estimated it to be as much as $2 million per year. He argued that, "It must be the worst kind of economy to hazard an expense of two million dollars for the sake of saving the charges of this armament." Refusal to build a navy would be far more costly, he added, should Algerian ships attack the North American coast, a prospect that he found quite likely. Similarly, Pennsylvania's Thomas Fitzsimons feared the possibility of a steep rise in the price of salt should American imports of that commodity from the Mediterranean be hampered by the defeat of the naval bill. He estimated the loss to the United States could be as much as $4 million annually. "We have been trying to buy a peace but without success," he explained, "and if we are not able to enforce it [with a navy] the price of buying it must be so much the higher." Building a navy would also have the advantage of stimulating the domestic economy by creating work for carpenters, shipbuilders, and other mechanics and creating a demand for naval stores.[24]

Finally, naval supporters emphasized the temporary nature of the proposed program. Their bill included a clause stipulating "that if a peace shall take place between the United States and the Regency of Algiers, that no farther proceeding be had under this act." Presumably, this clause meant that all shipbuilding would stop, that the funding for pay and provisions for naval personnel would be terminated, and that, in short, the navy would be disbanded as it had been following the American Revolution.[25] This stop clause, they argued, would eliminate any long-term expenses. In a lengthy pro-navy speech, William Laughton Smith of South Carolina described himself as "at a loss to discover" how "a bill providing six frigates, which were to exist only during the war with Algiers, could excite an apprehension of a large and permanent navy, and an enormous debt." Fitzsimons expected such a war would end quickly; indeed, he predicted, "As soon as Portugal is left to herself," that is, freed from the British pressure to abide by the truce with Algiers, "she will certainly protect us." Thus the naval armament would only be necessary for the short period that the truce continued. Still, William Smith argued, even a small permanent naval establishment might not be all bad. He saw "no reason why the United States, with an increasing population, much individual wealth, and considerable national resources, might not, without ruin, do as much, or why the equipment of a squadron, inferior to that of any of the petty nations of Italy, should involve us in insupportable expense."[26]

It would be a mistake to dismiss the Algerian crisis as mere pretext, even if both sides may sometimes have used the captivity crisis cynically to pursue their own agendas. Post-Revolutionary antipathy toward standing armies and the new nation's impecuniousness meant that it would have been difficult to create a navy without being prompted by some clear danger. Because of the political standoff between Anglophile and Francophile, however, a threat from either France or England (unless a clearly belligerent attack on American ships or soil) most likely would have led Congress into a political quagmire. In this context, the Algerian threat was ideal for pro-navalists. Rather than coming from a well-known European nation, it came from a country that most Congressmen viewed as extremely alien, even barbarous. Furthermore, because Algiers was such a minor power, American ineffectiveness in the crisis played into fears that the new nation was still not fully independent.[27]

Both opponents and proponents of the navy were concerned about dependence. Naval proponent William Vans Murray feared relying on Portugal would create "a disgraceful dependence on a foreign power," while naval opponent William Giles thought that the expense of a new navy should "increase rather than lessen our dependence" on foreign powers, at least until it was firmly established. Dependence was, however, a losing argument for anti-navalists so long as the press and the public emphasized the new nation's shocking weakness in the face of Algerian depredations. Considering the tenor of public opinion, it would be hard for Congress to deny that a navy, once established, would probably make the United States stronger, freeing them from the threat of the Algerians and other pirates. Finally, as William Smith argued with some apparent justification, the stop clause "was a complete answer to all the reasoning which had been indulged on the subject of navies and debts."[28] It was a stroke of genius on the part of pro-navalists, who could now maintain that there were no ulterior motives, that the naval bill was about Algiers and only Algiers, and not an entering wedge for a massive military establishment.

While the naval bill did much to define developing party lines, it also transcended partisanship. Madison later noted that, "The vote in favor of the measure was indeed so chequered, that it cannot even be attributed to the influence of party."[29] Party identification in this period of an emerging party system was sometimes tenuous and therefore often difficult to label with precision. Nonetheless, analysis of the House vote shows that without the support of six members identifiable as Democratic-Republicans who crossed party lines to vote for the naval bill, the measure would have failed. Conversely, only one Federalist appears to have broken ranks to oppose it.[30] Additionally, a Democratic-Republican, Samuel Smith of Maryland, was one of the most vocal pro-naval speakers during the debates. Smith, a leading Baltimore merchant, feared that fellow Democratic-Republicans, especially Madison, were too anxious to attack Britain with commercial discrimination at the expense of American commerce. "Our duty is not to injure others but to protect our own interest," he explained. His position no doubt was influenced by his own problems with North African pirates whom he had been bribing for years in order to protect his ships.[31]

Smith was part of a group of merchant Republicans who demonstrated the potential compatibility of support for a naval establishment with anti-English sentiment. Other pro-naval merchant Democratic-Republicans included Nicholas Gilman of New Hampshire and Richard Winn of South Carolina. Another, John Swanwick of Philadelphia, would be elected to serve in the next Congress, replacing pro-naval Federalist Thomas Fitzsimons. Interestingly, Swanwick, a converted Federalist, supported the naval bill *and* Madison's discrimination plan. He also actively solicited funds for the Algerian captives during the 1794 publicity drive.[32] While certainly no great friends of Britain, these Republican merchants were supportive of American commerce and believed that maintaining a navy was necessary for its protection. Had the naval bill been cast as a reaction to France or to England, they might have had more difficulty supporting it. But because it was explicitly aimed at depredations against American commerce by the "barbaric" Algerians, they could in good conscience cross party lines to support the establishment of a naval force that would protect the American public and provide the additional benefit of protecting their own commercial livelihoods.

No doubt the prospect of government contracts also enticed representatives from port cities to support the measure. Jefferson observed that, "where members may hope either for offices or jobs for themselves or their friends, some few will be debauched, and that is sufficient to turn the decision where a majority is at most small." Certainly, the administration hoped that would be the case. In a report prepared shortly after Congress authorized the navy, Secretary of War Henry Knox proposed that each of the six vessels be built in different ports spreading from Boston down to Charleston, an inefficient proposal due to the need to replicate personnel and equipment in each of the six cities rather than centralizing them in a single shipyard. "If the principles of economy alone were to predominate in determining the places where the said vessels were to be built and equipped, it is not improbable the arrangement might be different," Knox admitted to the president. But, he continued, "as the government is of the whole people, and not of a part only, it is just and wise to proportion its benefits as nearly as may be to those places or states which pay the greatest amount to its support." Captain Thomas Truxton, who would be assigned to Baltimore to oversee construction of what would become the USS *Constellation*, complained that this program appeared "to be going great lengths for the gratification of a few individuals."[33] The cause of fiscal efficiency, however, clearly was secondary to the broader need for political consensus. With opinions so nearly evenly divided over the need for the navy, it was crucial for the administration to gain public support from as many quarters as possible.

As Congress debated these issues at its capitol in Philadelphia they continued to be influenced by Americans in the Mediterranean. The committee report that initiated the debate indicated that the Algerian navy was relatively small and could be easily checked by a force of the size that Congress was considering based on reports from American diplomats in the Mediterranean as well as letters from O'Brien and other captives in Algiers.[34] The committee refused to make public the specifics of this classified information, but clearly it set the tone for the subsequent congressional debate. The Americans in the Mediterranean who communicated this information to the United States were by this time nearly unanimous in their agreement that a naval force was necessary, and in their reports they made this position very clear. While it would probably be too conspiratorial to view them as stealthy plotters attempting to influence Congress into undertaking a naval program, their steady pressure on this issue nevertheless should be considered an important early factor in pushing Congress toward authorizing a navy.

In March, two months after the initial committee report, Congress received new "confidential communications" from the Mediterranean that led some members to believe that the possibility of a peaceful settlement was increasingly likely. It is not clear exactly what was contained in these letters, but according to Congressman Giles, they indicated that the Algerian-Portuguese truce was "part of the system of the combination against France." Most likely, Congress was reacting to a petition sent by Captain O'Brien to the president in late December and, perhaps, to a letter sent in early January by James Simpson, the American consul in Gibraltar. O'Brien reported that Great Britain brought about the truce to "prevent the United States from supplying the French in their present glorious contest for liberty." Simpson, however, predicted the truce would not become permanent and Humphreys agreed. If this were the case, then a negotiated settlement seemed possible and, once the truce ended, future captures of American ships unlikely. Anti-navalists saw this information as vindication of their position, but pro-navalists might take heart in O'Brien's analysis that the United States had "no alternative [other] than to fit out with the greatest expedition thirty frigates and corsairs, in order to stop those sea robbers in capturing American vessels."[35]

Pro-navalists in Congress were also now influenced by the captives' published narratives and the public response to them. In particular, the account of Captain William Penrose, which was published in newspapers in March, seems to have struck a chord. In this rather standard sensibility-laden account of capture at sea and suffering in slavery in Algiers, Captain Penrose warned that the Algerians "have several cruisers out now, and there are several in the harbor equipping with utmost speed," presumably to capture more Americans. In the end he pitifully begged for a few dollars, which would be "the greatest favor any person ever conferred on me, for it is impossible to subsist long in this miserable situation."[36] "Who," wondered Congressman William Smith, "could, after reading the affecting narratives of Captain Penrose and the other unfortunates, sit down contented with cold calculations and dry syllogisms?" Instead, the captives' communications "ought to excite every possible exertion, not only to procure the release of the captured, but to prevent an increase of the number of these unhappy victims."[37] The method must be to build a navy, no matter the expense; for how could the "national disgrace" of the seamen's slavery be reckoned against the cost of a navy? Still, anti-navalist William Giles was unmoved by this argument. Unlike Smith, he contended that those who cared about Penrose's plight should in fact oppose the navy, for "a declaration of war under such circumstances, would irritate the barbarians and furnish additional misery to the unfortunate prisoners."[38]

Passing the naval bill by no means ensured the establishment of a navy. In June, Congress authorized spending nearly $700,000 to construct the six frigates and Alexander Hamilton's Treasury Department began to procure materials for the six shipyards. This task proved difficult for a department already burdened with the job of securing funds to pay the Algerians to release the prisoners as well as overseeing construction of the program of fortifications to protect the port cities. The biggest headache came from the administration's insistence on procuring live oak timber from Georgia and South Carolina for the ships. Unfortunately, by December hardly any of this wood had found its way to the waiting shipyards. Pierce Butler, one of South Carolina's U.S. senators, wrote the president, "I feel it a duty incumbent on me, to inform you, that there is a defect in the arrangements made for getting timber from this state." The local superintendent appeared to be doing his job, but Butler insisted, "There is a deficiency somewhere; and unless it is corrected, the ships might as well, were it possible, be built of bars of silver as of live oak." Hamilton's assistant, Tench Coxe, who was in charge of procuring revenue for the navy, took Butler's charges as an attack on his own integrity and wrote a long report to Hamilton rebutting any hint of corruption and arguing that the delay was due only to an unfortunate set of circumstances.[39] Whatever the causes, by the end of 1794 timber had only just begun to arrive at the Philadelphia shipyard, nine months after passage of the naval bill.[40]

While the administration attempted to give new life to the moribund naval construction program, peace in Algiers began to seem imminent. By March 1795, rumors that a treaty had been completed began to appear in the press. These rumors were premature, but they proved to be harbingers of an actual treaty, which was completed by Joseph Donaldson, the recently appointed American envoy to Algiers, on September fifth. News of the treaty and the fact that Captain O'Brien had been freed to transport it reached the United States in mid-November.[41] Under the terms of the treaty, the United States agreed to pay $642,500 to insure peace and to ransom the sixty-six remaining captives, as well as a $21,600 annual tribute to the dey in the form of naval stores.[42] Thus, as 1795 came to a close, the crisis appeared to be over, although official word of the treaty had not yet arrived in America, nor had the United States paid the tribute. In the meantime, due to the supply problems and changes in the plans for the vessels, the cost estimate for the six frigates had nearly doubled from $688,888 to $1,152,000. Consequently, the congressional oversight committee recommended that all available resources be used to complete two of the six frigates and that work on the other four be temporarily suspended.[43]

Had they followed the letter of the naval bill's stop clause, the president and Congress might well have stopped *all* construction at this point. Such a step would have had the added benefit of immediately curtailing the mounting expenses. Nonetheless, work on the two frigates continued through the first quarter of 1796. It was not until March 15 that the president acted, and even at this juncture, he did not order the construction halted. Instead, he tossed the ball into

Congress's court, noting that if the program were suspended immediately, "the loss which the public would incur might be considerable from the dissipation of workmen, from certain works or operations being suddenly dropped or unfinished, and from the derangement of the whole system." In short, the money already expended would be lost, and the United States would have no frigates to show for it. He therefore asked Congress to determine whether such a suspension would "comport with the public interest."[44]

Some navy proponents in Congress had no intention of letting the stop clause halt the construction program. William Laughton Smith, the most outspoken of the bunch, had proposed in January that the clause be removed from the legislation, thereby allowing the naval construction program to continue at full speed regardless of developments in North Africa. At that time, with the results of the negotiations in Algiers still unclear, no one was willing to follow Smith's lead, and the proposal died.[45] Now, with Washington's directive, Congress could no longer avoid the issue. The Senate committee formed to look into the matter split the difference, recommending in March that three of the six frigates be completed.[46] When the full House took up the matter in early April, the entire naval debate was reopened. Now the terms were somewhat different due to two important developments. First, construction of the six frigates was already well under way despite the astounding cost overruns and delays. Consequently, earlier objections to the building program based on cost, while still relevant, were now less convincing. The federal government had already dumped nearly a million dollars into the shipbuilding program; curtailing it would mean that the money had been essentially wasted, even if a portion might be recovered by selling off the building supplies already purchased.[47] As a result, legislators were now mostly unwilling to push for strict compliance with the stop clause. Instead, anti-navalists generally hoped that only two or three of the six frigates would be completed, while pro-navalists wanted to continue with all six.

The apparent end of the Algerian crisis also played a part in these debates. With the signing of the peace treaty and the seemingly imminent release of the captives, naval proponents could no longer use events in North Africa as a justification for a navy, or at least it was more difficult for them to do so. Some continued to argue that the dey could not be trusted to keep the peace and that other North African countries such as Morocco and Tunis remained a threat. Samuel Smith observed that if the United States were to complete three frigates and send them into the Mediterranean, "it would convince the Barbary Powers that we were . . . ready to chastise them, if they attempted to annoy our vessels further." Writing from Lisbon at the time of the congressional debate, David

Humphreys attempted to convince the Secretary of State that Morocco might well destroy America's Mediterranean commerce "unless we shall have some small naval force in readiness to prevent it." Nevertheless, the lack of a clear and present threat would make it impossible for pro-navalists to argue, as they had in 1794, that the crisis in the Mediterranean made it imperative to build a navy. In fact, one of the most extreme pro-navalists, William Laughton Smith of South Carolina, suggested that such arguments had always been something of a diversion. Despite the stop clause in the original bill, he remarked, "It was never seriously thought that building any of [the frigates] would be discontinued."[48] This statement was particularly curious, considering that at that time he had been a leading proponent of the stop clause. Whether or not Algiers had merely been a front for Smith and other pro-navalists, the revived debate could no longer focus on the Algerian crisis.

Instead, naval proponents argued along two new tracks. The first was described by Samuel Smith as the "right to expect protection," which applied to Americans at home and abroad. At home, the threat came from enemies to the west and on the coasts. Smith noted that Congress had recently spent "a million and a half to protect the frontier." Likewise, the naval program and the new coastal fortifications would protect the nation's seaports from its enemies. The new capital city of Washington, D.C., was particularly vulnerable to attack, according to pro-navalist James Swanwick, who had been recently elected as a representative from Philadelphia. Europeans perceived America's coast as "being wholly defenceless," and, Swanwick added, coastal property was vulnerable to "the attack of any marauding privateer."[49] This homeland defense argument was relatively uncontroversial. Congress had already agreed to fund new construction or repair work at a number of coastal forts. Even John Nicholas of Virginia, a staunch opponent of expanding the naval program, could agree with it to some extent. While uncomfortable with the idea of continuing to build the frigates that were approved "only with a view to the Algerines," he averred that he was nonetheless "willing to go into the equipment of two frigates for the defense of [the American] coast to guard against pirates."[50]

When naval proponents expanded the right to protection to apply to American ships at sea, however, they ran into more resistance. Many naval proponents stressed the importance of protecting the Mediterranean trade which, according to Samuel Smith, promised to be "greater than all the commerce we now enjoyed" should American ships be free to sail there. Swanwick interpreted the widespread public support for the Algerian captives as an endorsement of the Mediterranean trade. Recalling the "horror" with which "every description of persons throughout the union hear[d] of the capture of their fellow-citizens by the Algerians" and the rush to raise subscriptions for their return, he asked rhetorically, "Was this a showing of coldness with respect to commerce on the part of the people; No." Naval opponents were skeptical. While Josiah Parker of Virginia admitted that the Mediterranean trade might eventually prove lucrative, he "did not think the present time the most proper to engage in the business." Referring to the great expense of building a fleet, John Nicholas concluded that he "should not be for purchasing commerce at such a price," despite his support for frigates for homeland defense. While noting that he "wished to encourage commerce as far as the true interest of [the United Sates] would admit," John Williams of New York nevertheless "thought agriculture required their greatest attention," and therefore he opposed building frigates to protect overseas trade.[51]

The second track that pro-navalist arguments now followed was national reputation. As Theodore Sedgwick remarked, "If it was thought to be the interest of the nation when the act passed that six frigates should be built, it now became its honor not to abandon the object." Similarly, William Laughton Smith observed that not finishing the frigates "would give foreign powers a very unfavorable idea of [U.S.] stability and importance." On a more positive note, John Swanwick reported his pride when watching the activity at the Philadelphia shipyard and "hearing the remarks of foreigners on the vessels now building." That pride would turn to shame were the shipbuilding program terminated, "the materials offered at vendue, and the Government made to become auctioneers in fact of the materials of the national strength."[52] These comments reflected the widespread concern expressed by so many Americans during the Algerian crisis that the new nation was a weakling, incapable of joining the first ranks of the western powers.[53]

Anti-navalists generally resisted this argument. Future Secretary of the Treasury Albert Gallatin, serving as a representative from Pennsylvania, rejected this martial definition of honor in favor of a more fiscal approach. He tartly noted, "If the sums to be expended to build and maintain the frigates were applied to paying a part of their National Debt, the payment would make [the United States] more respectable in the eyes of foreign nations than all the frigates they could build."[54] John Nicholas believed that completing the six frigates would lessen "our consequence in the eyes of Europe," because "we would be showing to foreign powers that we did not understand the true means of defense which were in our power"—namely, payments to the Algerians. Paying for peace made more sense than finishing the frigates, because, as he explained, it was far less expensive. James Madison agreed that payments made more sense than frigates, and he went so far as to deny that the threat of a navy had any effect at all on the resolution of the Algerian crisis since, in the end, the United States had still been forced to pay for peace, and the price determined by the Algerian treaty did not appear to be any lower as a consequence of the inchoate naval program.[55]

In this debate, perhaps even more than in 1794, foreign policy concerns merged into and helped to define domestic partisan conflict. Now, as George Washington prepared to leave office for the last time, the emerging Federalists and Democratic-Republicans prepared for what would be the new nation's first truly partisan presidential election. In Congress, Federalists generally took the more bellicose pro-naval position and Democratic-Republicans were more inclined to use America's economic might rather than military measures to buy peace and put commercial pressure on European rivals.

This foreign policy divergence also reflected different economic philosophies. America's economy was broadly understood to be divided into three sectors: agriculture, commerce, and manufacturing. Federalists were already most closely associated with commerce. Alexander Hamilton, their fiscal genius, believed that stimulating commerce would eventually cause the entire economy to grow. Pro-navalists worked from similar assumptions in 1796. John Swanwick asked Congress, "When they considered the great advantages which foreign commerce bestowed upon the nation, and the profits it afforded to individual merchants, mechanics etc., and indirectly to the agricultural interests, ought they not to afford it every protection in their power?" Republicans, led by Thomas Jefferson and James Madison, tended to stress the importance of agriculture over the other sectors, reflecting to some extent the economic ideas of French physiocrats who believed European mercantilist doctrine had overemphasized foreign commerce at the expense of domestic development. Anti-navalists tended to agree. John Williams declared that, "The true interests of this country . . . were the agricultural[,] and every thing taken from agriculture to commerce, was taken from the greater and given to the less."[56] So, for Federalists, an understanding that Britain did not lurk behind the Algerian depredations, a strong interest in protecting overseas trade, and a more bellicose approach to foreign affairs all predisposed them to support the navy. Conversely, Democratic-Republicans' fear of English plots, relative disinterest in overseas trade, antipathy toward big government, and preference for economic coercion over military measures pushed them in the opposite direction.

In the end, the House and Senate agreed to split the difference and continue construction of three of the six frigates.[57] Not surprisingly, voting was generally quite partisan. The extreme pro-navalists, those who wished to continue construction of all six frigates despite the end of the Algerian conflict, were over-whelmingly Federalists, while extreme anti-navalists, who voted to reduce the number of frigates constructed from three to two, were overwhelmingly Democratic-Republicans. And yet, the party divisions had not entirely hardened. About one in six of the extreme anti-navalists was a Federalist, and a similar proportion of the extreme pro-navalists was Republican.[58] Furthermore, John Swanwick, the leading pro-naval orator was a Democratic-Republican, while John Williams, one of the most vocal anti-navalists, was a Federalist. Swanwick was a Philadelphia merchant understandably concerned with overseas trade, much like his fellow Democratic-Republican and pro-naval merchant from Baltimore, Samuel Smith. Williams, born in England, resided in Salem, New York, far from the port city and deep in the rich farm country along the Hudson River. A doctor and land-holder, his concerns naturally lay with agriculture rather than overseas trade. For Swanwick, Smith, and Williams, economic interest and regional concerns trumped party loyalty.

What was true for these individuals was broadly true of the other congress-men who crossed party lines. Of the five pro-naval Republicans, three came from north of the Mason-Dixon line and none from the Deep South, while sixteen of the nineteen anti-naval Republicans were from South of the Mason-Dixon line. While two of the five pro-naval Republicans were merchants, none of the nine-teen anti-naval Republicans was. Similarly, two of the four anti-naval Federalists were from inland districts and none was a merchant. Of course, regional origins and economic factors were closely linked to party affiliation; Federalists were more northern and mercantile while Republicans were more southern and agrar-ian. The dispute over the navy can be understood as one of the issues in the mid-1790s that helped to shape these cleavages, even if it was hardly the only one.

The issue of homeland security, highlighted the following month in the de-bate over funding the seaport forts, exhibited the limits of this burgeoning par-tisanship. John Swanwick gamely attempted to tie it to the naval question, com-menting that, "Whilst we discard all ideas of fleets, we ought to attend to our internal defence, without which, we should be too much exposed to the attacks of an enemy." By and large, however, pro-navalists and anti-navalists, Federal-ists and Democratic-Republicans all were united behind the forts due to their common hunger for pork. Federalist anti-navalist John Williams of New York asked for more funding to fortify New York City. Republican pro-navalists Swan-wick and Smith of Pennsylvania and Maryland feared the bill underfunded the ports of Philadelphia and Baltimore. Federalist pro-navalist William Laughton Smith of South Carolina felt Charleston had been slighted, and Republican pro-navalist Henry Dearborn of Massachusetts saw "no good reason why New York and Charleston should have large sums expended on them, any more than Boston."[59]

The sums were relatively large for the time. Between 1794 and 1796, Congress expended $132,234 on twenty coastal forts from Portland, Maine, to St. Mary's, Georgia. In June of 1797 the War Department estimated another $200,000 was needed to complete the job.[60] This money not only served to fortify harbors but also helped enrich local economies by providing construction projects and making port facilities more desirable. For example, Philadelphians hoped that reconstruction of their fortifications would include the erection of new piers in the Delaware River that would be of use to commercial vessels as well as warships. New York Representative Edward Livingston felt that was going too far. He viewed these piers as "a local advantage to Philadelphia, which ought to be done at their own expense, as much so as docks, or any other convenience for shipping."[61] Fortification of New York harbor, on the other hand, he insisted, was in the national interest. Washington had begun the navy and fortifications program partly as a project to tie the localities to the nation in their desire for federal money. In this sense he may have succeeded all too well.

Back in 1794, when the fortifications issue was first raised, there had been a fair amount of concern that the Algerians might eventually attack American harbors. Charlestonians in particular felt vulnerable to Algerian attacks by way of the West Indies.[62] But by 1797 nobody in Congress seemed to worry much about Algerian cruisers in American waters. Instead, their concern was the vulnerability of American ports to European fleets. Edward Livingston feared the "approach and attacks of an *enemy's fleet* in case of war," and his fellow New Yorker Jonathan Havens feared New York harbor "could not be put in a complete state of defence against a *large maritime force* unless fortifications were to be erected at the Narrows." James Swanwick feared "any *fleet* which would ever come to attack [Philadelphia] would have no dread of the existing fortifications."[63] The emphasis on large fleets rather than occasional corsairs reflects a shift in concern from North African pirates to European naval giants. Much as in the naval debate, the Algerian crisis had served as an entering wedge, allowing the initial funding of the fortification program, which would continue well after the Algerian threat was over.

And now the Algerian crisis really was ending. Nearly a year and a half after the peace treaty had been drawn up, the remaining Algerian captives were finally returning home. Their journey had been a long and difficult one. After suffering through two to eleven years of captivity—the last part spent worrying that the treaty might fall through if their government could not secure funds for their release—the captives were finally freed in June 1796. Unfortunately, the plague broke out on the ship carrying the largest group out of Algiers, and when they arrived in Marseilles they faced a long period of quarantine. Consequently, they did not arrive in the United States until February 8, 1797, when their ship docked at Marcus Hook, near Philadelphia. Hundreds of well-wishers filled the roads to greet them as they made their way to Philadelphia. The press of the crowd grew so great that the former captives were barely able to push their way into the India Queen's Tavern for refreshments. The captives' celebrity was, however, short lived. Those from Massachusetts looked forward to receiving their share of the money raised for them several years earlier at a theater benefit.[64] For the most part, though, the captives were soon yesterday's news. The Algerian crisis had been resolved for well over a year, and the war in Europe, especially the growing hostility of France toward the United States, was now a far bigger and more immediate concern.

While the Algerian crisis slipped into the past, the problem of the frigates remained very much in the present. Congress once again was forced to debate the matter due to the shipbuilders' incessant need for funding. On March 2, 1797, as Philadelphians awaited what would be the last presidential inauguration in their city, William Laughton Smith proposed appropriating an additional $172,000 to complete the three frigates. Predictably, the measure stirred controversy. This time, however, virtually nobody said a word about North Africa. Instead, the debate centered on partisan concerns about political power. Albert Gallatin, a leading Republican from Pennsylvania, expressed some support for building the frigates but said he was concerned that the president "could man the vessels and send them to sea independent of Congress." This concern was no doubt prompted by the imminent inauguration of a frankly Federalist John Adams, who would replace the nominally nonpartisan and difficult to reproach George Washington. Gallatin's concern was heightened by revelations that Washington had already increased the size of the frigates on his own authority. Consequently, Gallatin proposed that Congress only authorize the hulls of the frigates to be completed, thereby preventing the president from manning them and sending them to sea without asking Congress for further appropriations. In effect, this move would force the Federalist president to yield to the Republican Congress before he could activate the nascent navy.[65]

As party differences hardened, the voting split more clearly along partisan lines than ever. Only two Federalists (5 percent of the total) voted in favor of Gallatin's proposal. This figure was surprisingly low considering that in 1796 roughly 16 percent of the extreme anti-navalists had been Federalists. The Republicans were less disciplined, however. Six of them broke ranks, thereby narrowly defeating the measure. The defeat of Gallatin's amendment allowed Congress to vote on the main question—whether to allocate the funds to complete the frigates. Here, too, Federalists remained remarkably unified, with all but one voting in favor of the bill. They were joined by fifteen defecting Republicans (26 percent of the total), which allowed the bill smooth sailing. Without these Republicans, the new frigates would have been sunk by four votes.[66] The partisanship intensified in a special session of Congress called by President Adams in the wake of the X,Y,Z Affair, which ratcheted anger toward France up several notches, making war seem far more likely. Adams and the Federalists proposed a program that would help prepare the United States for military conflict. Finishing the frigates and the fortifications was an important element of this plan, which also called for recruiting a provisional army, arming merchant vessels, and budgeting more money for defense.[67] Republicans now alleged that Federalists had long been attempting to drag them into war. Referring to the continual requests for appropriations for the frigates, John Nicholas of Virginia complained that he "did not like to be drawn from step to step to do what, if the whole matter had been seen at first, they might not have consented to." His fellow Virginian and long-time anti-navalist, William Giles, was more explicit. He was sorry to say that he "was more and more convinced that it was the constant aim of some gentlemen in that House to increase the expense of our Government" through the naval program. "The propriety of establishing a navy," he explained, "was first begun under an alarm, and it had been continually carried on by the same means." In other words, the Federalists had used first the Algerian crisis and now the French crisis to push through their big government agenda.[68]

Yet, in the end, enough Republicans continued to support the navy to allow construction to go on. In fact, the frigates and the forts were the only aspect of Adams's program that they did not defeat.[69] Jefferson felt that the whole session was a "folly," merely a Federalist ploy to involve the United States in a war with France.[70] Given the partisanship of the session and the Republicans' political strength, it seems remarkable that the navy survived at all. The most likely explanation is that once it had begun and gained momentum, like most government programs, the navy became difficult to kill. So much had been expended already that spending a little more seemed more prudent than wasting all of the money already invested. Republicans like Giles saw all this as evidence of a

Federalist conspiracy reaching back to the Algerian crisis. But, as South Carolina Federalist Robert Goodloe Harper pointed out, there was no reason necessarily to suspect conspiracy or even much planning. Harper argued that the frigates were not "commenced from an idea of laying the foundations of a large Navy Establishment," but they were rather the product of "particular circumstances." He added, "Shall we at a time when we are threatened with danger abandon them?"[71] Whether due to conspiracy or merely happenstance, the navy was saved because it had already been begun during the Algerian crisis. Should Republicans have been asked to begin a navy from scratch, potentially to fight their French friends, the task would have been far more difficult.

As the first full year of John Adams's presidency began, the naval program faced some peril. Congress initiated an investigation into the tremendous expenses associated with the frigates, eventually discovering that over $1.1 million had already been spent on them. At least one congressional pro-navalist claimed that the "excessive expense" had cooled his ardor for the navy.[72] Despite these developments, increasing friction with France was now fortifying Congress's inclination toward an expanded navy. In April 1798, the War Department recommended a vastly expanded military response to the French threat in order "to preserve character abroad, esteem for the government at home, safety to our sea property, and protection to our territory and sovereignty." This program called for the construction of twenty new naval vessels of varying sizes in addition to the three frigates being readied for sea. It also recommended expenditure of an additional $1 million on the seaport forts, although the Secretary of War commented that some of this money might be saved if the navy were enlarged enough to provide adequate patrols. The congressional debate hinged on concerns over expenses and whether the navy was to be used as an offensive weapon—potentially further entangling the United States with European wars—or primarily as a means to defend American ports and ships. Eventually, Congress authorized twenty-two new naval vessels, the largest naval expansion to date: twelve twenty-two gun ships and ten small galleys, as well as new gun foundries and a new Department of the Navy to be led by Benjamin Stoddert of Maryland.[73]

Completely absent from these debates and preparations was any mention of Algiers or North Africa. Four years earlier, during the initial push for a navy, David Humphreys had written of "victims to pirates." By 1798 those victims were largely forgotten, having returned to their families and relative anonymity. But Humphreys's martial sentiments—"Blow YE THE TRUMPET! Sound—oh, sound the alarms—To arms—To arms—brave citizens! To arms"—were now more relevant than ever, if directed against France rather than Algiers. Nevertheless, the Algerian crisis had played its part. By creating outrage against a universally despised enemy, it had more or less united the nation and Congress behind the idea of building a navy, and, in the process, creating a greater American presence abroad. As America faced the intensified French threat, it already had a naval establishment, a system of forts, working shipyards, and three new frigates. With this foundation in place, naval expansion would be a relatively simple matter. Once the quasi-war against France fizzled out, this growing navy and the attendant national ambitions would refocus away from France and back to the Barbary coast.

PART THREE

CAPTIVITY AND
THE AMERICAN EMPIRE

CHAPTER SEVEN

Masculinity and Servility in Tripoli

Not quite all of the former captives disappeared into anonymity; a few returned to Barbary to serve as the United States' first African experts during a second round of captivity crises. Captain Richard O'Brien had been America's de facto consul in Algiers throughout much of his eleven years of captivity and had gone to great pains during that period to demonstrate his knowledge of Algerian affairs. John Barry, captain of the USS *United States,* one of the newly constructed ships intended to patrol the Mediterranean, offered O'Brien the position of lieutenant, no doubt due as much to his understanding of Barbary culture and geography as his seamanship. O'Brien refused the offer in favor of an even better position: consul general to Algiers. When informing the dey of O'Brien's appointment, President Adams noted that the captain's "intimate acquaintance with the manner of transacting public affairs at Algiers may render him particularly useful to his country as well as acceptable to your excellency."[1] In 1799 O'Brien would be joined by his fellow ex-captive and the dey's former chief Christian secretary, James L. Cathcart, who was appointed U.S. consul to Tripoli. William Eaton, a prickly but courageous Dartmouth graduate and career soldier with no previous Mediterranean experience who was appointed U.S. consul to Tunis in 1798, soon joined them.

Using his characteristic naval metaphors, O'Brien wrote that he, Cathcart, and Eaton "might be compared unto three lighthouses erected on three dangerous shoals, said lighthouses erected to prevent valuable commerce running thereon." Unfortunately, while the "lighthouses" did generally manage to keep American commerce safe at first, they appeared to be poorly synchronized from the beginning and soon could not work together at all. Although a number of factors were at play, ultimately the problem was that Eaton could not respect the others due to the very thing that had brought them to the State Department in the first place: their experience in Algiers. American negotiators, Eaton complained to the Secretary of State, had thus far been "Frenchmen, apostate Americans, and slaves." Clearly, the last of these categories referred to Cathcart and O'Brien. Rather than valuing his colleagues' expertise, he suspected that O'Brien and, to a lesser extent, Cathcart retained a servile mentality toward the North African rulers as a result of their years in captivity. Eaton added that he did not "mean a criminal reflection" by complaining of "slaves." Many otherwise brave warriors, he explained, would tremble "in passing the graveyard for fear of ghosts," and, likewise, many slaves might not "shrink at the thunder of a broadside of a man of war," but they would still "tremble at the nod of a turban."[2]

Eaton's equation of the former captives' slavery with cowardice suggests a deeper concern with their masculinity. In every corner of the new republic and at nearly all social levels, Americans equated manhood with independence and the mastery of passions (including fear) and femininity with submission and un-restrained passion (including cowardice).[3] In the South, honor culture dictated that planters gauge the reaction of their peers to their own behavior and take umbrage at the least slight to their honor. A planter who submitted to invective without taking action would be considered unmanned, and the greatest insult was to be labeled a coward. Furthermore, honor applied only among equals, so that inferiors were by definition excluded from this masculine culture to the extent that their insults were deemed so insignificant that they could be ignored with no damage to the superior's honor. Slaves, therefore, existed in a realm as far as possible from that of honor culture.[4] Not only would an insult from one of them be insignificant, but the very dependence of their position as chattel symbolically unmanned them. This emasculation comported well with planter notions of paternalism, which held all slaves to be essentially children and male slaves to be "boys" no matter what their age. Thus, a former North African cap-tive would be suspect within the masculine world of honor, independence, and brave manliness.

Independence, mastery, and masculinity were also closely linked in urban mercantile and artisanal culture. Merchants facing bankruptcy, having lost con-trol of their affairs, portrayed themselves as essentially unmanned. For artisans, too, the goal was mastery. Apprentices and journeymen served masters while attempting to gain a competency and become independent masters themselves. In the urban setting it was possible, even desirable, to rise from dependence to independence. As master printer Joseph Buckingham wrote, "chains and fetters may be made of gold as well as of iron, but neither the one nor the other can keep down the energies of an intelligent, well-cultivated independent mind." However, those who failed to attain mastery, such as clerks, economic failures, and long-time dependents, were frequently viewed as less than manly.[5] Similarly, aboard ship, common sailors who served the officers were often compared to African American slaves. However, as with successful artisans, mastery of work skills could help to restore a modicum of manly dignity to these shipboard "slaves." Unlike artisans, sailors were subject to impressment, which was even closer to slavery and therefore more emasculating, although they might attain a bit of redemption through battling their captors. As an impressed American seaman named Horace Lane crowed, the British sailors who had earlier "made him a slave in their navy," received their comeuppance when afterwards "British seamen by the scores had to fall" in combat against the American privateering vessel whose crew he had joined.[6]

Barbary captivity, which was yet another step closer to slavery, emasculated its victims even further. Captivity itself had been feminized by a century-long American literary tradition of narratives that were, in large part, stories of damsels in distress. From at least the time of Mary Rowlandson's capture by Indians in seventeenth-century Massachusetts down to the sensibility-laden tales of O'Brien's and Cathcart's day, most captives, and certainly the most popular literary ones, were women. Indian captivity narratives in particular hewed to this pattern, particularly such famous examples as those of Mary Rowlandson, Eunice Williams, and Mary Jemison, and often with a not-quite hidden subtext suggesting that captivity might also have implied forbidden sexual familiarity.[7] In the North African genre, too, despite that all the actual captives were men, the biggest selling narratives tended to be fictional accounts of women like Mary Velnet / Maria Martin or the ladies in Susanna Rowson's *Slaves in Algiers* who were in constant peril from their "barbarian" captors.[8] In the Velnet/Martin narrative and Mrs. Rowson's play, the women were ultimately rescued by male captives. Men, who were captured, these plot twists imply, could become heroes by revolting against or at least tricking their North African captors to escape submission.[9] Subordination to North Africans was particularly worrisome because of American perceptions of Muslim and Barbary sexuality. Lacking Christianity and the Enlightenment, not to mention manly restraint, North Africans were viewed by Westerners as slaves to their passions who gave in to impulses for all sorts of lascivious behavior, ranging from sex for pleasure rather than propagation to pederasty, polygamy, and homosexuality. O'Brien himself had noticed and commented on one dey's predilection for young boys.[10]

Thus for Eaton, and no doubt for other American men, O'Brien and Cathcart had been symbolically emasculated by their experience as Algerian captives. As "slaves" to a man who was himself slave to his passions, they certainly had lost, at least temporarily, all claims to manly independence. Unlike their fictional counterparts or the impressed seaman Horace Lane, they never succeeded at or even really attempted escape or revenge, another strike against them. O'Brien had once been a ship's master and Cathcart a skilled sailor, so perhaps like bankrupted merchants or striving apprentices, they might be able to regain their manly independence in time, but for Eaton at least they still needed to prove that they no longer submitted to their former masters and that they had not been corrupted by their long exposure to the allegedly more passionate, feminized Algerian culture.

The former slaves' alleged passivity, cowardice, and subordination posed a serious problem for the United States as well as for Eaton. Eaton and many of his countrymen hoped that the new nation, buoyed by the naval buildup of the 1790s, would begin to show strength in the Mediterranean to make up for its disgraceful servility in the Algerian crises. As consuls, Cathcart and O'Brien represented the new nation literally and figuratively. If they were emasculated slaves rather than independent warriors (as Eaton imagined himself), could not the same be said of the nation that they represented? As it was, the United States remained technically subordinate to the dey due to its treaty obligations to provide Algiers with annual "tribute" payments. Algiers' displeasure at the new nation's habitual tardiness in this matter prompted new diplomatic efforts with the dey rather than the sort of aggressive saber rattling men like Eaton would prefer. No doubt this weak position emboldened Tripoli's bashaw, Yosuf Karamanli, to declare war on the United States in 1801 and to demand an annual tribute from the new republic.[11] These developments prompted conflict within the new nation's diplomatic corps and among the public at large. American policy for the most part was to rely on timely payments and diplomatic expertise of the sort offered by Cathcart and O'Brien. Eaton viewed this approach as mere servility, a continuation by a different name of American slavery in North Africa. He and other like-minded Americans hoped the new republic could overturn with its navy the entire system of tribute. President Jefferson seemed to be on his way to acceding to their wishes when he sent out a small squadron to intimidate the bashaw in response to Tripoli's declaration of war.

While all three "lighthouses" agreed that the United States needed a naval presence in the Mediterranean, their specific approaches varied. O'Brien had called for a naval buildup when still a captive. Eaton certainly agreed. Not long after arriving in North Africa, he wrote, "Without force we are neither safe nor respectable here." But he went further than his predecessors in criticizing the basis of U.S. diplomacy. Hitherto, he wrote, America had relied on assistance from the Algerian government, to which it paid tribute, and upon "a brace of Frenchmen and their Hebrew co-adjutors," who were allied with the dey of Algiers, to negotiate with the other North African regencies. As a result, "We are plundered and disgraced without securing our object, while our agents have shared the booty." Fundamentally, the problem was that the American representatives acceded to the corruption of this system. The United States, Eaton believed, could not succeed in North Africa until it decided to fight the corruption rather than go along with it. This attitude marks a subtle break with previous American policy. That former "slaves" were given positions in Barbary reflected a general assumption that those most familiar with the North African system were best qualified to negotiate there. Besides Cathcart and O'Brien, former captives Timothy Newman and William Penrose received lower level appointments in North Africa. Other countries followed a similar policy. For example, the Spanish consul to Tripoli had also been a slave in Algiers.[12] Westerners had played along with the African regencies' policy of declaring war on European nations, capturing their civilians, and ransoming them back to their governments, or using them as hostages for peace negotiations usually involving the payment of tribute for centuries.[13]

Eaton rejected this entire system. When O'Brien or Cathcart called for more naval power, they saw it as a way to negotiate more favorable terms with the Barbary powers. When Eaton called for more naval power, he saw it first as a means of asserting American strength. "Nobody here acquainted with our concessions [tribute]," he wrote, "could be persuaded that we are the same Americans who, twenty years ago, braved the resentment of Great Britain . . . There is indeed no nation so much humiliated in matters of tribute." Thus, the United States must "reform" its method of negotiation with Barbary so "as to remove the impressions that weakness and fear have dictated the measures to which we have hitherto yielded." From this perspective, former slaves such as Cathcart and O'Brien might be skilled negotiators, but they could not possibly be the proper men to create the new impression of a strong, imperious United States.[14]

To make matters in North Africa more complicated, Cathcart and O'Brien hardly provided a unified front. Friction between them dated back to their ordeal in Algiers. Cathcart, technically O'Brien's inferior (he served as a sailor aboard the *Maria*), rose higher in the dey's court, eventually becoming chief Christian secretary, the most influential position available to a slave. Subsequently, he appears to have resented receiving directives from his shipboard superior but civilian subordinate. This tension was badly exacerbated in 1799, when the former captives returned together to the Mediterranean to assume their diplomatic posts. O'Brien, unmarried at age forty-seven, was alone. Cathcart traveled with his wife, Jane Woodside, and her English friend, Betsy Robinson, described by a contemporary as "of good appearance [and] about 20 years old." After falling out with the Cathcarts, Miss Robinson found sympathy with O'Brien, who married her a little more than a month later, amid charges from Cathcart that O'Brien had "seduced his maid from him."[15]

Over the next few years, relationships among the three "lighthouses" further deteriorated as their nation's position weakened. The initial catalyst was the arrival of the U.S. frigate *George Washington* in Algiers in September 1800. The ship, commanded by Capt. William Bainbridge, bore tribute for the dey as stipulated by the American-Algerian treaty that Eaton despised. When it arrived, the dey insisted on commandeering it for a mission to Constantinople. Consul O'Brien had been afraid the dey might attempt such an action for some time, but, given the lack of U.S. naval power and his own lack of funds, he and Captain Bainbridge saw no way to avoid it. Moreover, O'Brien feared that if they refused, Bainbridge and his 131-man crew would suffer "detention and slavery." As a precedent, O'Brien noted that, in 1795, American negotiators had seen fit to promise the dey a frigate when he demanded it. That precedent, though not initially authorized, had been retroactively approved by the U.S. government. He added that, while this action was taken when there were still one hundred American slaves in Algiers (including O'Brien) the number of potential slaves aboard the *George Washington* "is greater at present [and] in the power of a despotic government bound by no treatie or equity."[16]

Neither Bainbridge nor O'Brien was pleased by the ironic prospect that the first American ship to arrive in Turkey, and one named for George Washington no less, would sail under Algerian colors. However, they saw no alternative other than war—which would mean the capture and enslavement of the Americans in Algiers, and, without a stronger naval presence, still more tribute to be paid to the dey. Even more alarming to Bainbridge was the prospect of losing America's Mediterranean commerce due to further captures by an enraged dey. Bainbridge reflected that if only "the United States [knew] the easy access of this barbarous coast called Barbary, the weakness of their garrisons, and the effeminacy of their people, I am sure they would not be long tributary to so pitiful a race of infidels." O'Brien was humiliated and disgusted, "too heartsick and tired of Barbary to stay any longer." His chief hope was that once the *George Washington* returned safely he could "leave this country whether the United States sends a consul or not."[17]

When Eaton learned of the affair, he was even more angry and embarrassed by such dishonorable effeminate behavior. His country's passivity drove him to declaim, "How art thou prostrate! Hast thou not yet one son whose soul revolts, whose nerves convulse, blood vessels burst, and heart indignant swells at thoughts of such debasement!" "Shade of Washington," he continued, "Behold thy orphan'd sword hand on a slave—A voluntary slave, and serve a *pirate!*" Fearing that he might now face the same maneuver in Tunis, he fretted, "Shall Tunis also lift his thievish arm, smite our scarred cheek, then bid us kiss the rod! *This is* the price of peace!" In an implicit swipe at O'Brien, he added, "But if we will have peace at such a price, recall me, and send a *slave*, accustomed to abasement, to represent the nation." Finally, he concluded, "Frankly, I own, I should have lost the peace, and been empaled myself rather than yielded this concession."[18] By using such charged language to imply that O'Brien had been content to roll over and take whatever the Algerians dished out, Eaton could hardly have been more insulting of his colleague's masculinity.

Eaton's fears of a repetition in Tunis were soon realized in December when the bey of Tunis, perhaps emboldened by the example set by Algiers, attempted to commandeer an American ship to Marseilles. Through ardent negotiation (and some well-timed lies), Eaton was able to convince the bey to step back from his demands that the United States give him the use of the ship and instead agree to purchase it at only slightly less than its owner felt it was worth. This, Eaton concluded, was a "small sacrifice" to insure "that no dishonorable concessions have been yielded to this government."[19] Eaton believed that, unlike O'Brien, he had passed the test and retained his honor.

In Tripoli, Consul Cathcart was also growing increasingly vituperative on the subject of O'Brien, who, as consul-general for the Barbary coast was once again his superior. Cathcart chafed at his subordinate position which was "couch'd in such terms as will not authorize my taking one decisive measure unless first approved by a man who has done nothing (this two years past) but write nonsense dictated by the perfidious Jews at Algiers." Referring to O'Brien's eccentric nautical writing style, Cathcart described his superior's letters as "a complicated chaos of contradiction, misrepresentation, ignorance and duplicity mixt together with rocks, shoals, anchors, cables, masts, rigging and a thousand other absurdities which would puzzle Lawyer Lewis or anyone else to understand." The only constant in O'Brien's instructions, Cathcart complained, was his "desire of throwing the whole of our affairs both at Tunis and Tripoli into the pusillanimous

Jews as they are at Algiers and of writing unintelligible metaphors no more to the purpose than the proverbs of . . . Sancho Panza were."[20] Cathcart no doubt viewed O'Brien's alleged subservience to "pusillanimous" Jews as another aspect of his continuing dishonorable servility. While few actual Jews lived in the United States at this time, the public was familiar with theatrical stereotypes, which, with occasional exception, still portrayed Jews as comic weaklings unable to master their inordinate passion for money.[21] These stereotypes were not far removed from perceptions of Muslims as slaves to a somewhat different set of passions, and certainly one who served the Jews could hardly be seen as an independent honorable man.

Soon Eaton, too, began to suspect that O'Brien was a pawn of the Algerian Jewish merchants. He and Cathcart had begun discussing a plan to assist the bashaw of Tripoli's brother in a coup to create a government friendly to the United States. O'Brien apparently derided the idea as "insane." In response, Eaton wondered why "every commander as well as everybody else who has *acted* on this coast comes into this measure; and that those only who have scarcely or never been here take on themselves to reject it!" He added, in an apparent reference to O'Brien, "I flatter myself that the sink of Jewish perfidy in Algiers will not always have the address to blast the measures and disgrace the flag of my country!" O'Brien wrote a number of letters to Eaton and others attempting to explain that the British and Turks rather than the Jews were running the show in Algiers. To Eaton he wrote, in his characteristic style, "You have got into the eddies and took it for the tow stream." In response, Eaton began writing insulting comments on his copies of O'Brien's letters such as, "A Jew advocate," and, "He can't help advocating the cause of the Jews."[22]

While continuing to bicker, all three consuls constantly feared that one of the Barbary powers might capture more American vessels. They frequently warned American ships of the danger, but despite these efforts, their fears were soon realized when, in the spring of 1802, a corsair from Tripoli captured the American merchant ship *Franklin*, bound to Marseilles with a nine-man crew and a cargo of wine, oils, silks, perfumes, hats, and other items. Luckily, five of the crew who were not American citizens were quickly liberated, including three British nationals and two others described only as foreigners. That left only Captain Andrew Morris and three seamen, one white and two black, as "slaves" in Tripoli. Following the precedent set by O'Brien and the other captives of the 1780s and 1790s, Captain Morris wrote to Cathcart to report his misfortune and touch the consul's sensibilities, describing a pitiful captivity "deprived of the converse of a wife, family, and friends, and what is dear to every American, liberty." The capture, according to Morris, was a cause for national humiliation, especially due to the ineffectual presence of an American frigate that did nothing as the *Franklin* was towed underneath its nose into the port of Tripoli. Like earlier captives, he also managed to write home, to friends in Philadelphia whom Morris expected would reimburse Cathcart for any assistance he might render. Like his predecessors, Morris seemed most comfortable when offering his expertise as a ship's master. Having viewed firsthand the weakness of the American blockade of Tripoli, he warned that other American ships were in danger and provided details of the Tripolitans' operations. Like all of his predecessors, he urged vigorous naval action. To Cathcart he wrote, "One summer spent with vigilance by enterprising officers would convince the Bashaw that America was in earnest [and] obtain me my liberty and an honorable peace for my country."[23]

Luckily for Captain Morris, the *Franklin* incident ended quickly without creating the same shock and concern as the earlier Algerian incidents. As soon as he heard of the *Franklin* capture, O'Brien, who was now well versed in the Barbary customs of haggling and gift giving, promised the dey of Algiers a $5,000 payment to intervene with the Tripolitans. The dey lavished the bashaw of Tripoli with gifts, including bushels of wheat, pistols, a gold-sheathed sword, a caftan, and other items that clearly exceeded the $5,000 limit. In response, the bashaw freed the prisoners and agreed, at the dey's urging, to a peace treaty with the Americans at a cost of $120,000, thirty thousand of which would go to the dey of Algiers. Although not empowered to make such a deal, O'Brien thought the offer promising, considering that the usual haggling process might drop the price of peace still lower. Fearing further captures, he recommended the United States quickly send more naval power to the region while negotiating with the dey and the bashaw.[24]

Both the capture and O'Brien's response infuriated Eaton. As consul to Tunis he had the duty to notify the *Franklin*'s owners of their ship's capture. He wrote them a remarkably caustic letter, in which he took the unusual and tactless step of excoriating his own superiors' policy. The *Franklin*'s owners must have been distressed to read Eaton's speculation that the ship's crew would be "cried for sale at public auction, like so many cattle; or, perhaps, stationed on the batteries to slay and be slain by their countrymen." This fate, Eaton continued, would have been unnecessary had the government only listened to his pleas for more small naval vessels to tighten the blockade against Tripoli. Instead, U.S. policy verged on a "farce" with "our citizens dragged to slavery and goaded to a lingering death under the bastinade of merciless robbers"—certainly another unpleasant image for the *Franklin*'s owners. For Eaton, the worst of it was the humiliation faced by the United States due to the capture and the anticipation of having to pay tribute to Tripoli, as well as the probability of further demands from the bashaw and further insults afterwards. "If America can yield to this and look the world in the face without a blush," he wrote, "let her blot the stars from her escutcheon and veil with sack-cloth the sun of her former glory."[25]

Eaton believed he had found a way to avoid such servile humiliation. As soon as he learned of the *Franklin* capture, the consul began attempting to negotiate for the crew's release with the captain of the cruiser that had captured them and was temporarily anchored in Tunis. Unfortunately, the captain refused to allow Eaton near the "slaves" and also refused the bribes proffered by the American consul. Eaton next remembered that the United States had recently released several Turkish prisoners to the bashaw of Tripoli who, in gratitude, had promised to free the next several American captives caught by Tripoli. By August, Eaton had registered a formal request to the bashaw to free the *Franklin* captives based on this earlier promise. This plan offered a means to free the captives without the United States paying a cent or losing any prestige with the North Africans. Not surprisingly, Eaton was furious when he learned that O'Brien had paid the dey of Algiers to act as an intermediary. Eaton feared that O'Brien's action would prove counterproductive because Tripoli would resent the implication that it was subject to Algiers. He went so far as to write the bashaw of these concerns, assuring him that, "We believe it would suit better both the independence of your [Excellency's] character and the interest of the parties that all our negociations should be direct and without the intervention of any other power."[26]

Lying behind Eaton's insubordination was his fear, shared by Cathcart, that the allegedly servile O'Brien was somehow attempting to make the United States more dependent upon the dey of Algiers and, still worse, upon the Jews who allegedly controlled the Algerian regency. Eaton suspected that O'Brien's refusal to communicate with him was a symptom of the brewing conspiracy. O'Brien, he concluded was "literally the echo of the Jewish Sanhedrin" at Algiers. To the Secretary of State he wrote, "I should be at a loss to account for [O'Brien's] taciturnity on the subject [of the *Franklin*] with me if I did not perceive in the transaction a perseverance of the original project of placing the affairs of the United States in these regencies in the control of a cordon of Algerine Jews stationed at the different capitals." These suspicions apparently reached back to at least 1800 when Cathcart and Eaton began to speculate that O'Brien had become personally indebted to the Algerian Jews who had once brokered Cathcart's and O'Brien's release, and that he was therefore compromised as an American official.[27] Thus, in Eaton and Cathcart's view, the corrupt O'Brien sought to keep the new republic dependent upon Algiers by giving the Algerian Jews control of its North African affairs when a true and honorable man would have instead tried to rescue his nation from servility to the dey and asserted its mastery of North Africa.

Cathcart also criticized O'Brien's efforts to ransom the captives, which he feared would set a "pernicious precedent." Like Eaton, he castigated O'Brien for his apparent preference for servility over bellicosity. Yet Cathcart clearly had not mastered his job or his own passions. Without a diplomatic portfolio since his expulsion from Tripoli after the bashaw declared war on the United States, Cathcart was supposed to replace O'Brien in Algiers, but his attitude caused the Algerian regency to refuse him. In a letter to President Jefferson, the dey explained that he "wanted an American with a clean face" and that he "would never accept of any such character" as Cathcart who, he explained to O'Brien, was "an enemie to Algiers and Tripoli and of course not a fit person as agent for the U[nited] States in Barbary." Cathcart's character, he wrote, "does not suit us as we know wherever he has remained that he has created difficulties and brought on a war." For his part, Cathcart probably hurt himself with his hostility and arrogance toward the North African rulers. He once described a Barbary consul's position as "of all others the most humiliating and perilous . . . exposed to every species of insolence and degradation that a fertile brain'd Mohammetan can invent to render the life of a Christian superlatively miserable, that dare oppose his will, one moment menaced with chains, the next with death and damnation, in a state of constant vigilance concern and perplexity." Cathcart's inability to control himself or the "savages" was particularly ironic in light of the advice he once offered Eaton to "work upon [the North Africans'] passions [and] make use of their absurdities and superstitions as lawful weapons."[28]

The three-cornered dispute came to a climax when Cathcart and Eaton met with O'Brien in Algiers in late March 1803. Eaton had been asked to leave Tunis by the bey because of his own aggressive demeanor. Cathcart feared that this development would serve as a precedent for "the Jews and Mr. O'Brien" to allow the dey to refuse Cathcart. On March 20 O'Brien and Cathcart, brother captives for more than a decade, were reunited in Algiers. They barely spoke to each other. O'Brien handed Cathcart a letter that he said was a reply to Cathcart's complaint's about his actions in the *Franklin* dispute. Cathcart took umbrage at the perceived insult, later recalling that this note "contain'd little but insolence which I treated with contempt." O'Brien reported to Commodore Morris that the dey refused to accept Cathcart and that it would be unwise to anger the dey by forcing Cathcart on him, particularly since Algiers was on the verge of concluding a peace with Portugal, which would give the dey free reign to capture his enemies' ships, much as he had in 1793. At this point, Cathcart, unable to restrain himself, interjected, "true . . . and all the presents we will ever give him, will not prevent his cruising against us when that [peace with Portugal] takes place, but he will never have it in his power to act the tragedy of 1793 again, so long as the United States has vessels of war to oppose his depredations."[29]

Cathcart alleged that O'Brien never intended to step down from his Algiers post. His spurious resignation had merely been a ploy to disguise his real goal: the removal of Eaton from the Tunis post. With that goal achieved, Cathcart presumed O'Brien would work in league with the Jews to block his appointment to Algiers and thereby leave O'Brien in his old position despite his "resignation." Cathcart suggested that the State Department should now "write to the Jews to stop Mr. O'Brien's credit." Were that to occur, then "the Jews having no longer an interest in Mr. O'Brien's remaining there will cease to oppose my admission." If the government were not willing to take this step, Cathcart added, he would accept a diplomatic appointment to Spain instead.[30] He never received that appointment, nor did he ever serve as consul to Algiers. Instead, President Madison appointed Tobias Lear, a former personal secretary of George Washington who had been at the first president's deathbed. In his instructions to Lear, Madison emphasized that the new nation's "universal toleration in matters of religion" should be used to differentiate it from European nations with established Christian churches. In other words, Lear should make clear that the United States had no religious agenda to pursue with the Islamic states of North Africa, an important point when the European states were still strongly Christian. One wonders whether this might also have been a subtle jab at the anti-Jewish, anti-Muslim harangues of Eaton and Cathcart. At any rate, Madison proceeded to appoint Cathcart consul to Tunis, explaining that the failure to appoint him to the higher-ranking Algerian post should not be viewed as a mark against his previous conduct but only as a pragmatic accommodation to Cathcart's "personal unacceptableness to the Bashaw."[31]

Cathcart never served in that post either. The bey of Tunis refused to accept him, setting Cathcart into yet another rage, and, according to his chargé d'affaires, George Davis, nearly precipitating "an immediate war." Davis put the blame squarely on Cathcart's "extravagant passions, folly, and ill judged communications to the Bey." Ironically, by attempting to demonstrate his lack of "slavishness" to the North Africans, Cathcart had revealed himself to be a slave to his own passions and thereby validated Eaton's concerns about his manliness. For his part, Cathcart again blamed the Algerians and the Jews. He maintained that the bey's rejection of him was "in consequence of a request from the Dey of

Algiers in compliance with the will of the Sanhedrin and their most righteous secretary," by which he presumably meant O'Brien. Regardless of who was responsible, Cathcart had no choice but to resign his post in September 1803. In his resignation letter, he asked Secretary of State Madison to find him a new position in the recently acquired Louisiana Territory.[32] Although no longer a government official, he would continue to foment conflict in North Africa for some time.

Shortly after Cathcart's resignation, disaster struck. The U.S. frigate *Philadelphia*, commanded by William Bainbridge as part of a small American "squadron of observation" under President Jefferson's more aggressive Mediterranean policy, floundered onto a sandbar in Tripoli harbor in October. Unable to budge their vessel, the captain and crew eventually surrendered to the Tripolitans who surrounded the ship. The North Africans marched the 307 officers and crew members into town and held them as slaves, thus initiating the largest captivity crisis in America's contentious history with Barbary.[33] The Tripolitans soon managed to float the *Philadelphia* off of the sandbar, thereby providing themselves with a powerful modern vessel with which they might capture even more ships.

Cathcart, now a private citizen in Livorno, Italy, immediately attempted to take action to aid the captives. As a former captive, he claimed a deep sensibility to their plight. He quickly established a line of credit for them, sent three thousand Spanish dollars in cash for their use, and began to make arrangements to provide them with clothing, always a necessity for Barbary captives who were stripped of their worldly possessions at the time of capture. He wrote to Secretary Madison of feeling "grief as poignant as any of the sufferers can possibly feel for this most unfortunate event."[34] No doubt his grief was sincere, for, with the possible exception of O'Brien, no one in the government could better understand the suffering and terror that the captives were experiencing in Tripoli. He wrote to Captain Bainbridge, now a captive in Tripoli, that he hoped reports that the United States was paying a ransom for the captives were false. "I have been eleven years in captivity myself," he wrote, "and yet, I solemnly declare that before I would see my country obliged to accede to all the impositions which will be the consequence of concluding a precipitate peace with Tripoli, that I would suffer to undergo as long a captivity again and would glory in my chains."[35] Such lofty sentiments failed to inspire or reassure Bainbridge, who would soon advise the government to come to a quick settlement with Tripoli. To Secretary Madison, Cathcart expressed his wish that Bainbridge and his crew had blown themselves and their ship up rather than surrender it to the Tripolitans. "How glorious it would have been to have perish'd with the ship," he wrote. Instead, he added, both the *Philadelphia*'s crew and the nation would be again constrained in chains. "How apt are we all to prefer a precarious, nay an ignominious life of slavery to a glorious death which would transmit our names to posterity and have establish'd a national character which time could not efface," wrote a man who had endured, and even flourished as the dey's chief Christian secretary and a wealthy tavern owner during a twelve-year period of "slavery" in Algiers.

It was not long before Cathcart's efforts offended his former diplomatic colleagues, who viewed him as interfering with their official roles. Lear wrote Bainbridge that Cathcart's style was "arrogant and dictatorial." He added, "Mr. C. should consider that he is now but a private citizen; and further, he should re-member, that his conduct has given disgust (whether rightly or wrongly) to the Barbary powers; and therefore it could do no good to our affairs for him to as-sume an agency in them." Bainbridge agreed, expressing his hope that Cathcart would not be involved in peace negotiations and speculating that the former consul "must be deranged in his intellectuals, or lost to all reflection."[36] In his report to Secretary Madison, Tobias Lear, now technically in charge of all Bar-bary diplomacy, considered Cathcart's aid to the captives to consist "more of ostentation and vanity than anything else." Cathcart, he sniffed, "arrogates to himself almost the directions of all our affairs in Barbary." Clearly, he feared that Cathcart's work would reflect badly on his own efforts, for after criticizing Cathcart's initiative he quickly added, "I flatter myself that the relief from this quarter reached them as soon as from any."[37] While Cathcart no doubt hoped to emerge as a hero for assisting his countrymen, once again his fellow diplomats saw him as a hothead and a blowhard, certainly not the ideal of a self-controlled man of effective action.

The true hero of the episode and the apparent embodiment of that ideal was Lieutenant Stephen Decatur. In a daring action he and his crew sneaked into Tripoli harbor aboard a captured Tripolitan ketch renamed *Intrepid* and set fire to the *Philadelphia* under the noses of the bashaw and his navy.[38] They escaped without harm and to universal acclaim. Showing true sangfroid, and none of the bluster exhibited by Cathcart, Decatur simply signaled back to his commander, "Business, I have completed, that I was sent on." One American midshipman recalled, "At Naples you could hear of nothing but the '*brave Decatur.*'" Perhaps if he had failed, Decatur, like Cathcart, would have been viewed as merely hasty and overly passionate, but, as the midshipman noted in a pun on the name of Decatur's vessel, the new hero was understood to exhibit "an intrepidity which nothing but success could rescue from the imputation of rashness."[39] Heroes were intrepid, while failed would-be heroes were merely rash.

Meanwhile, O'Brien's star was also on the rise. Lear commended him for his work in Algiers, praising his ability to "keep the Dey in good humour, when we have been so tardy in our annuities." Both Bainbridge and Commodore Preble requested his assistance in Tripoli, while rejecting Cathcart's offer to help.[40] For all Cathcart's criticism of O'Brien as a tool of the dey and the Jews, the former captives' positions on Mediterranean policy do not seem to have differed all that greatly. Both former slaves wanted to see a strong U.S. navy that could force the North Africans into submission.[41] O'Brien, however, remained willing and able to work with the North Africans without becoming a slave to his passions. He urged George Davis, now the U.S. consul in Tunis, to negotiate a tribute with that country in order to prevent war with a second North African state, and he even authorized Davis to bribe the local authorities. To Cathcart, this approach reeked of weakness and a slave mentality, but to others it was a pragmatic way to make peace when, after all, the United States did not appear to be in a strong enough position to dictate terms unilaterally. Commodore Preble defended O'Brien's approach. He wrote Cathcart, "I can assure you, that you mistake that part of [O'Brien's] character which leads you to believe he wishes us to purchase or beg a peace." Quite the contrary, he continued, O'Brien was "as anxious that we should beat them into it, as I am myself."[42]

If the stylistic contrast between O'Brien and Cathcart was great, the contrast between O'Brien and Eaton was still greater. Like Cathcart, Eaton had been kicked out of a Barbary regency because of his belligerence. He accused the bey of Tunis's male lover of theft to the bey's face and chided the Tunisian ruler for the "violence and indignity" Eaton had received in Tunis. After turning Eaton out, the bey reportedly explained that the American was "too obstinate and too violent."[43] On his later return to Barbary as a special agent, Eaton was disappointed to find that the bey of Tunis was no longer threatening violence to American shipping. "I candidly confess I entertained an individual wish that we should find affairs at Tunis in such a situation as to afford me an opportunity of gratifying a righteous resentment against that Regency," he wrote Cathcart. This was too much even for Cathcart. When he forwarded Eaton's letter on to the Secretary of State, Cathcart distanced himself from his friend's aggressive stance with the disclaimer that, "I don't subscribe to [Eaton's] opinion as I have been always disposed to let the Barbarian chiefs alone while they remain friendly to us but when they infringe existing treaties to chastise them for their arrogance."[44]

Eaton's new mission in North Africa was to implement a bold plan he and Cathcart had crafted earlier. Essentially, they hoped to support a coup against the bashaw of Tripoli and bring his brother, Hamet Karamanki, to power as a puppet, or at least as a strong supporter of the United States. After the *Philadelphia* capture, Eaton touted this plan as the only way to preserve the nation's honor and to free the captives without paying a cent in tribute. "As an individual," he wrote, "I would rather yield my person to the danger of war . . . than my pride to the humiliation of [negotiating] with a wretched pirate for the ransom of men who are the rightful heirs of freedom."[45] Probably because of his difficult personality, Eaton had nearly as much trouble gaining support from his own government as he would marching through the desert. One problem was that his plan, if successful, had the potential to prove disastrous for the captives. The Danish consul in Tripoli wrote that the scheme was "very base" because "you sacrifice your prisoners [lives] here in case of success." For his part, Eaton pursued his plan with extraordinary, perhaps monomaniacal dedication, convincing a skeptical Hamet and a ragtag, disagreeable band of mercenaries to march across four hundred miles of desert from Alexandria to capture the province of Derne in a journey resembling the later trek of Lawrence of Arabia. Almost miraculously, Eaton and Hamet were able to meet up with the United States navy to capture Derne in a pincers action. Quite justifiably, Eaton's success was widely celebrated in the United States, and he became second only to Decatur as hero of the conflict in Barbary. Had he failed, no doubt, he would have been viewed as another Cathcart—rash and hotheaded rather than heroic and manly.

Sadly, the sequel did not go well for Eaton. Despite his urgings to the contrary, the capture of Derne allowed Lear to negotiate an inexpensive settlement with the bashaw, eventually freeing the captives at a cost of $60,000. This was far too much for Eaton, who stuck to his position that the United States should not pay a cent. To make the pill even more bitter, rather than setting Hamet up as bashaw and reuniting him with his family, which had been held hostage by the current bashaw, the United States withdrew all support for him except for a small stipend. Eaton viewed this action as deeply treacherous and dishonorable; after all, he had urged Hamet into action with the promise of power and an end to his family's captivity. While Eaton had, to his mind, pushed for a manly contest against the Barbarians and had come very close to pulling off a victory without paying tribute, the United States, he believed, had once again chosen the route of servile dishonor by paying off the bashaw. Eaton succumbed to alcoholism, which, combined with his difficult personality and various political machinations, soon transformed the hero into an embarrassment to those who had once glorified his name. He died in poverty and relative obscurity at the age of forty-seven, still bitter about his nation's treatment of Hamet and himself.[46]

The administration clearly had not shared Eaton's visceral outrage that the United States would negotiate with and even pay "tribute" to the "barbarians." In this regard O'Brien, rather than Eaton or Cathcart, was more in the diplomatic mainstream. It was not that Eaton despised the North Africans more or less than the other Americans involved in Mediterranean affairs. Most other politicians and diplomats simply did not envision the United Sates acting much differently than it did. After all, as O'Brien frequently reminded his correspondents, many smaller European powers also were in the habit of paying "tribute" to ransom captives and maintain the peace. Even England made some payments to the Barbary powers.[47] Although Eaton was probably correct that the U.S. consuls sometimes did not act as energetically as they might, to most Americans and Europeans the United States simply did not seem to have the power to terminate the centuries-long system of tribute and captivity. Thus, while Eaton hoped to use Hamet to destroy what was to him a servile system of tribute, the administration was happy enough to use him as a bargaining chip to gain a less expensive settlement.

Like the diplomats, the captured crew of the *Philadelphia* also worried that servility to the "barbarians" would compromise their manhood. One notable difference in the language of the Tripoli captives' letters compared to their predecessors in Algiers, was their refusal to describe themselves as slaves. Describing oneself as a slave was an excellent way to gain public sympathy by tapping into the language of sensibility and by appealing to abolitionist sentiments.[48] In doing so, the Algerian captives had represented themselves as helpless victims in need of charitable benevolence. The *Philadelphia* captives—at least those whose letters survive—were reluctant to assume this position. The most likely explanation is that, unlike earlier captives, they were members of the U.S. Navy rather than the civilian merchant marines traditionally held as Christian slaves by North Africans. As warriors, they believed they fit into a separate and more honorable category.

Consequently, the officers of the *Philadelphia* spent a great deal of effort defining themselves as prisoners of war rather than as Christian slaves. While Captain Bainbridge occasionally used both terms to describe the captives, it is clear that he preferred the former.[49] The difference was neither arbitrary nor trivial. To be a slave meant to be forced to work for the Tripolitans like a civilian captive. To be a prisoner of war, for the officers, meant to be confined as a gentlemen—with all the honorable connotations implied by that term, with at least a modicum of comfort, and certainly without working—until the warring sides reached a settlement. Shortly after the capture Bainbridge wrote Commodore Preble, "the officers as yet, have not been made to work, myself never will." Preble approved of this approach, writing to Bainbridge that, "Whether you will be slaves or not depends on yourselves, your determination not to work will be proper, and if the Bashaw should attempt compulsion by punishing you for a refusal, I shall retaliate on his subjects which I now have, and which may hereafter come into my possession." He soon recast this advice into an order, threatening that any captive who voluntarily assisted the Tripolitans would be put to death and writing that, "You ought not to let the threats of those, into whose hands you have unfortunately fallen intimidate you, but obstinately persist in your rights of being treated as prisoners and not as slaves."[50]

In general, the officers did manage to avoid hard labor, and they were, by their own accounts, relatively well treated. Cathcart's former house, where they lived most of the time, was "large, airy and commodious, with lengthy piazzas, in which we walk a great deal." The food, though "not sumptuous" was "extremely palatable and wholesome," and included eggs, muffins, boiled beef, mutton, soup, and, occasionally, tea. Officers were allowed to keep their personal servants that they had brought on to the *Philadelphia*. The ship's doctor, Jonathan Cowdery, although contemptuous of the "haughty" and tyrannical ruler, nonetheless confessed that he was well treated by the bashaw, who employed his services during various epidemics. One midshipman complained that he was not given *enough* work. "It is true," he wrote, "we have been treated with more lenity than we had reason to expect from a Barbary prince, but how much better would it have been for us to have been put to hard labour . . . then we could feel the fresh air, which is so essential to human nature." Conditions did occasionally deteriorate, most notably on two occasions when the officers were moved out of Cathcart's house and into the "castle" where the crew was imprisoned. This temporary precaution was taken just after Decatur burned the *Philadelphia* and the American squadron bombed Tripoli, when the bashaw may have feared further attacks or an attempt to free the captives. At any rate, this reversal was temporary, and afterwards one captive wrote they were "treated with more humanity than they were before the bombardments."[51] Nevertheless, the officers demonstrated their bravery by attempting to escape at least once and planning to do so a second time.[52]

The crew members, unlike the officers, did not or could not claim prisoner of war status. Dr. Cowdery lumped them together as slaves of the bashaw along with some Neapolitans and "negroes." These "slaves," he wrote, complained much "of hunger, cold, hard labour, and the lash of the whip." They also suffered from diarrhea and dysentery, which Cowdery was able to cure with carbonate of soda. Several crew members, including Bainbridge's former coxswain, attempted to improve their status by converting to Islam—or "turning Turk" as it was commonly described. This practice of becoming a "renegadoe" was a common one; indeed the bashaw's prime minister was a former Christian. Although Bainbridge roundly condemned these turncoats, given their miserable lot as the bashaw's slaves, it is surprising only that more did not follow this path.[53] As 1804 progressed, the crew's plight improved a bit. The Secretary of the Navy ordered that their families in America should receive their pay while they remained enslaved. That measure, however, did little to help the three-quarters who were not American citizens. In May the crew was moved into a new, more commodious prison where, Bainbridge claimed, "they now enjoy much purer air than the officers."[54] Still, their general situation remained far inferior to that of their superiors. In a hierarchical organization such as the navy, where even in the best of times the crew had virtually no freedom, that these men were "slaves" may even have seemed proper, or at least unremarkable, to some officers.

Despite his captivity Captain Bainbridge was able to maintain his importance and dignity as a man of affairs, acting in essence as the American consul to Tripoli. In so doing, he followed in the footsteps of Captain O'Brien, who had played a similar role when a captive in Algiers. But by 1803 the diplomatic corps and navy were much larger than in 1785, providing Bainbridge with more correspondents and a more powerful government apparatus than O'Brien had. Bainbridge wrote diplomatic and naval officials about the prisoners' conditions, the strength of the Tripolitans, and, most importantly and persistently, the best way to negotiate peace and free the captives. At one point he even entertained the hope of serving as an official negotiator for the United States in talks with Tripoli.[55] Although Bainbridge frequently complained that his correspondents did not respond, the administration nevertheless seems to have paid attention to what he had to say. Not long after he was captured, he outlined a scheme for blowing up the *Philadelphia* while it lay in Tripoli harbor. Eventually, Lieutenant Decatur carried out the operation more or less the way Bainbridge planned it, thereby becoming the great hero of Tripoli and saving the United States from the humiliation of being attacked by its own ship.[56] Bainbridge's suggestion that O'Brien be sent to negotiate with the bashaw was also followed, although Bainbridge was ultimately not happy with the results. His harsh criticism of the Eaton-Cathcart plan to support the bashaw's brother—whom he termed a "poor effeminate fugitive" and a "pusillanimous being"—probably helped Consul Lear and the administration to decide to keep their distance from the man whom the United States still officially considered the rightful bashaw of Tripoli.[57] Of course, unlike captive O'Brien, Bainbridge already was a high-ranking naval officer personally acquainted with many of the major players in the Mediterranean and in Washington. No doubt his position made his advice more valuable and influential than it would otherwise have been.

The bashaw was probably aware that Bainbridge was playing a crucial role in intelligence and policy discussions. Bainbridge and others always assumed that their mail was being read and frequently interrupted. The bashaw apparently even read the newspapers that the captives' friends sent to them. Word of the U.S. government's funding for Mediterranean operations in one such newspaper may have helped convince the bashaw that if he did not agree to peace the United States would be ready and willing to continue to attack Tripoli.[58] To avoid this surveillance, Bainbridge began to write his letters in code. This device had the advantage of secrecy but the disadvantage of signaling to the Tripolitan censors that he was up to something secretive. Eventually, with the assistance of the Danish consul to Tripoli, Nicholas Nissen, he devised a means of writing sensitive messages in lime juice, which was invisible to the Tripolitans but could be made visible by those in on the secret when they held it over a fire. Although Bainbridge occasionally feared that the Tripolitans were catching on to the code, they do not appear to have ever broken it.[59] Despite his captivity, Bainbridge became something of an invisible fourth lighthouse—to modify O'Brien's metaphor—warning the administration of treacherous shoals and providing other valuable information.

When Bainbridge and his men were finally freed in June 1805, their countrymen applauded without, perhaps, quite offering up the full three cheers. While the Algerian captives were treated as heroes and charity cases, the position of the *Philadelphia*ns was more ambiguous. Captain Bainbridge's very presence commanded sympathy. One of the first sailors to see him freed in Tripoli wrote that Bainbridge "exhibited a spirit of joy and gladness, mixed with humility which I never saw before in all my life. His first entrance . . . was truly a specimen of joy to excess, but his pale meagre countenance showed how the confines of Barbary fiends would dilute the whole system of a Christian." As usual, however, the experience of the crew was different. They embarrassed their officers by promptly, and understandably, getting drunk. As Captain John Rodgers, who was assigned to transport them, observed, the crew was not able to leave on schedule "as the intoxication of liberty and liquor has deranged the faculties as well as [the dress] of many of the sailors, and Capt. B[ainbridge] wishes them all on board quite clean and in order."[60]

For many of the crew members, liberty proved fleeting. Three were quickly impressed by a French ship, while most of the others were distributed among the crews of other American vessels where, while no longer prisoners, they remained subject to strict naval discipline. The officers and some seamen sailed on to Malta and then back home, arriving in Virginia in September. Newspapers and, presumably, private citizens greeted them warmly. One account offered them "the sincere hope that the pleasures they will meet in their native country, and in the embraces of their friends, will compensate in a measure their past sufferings."[61] But there do not seem to have been any parades or celebrations or even much more newspaper coverage, and other than Captain Bainbridge, the captives were mostly forgotten. In time-honored tradition one of them, Dr. John Ridgley, was appointed agent and later consul to Tripoli.[62] But the real heroes of the Tripoli War were Stephen Decatur and, for a time, William Eaton. Surely, this focus reflects dissatisfaction with the new nation's repeated victimization in the Mediterranean, of which the captives were a continual reminder. It probably also reflects the relatively short period of their captivity (compared to O'Brien and Cathcart's) and the fact that military men make less attractive victims than "innocent" civilians. Most of all, Eaton and Decatur represented America's new and (many hoped) growing strength and manly vigor, while the captives represented the old story of weakness and ineffectiveness.

The United States persisted in its effort to delineate between prisoners of war and slaves even after the Tripoli crisis ended. Article 16 of the peace treaty, which Cathcart had first suggested some years earlier, stipulated that should war resume "the prisoners captured by either party should not be made slaves; but shall be exchanged rank for rank"—that is, as prisoners of war. Only if one side captured more prisoners than the other would the excess captives be ransomed, and even then the treaty stipulated that they must be exchanged within a year.[63] Essentially, Cathcart's provision sought to transform the nature of American-Barbary relations from a slave-master relationship to a more equal footing. Much as Eaton had hoped to use force to end American enslavement, the treaty attempted to change America's subservient position through diplomatic means. Importantly, it did not specify that the captured ship must be a war ship. Thus, even merchant ships such as the *Franklin* or those captured by Algiers in the 1780s and 1790s were presumably included. The system of Barbary captivity was predicated on the idea that either civilian or military ships might be captured in time of war and their crews ransomed back to their homelands. This treaty provision, therefore, would appear to have revised the entire nature of this system in favor of the United States, preventing a long captivity crisis like the Algerian situation or that of the *Philadelphia* from occurring again with Tripoli.

Back home, issues of manliness, servility, and honor also shaped the political discussion of the crisis in Tripoli. Politics had been and remained a male sport, but by this time it was also becoming a contest between Federalists and Democratic-Republicans as the first party system matured and spawned a partisan press. In these newspapers the political conflict arising from the *Philadelphia* was most evident as both parties attempted to spin the crisis to make themselves appear more masterful, honorable, and manly and their opponents more impotent, incompetent, and servile.[64]

Because their leader, Thomas Jefferson, was president, Democratic-Republicans naturally tried to minimize the importance of the *Philadelphia* capture in order to protect their administration from criticism. One subtle way they did so was by scrupulously refusing to refer to the captives as *slaves* in partisan gatherings as well as in the Republican press. Thus, the Tammany Society of New York referred to "our brothers in captivity"; the 110th Pennsylvania Regiment toasted "our captive brethren in Tripoli" at a celebration of the administration's Louisiana Purchase; and another militia company, the Republican Blues, toasted "our fellow citizens now captives in Tripoli." On July 4 a popular Republican toast was to "our fellow citizens in Tripoli."[65] Citizens, even those in captivity, do not sound nearly as degraded as slaves, and the administration, which already had a domestic slavery problem, certainly did not want anyone to infer that it was responsible for white slavery in North Africa.

By contrast, the opposition Federalist press more frequently described the captives as *slaves*. This nomenclature not only made the crisis seem more profound but also highlighted the connection between the Jeffersonians and servility. Boston's Federalists toasted "our brethren in captivity at Tripoli," prayed that "their country's sympathy [would] break their chains," and then, to hammer the point home, sang a rendition of the song "Galley Slave." A poem in the *Boston Gazette* lamented that the captives were "the slave[s] of slaves." Another poem in the same journal referred to them as "brave men . . . doom'd to slavery's chain."[66] By employing such language, Federalists made the captives' condition appear as dire and pathetic as could be, thereby emphasizing America's weakness and implying that Jeffersonians were the source of this weakness.

In antebellum America, slavery could never be a mere metaphor, and during the *Philadelphia* crisis some Federalists linked the so-called slavery of the *Philadelphia* crew to the actual slavery of African-Americans. One Federalist poet connected Jeffersonian Republicans' predilection for domestic servitude to their alleged callousness toward the "slaves" in Tripoli. In an apostrophe to the captives, he declared: "The proud Virginian, who by slaves grows great; / The Carolinian, rich in ricy fields; / The Georgian too that rides in ample state— / No men or treasure for your ransom yields." Referring to the southern Republicans' dependence on their slave population for their representation as a result of the infamous three-fifths clause in the Constitution, the poet continued, "From those who to our country's councils come, / And have their suffrage from their numbered slaves, / Ye've nought to hope but slavery for your doom, / They'll neither ransom, fight, nor tempt the seas." The poet's message was clear: Democratic-Republicans, enervated and corrupted by their dependence upon slaves, could not be relied upon to attack slavery in Tripoli. It was only New England's vigorous, independent Federalist sons, who "would all alike their glorious aid impart, / And from their base Tripoli's ramparts sweep."[67]

Federalists also criticized Republicans for their alleged parsimony in funding the navy. William Coleman's *New York Evening Post,* among the first of the Federalist newspapers to take this tack, argued that if the administration had built more naval vessels for the Mediterranean squadron, the *Philadelphia* would have been protected by a convoy of American ships rather than finding itself alone and vulnerable when it ran aground in Tripoli harbor. The *Boston Gazette* soon published a letter making a similar point about Jefferson's parsimony and wondering, "Can it be the wish of our *economical* administration in this manner to avoid the expense of ransoming these unfortunate men?" A writer in the Federalist *Fredericktown Herald* averred, "Every man will see in a moment that the loss at least of the men [of the *Philadelphia*] is entirely owing to the niggardly policy of our rulers," and a writer in the *Charleston Courier* blamed Jefferson's "parsimonious plans" for the continuing crisis.[68] William Eaton's comment that the particularly frugal Republican Treasury Secretary, Albert Gallatin, "Like a cowardly Jew shrinks behind the counter" suggests that, for some, frugality was linked to the cowardice associated with Jewish merchants and that these attacks on Republican parsimony were also implicit attacks on Republican manliness.[69]

Predictably, Republicans were not happy about this criticism. The Republican *Aurora* accused Federalists of "mak[ing] the loss of the *Philadelphia* a *party business*" rather than blaming the dangerous shoals of Tripoli harbor. "We observe," the *Aurora*'s editors wrote, "some of the Solomons of the Federal party follow the example of Coleman in efforts to prove that the loss of the Philadelphia is attributable to Mr. Jefferson, who ought to have been *philosopher* enough, according to these wiseacres, to know that there were rocks in certain parts though they had never been laid down in the charts."[70] Nevertheless, Republicans themselves soon politicized the issue further by attacking the competence of Commodore Preble and Captain Bainbridge who, to the Republicans' glee, turned out to be Federalists. The Republican *Aurora* further revealed that Bainbridge himself had taken full responsibility for sending a schooner out of Tripoli Harbor, thereby leaving the Philadelphia alone when it became stranded. "If, then, the loss of the frigate and captivity of the crew are attributable to the absence of a second vessel the fault can no longer be attributable to the administration," the *Aurora*'s editors crowed. Cleverly questioning Bainbridge's ability while denying they meant to do so, they added, "We by no means wish to implicate Mr. Bainbridge, with us no doubt exists but all that happened was accidental, but if different opinions shall be entertained, he must thank the Federalists for their scrutiny." Still, "Since Mr. Bainbridge has assumed all the blame, and he is a Federalist, we shall hear no more from Mr. Coleman or others on the subject," they concluded. Preble, too, came under attack from the *Aurora*, which argued that, as Bainbridge's superior, he bore some responsibility for the debacle.[71]

In response, Federalists attempted to make a hero of "their" commodore and cast further aspersions on the Republican administration. One Federalist claimed, "the gallant Preble was obliged by want of adequate force, to withdraw from the shabby walls of Tripoli. Himself and his gallant officers and men, revered with glory—his national councils covered with shame." A similarly minded Federalist wrote of a Mediterranean squadron "commanded . . . by skillful and enterprizing officers, and manned by brave and experienced seaman, but utterly incompetent, in point of strength, to reducing the enemy." All this occurred, he noted disapprovingly, while "tens of millions of the public treasure [were] squandered in the purchase of a trackless wilderness," namely, the Louisiana territory.[72] In 1805 when Jefferson relieved Preble of command and brought in a fresh squadron commanded by Commodore Samuel Barron, the Federalist press took the opportunity to print various encomiums to Preble, who had pursued an aggressive strategy against Tripoli after the *Philadelphia* capture. The *Boston Gazette* published in full a tribute to the commodore signed by his subordinates in the Mediterranean, including the great Republican hero, Captain Stephen Decatur. The paper also published praise from a British commodore who wrote that Preble's "bravery and enterprise cannot fail to mark the character of a great and rising nation." There was even praise from the pope, who averred that in subduing the Tripolitans Preble had "done more for the cause of Christianity, than the most powerful nations of Christendom have done for ages."[73]

In some ways similarities outweighed differences in this conflict. Both parties assumed that naval force of some sort was the way to regain national honor and end American slavery in North Africa. Both sides also shared the strategy of subtly impugning the manliness of the opposition. In this climate, neither party could risk losing face by suggesting a negotiated settlement, so instead they debated the cost of action. In the wake of the *Philadelphia* capture, Congress deliberated on a bill to raise more funds for the Mediterranean fleet by temporarily elevating import duties. Somewhat contradictorily, considering their usual attacks on Republican "parsimony," some Federalists saw the proposal as too expensive.[74] Republicans maintained that the tax was necessary to pursue the fight against Tripoli effectively. Treasury Secretary Gallatin noted that the government had only $150,000 on hand, far short of the necessary sum. Furthermore, the new imposts would be temporary and would be rescinded within three months of ratification of a peace treaty with Tripoli, provided the United States remained at peace with the other Barbary powers.[75]

The Republicans managed this debate cleverly. By acting promptly to raise more funds for the Mediterranean squadron, they co-opted any lingering Federalist criticism of their alleged weakness or parsimony. Any Federalist opposition would now look unpatriotic if not duplicitous. Federalist opponents were, therefore, quite defensive. Raising the impost was no doubt distasteful to many of them. Centered in the Northeast and more closely tied to the overseas merchants affected by the impost than were the Republicans, Federalists feared that their constituents would be disproportionately burdened by the Republican plan. But the Republicans had them trapped, and in the end the impost bill passed unanimously. Before reluctantly voting his approval, Benjamin Huger, a Federalist from South Carolina, could not help noting for the record that "those most averse to this mode of raising revenue from its inequality and oppression, were, notwithstanding, ready to vote for carrying the great object of the bill into effect."[76]

Such was the power of captivity that it seemed always to push Congress and America generally toward a more aggressive military policy. This tendency was already emerging during the Algerian crisis, and it became much clearer in 1804. While politicians might be able to resist calls for military intervention to protect trade or to fortify distant and thinly inhabited frontiers, in a democratic republic they simply could not resist the moral imperative to rescue captive citizens. Given the connection between action and masculinity that had been raised by Americans in North Africa and by the partisan press, it became nearly impossible to oppose naval expansion. American men at home and abroad clearly feared that their nation's perceived weakness might reflect poorly on their own masculinity, and in a republic in which a large percentage of the male population participated in the polity and was beginning partly to define itself through such participation, any perception of national impotence reflected on the new republic's men. Increased saber rattling and heroic efforts to rescue their captive countrymen were a way of correcting this perception and restoring honor to America and her sons. Time and again Barbary captivity played into the hands of those who hoped to enlarge the navy, some of whom no doubt also hoped to enlarge America's role in Mediterranean and world affairs generally. Thus, even while continuing to feed party divisions, the crisis in Tripoli also inexorably pulled both parties into deeper involvement in overseas affairs.

CHAPTER EIGHT

Between Colony and Empire

For most of its early history, North America was the subject of literary explorers, conquistadores, travelers, and armchair geographers ranging from Christopher Columbus to Richard Hakluyt to Captain John Smith, all of whom produced important books about the New World. It was only in the late eighteenth century that residents of North America themselves began to produce such literature about other continents, and this development was largely associated with the effort to describe North Africa to a public shocked by the capture of their countrymen. This genre could best be described as popular Orientalism—depictions of the exotic Islamic East written by amateur authors, frequently former captives, for the general public. Following Edward Said, most scholars who discuss Orientalism see it as a handmaiden to empire. That is, knowledge of "Orientals" and their lands becomes a tool and incentive for imperial expansion. The circumstances for Americans of the early republic, however, were more complicated. Their own home had recently been a colonial subject of European geographers interested in the "savage" other, but they were mostly the descendants of colonizers, and, as such, were heirs to an already established British Orientalist tradition. The popular Orientalism of the early national United States reflects both aspects of this heritage and also serves as a sort of map and instrument of the new nation's transition from colony to proto-empire.

American Orientalists blended two well-established genres: travel literature and captivity narratives. Travel literature had a long history in England and was itself a hybrid, blending history, geography, and natural history into what has been described as "chaotic variety."[1] Whatever the subject matter, it was usually written in the language of expertise to instruct the reader, or at least that was its avowed purpose.[2] At perhaps the most fundamental level it was a sort of professional stock in trade—or a system of knowledge—to assist those men (almost always men) at the leading edge of empire in their day-to-day business of conquest or trade. However, by the late eighteenth century, travel literature was becoming more overtly sensational, presumably designed to attract armchair travelers of all types and both genders. Nonfiction authors increasingly brought more of their own thoughts and experiences into their work, making them, in Mary Wollstonecraft's words, "the little hero of each tale."[3] Fiction writers, particularly Laurence Sterne in the aptly titled *A Sentimental Journey*, brought the newer language of sensibility into the genre. American authors in the early republic reflected these trends with their frequently lurid and sensational accounts.

Captivity narratives, too, were becoming more lurid and melodramatic, but unlike travel narratives, they were a more distinctively American genre. Although recent scholarship has shown that they were becoming more common in Britain, where *Gulliver's Travels* clearly reflected their influence, it was in North America, located at the interstices of European and Indian worlds and the confluence of "civilization" and "savagery" that such narratives were most common, particularly those describing the capture of women by Indians.[4] In addition to the ever-present threat of Indian captivity in pioneer life, Americans also were frequent victims of captivity at sea—whether from European navies or Caribbean pirates—and African Americans were beginning to tell their own stories of captivity at the hands of European Americans. Because the literature about North Africa was also prompted by captivity, this genre often served as a template for the first American Orientalists.

These American authors saw another connection between Barbary and Indian captivity: in both cases the writers viewed the captors as savages. The first major American accounts of Algiers, written by Mathew Carey, John Foss, and James Stevens, described parallels between Algerians and Native Americans. Carey compared Algerian Arabs to the "North-American savage," while the complexion of the "Moors" reminded Foss of the "Indians in North America." Stevens compared Algerian Turkish haughtiness and the "horrible yells" of the corsairs to Native Americans.[5] They were hardly the first authors to make such comparisons. Captain John Smith, who had been a captive in Constantinople before exploring Virginia may have been the earliest Englishman to make the connection, but comparisons between Native Americans and Turks were common among Virginians in the colonial period.[6] Finally, the frequent newspaper connection between outrages committed by "savage" Indians against Americans in 1794 and the contemporaneous outrages committed by "savage" Algerians against American shipping reflected and reinforced the connection between Native Americans and North Africans.[7]

The first American Orientalists relied on the Indian captivity narrative model, in which Americans were largely passive victims, and upon English travel narratives, from which they sometimes stole long passages whole cloth. The first, most influential and, probably, most popular of these writers was Mathew Carey, author of *A Short History of Algiers* (1794).[8] Carey set the precedent for the genre by blending instructive travel literature and sensational captivity sections. Accessible and relatively concise at five short chapters plus appendices, Carey's book opens with two chapters providing general descriptions of the geography and mores of Algeria. He emphasizes the region's decline from the glory days of Carthage and the modern inhabitants' savagery and ignorance. For example, in describing the geography of Algeria, he notes that most rivers there might be used for transportation "were the inhabitants of a more intelligent and industrious character," but due to the "gross ignorance of the natives," not one was even bridged. Such arguments resemble contemporary descriptions of Native Americans as lacking civilization because they lived in a supposedly unimproved wilderness.[9] The next two chapters trace Algeria's history from the rise of King Barbarossa in the sixteenth century to the Spaniards' failed attack of 1775. Carey discusses the Algerians' contact and conflict with Europe without much consideration of their internal history other than a few entertaining accounts of their bloody political struggles—usually focusing on the murders of various leaders.

One might be tempted to see Carey's book as taking the first step to develop the new nation's knowledge of North Africa in order to establish and justify hegemony over "Oriental" people, working much like early European Orientalism as described by Said.[10] The problem with this interpretation is that virtually every word of these first four chapters is lifted from older British sources. Carey took the two historical chapters (49 pages out of a 106 page text) nearly verbatim from the entry for Algiers in John Seally's *A Complete Geographical Dictionary or Universal Gazetteer of Ancient and Modern Geography* (1787). The next two chapters copy a variety of sources, most notably Thomas Salmon's *Modern History* (1744–46).[11] Only the short fifth chapter on Algerian-American relations is substantially in Carey's own words. Thus, most of Carey's work might be understood as reflecting established currents of British Orientalism rather than developing an American school. To accuse Carey of plagiarism, however, is to miss the point. While Carey's borrowing appears rather extreme, it is probably typical of the way knowledge was disseminated in the eighteenth-century. While twenty-first-century copyright laws criminalize plagiarism, in the eighteenth century ownership of words was far more flexible. Much like today's World Wide Web, sentences and paragraphs were fungible and passages or chapters from one work were frequently cut and pasted into others. For example, Carey copied a passage on the Spanish king Charles V's siege of Algiers nearly verbatim from Sealley's 1787 geographical dictionary.[12] In turn, Sealley, who seems never to have traveled outside of Europe, most likely took this passage from an anonymously authored work published a generation earlier.[13] In this sense, Carey was heir to a long tradition and was as much a colonial dependent on the wisdom of the mother country as an imperialist offering the tools to control new territory. Carey's dependence on British predecessors reflects an ongoing American scientific and literary colonialism that extended well beyond independence.

Carey was not, however, entirely derivative. A close comparison of his text to its predecessors offers some hints of a distinctive American attitude. For example, the large section on Algerian mores, mostly lifted from Salmon's popular (and frequently copied) work focuses on brutal punishment. Salmon, a world traveler who may or may not have visited Algiers, provides a long paragraph on Algerian "punishments," beginning with the bastinado—always fascinating to English Orientalists. Carey copied most of this paragraph, omitting only a detailed definition of the bastinado (of which he may have assumed his readers were already aware) and, more tellingly, two of Salmon's caveats. Carey includes Salmon's description of the "worst of all deaths," which occurred when a Christian slave was thrown from the walls of Algiers onto iron hooks "on which they are catch'd by the jaws, by the ribs, or some other part of the body, and hang in the most exquisite torture for several days," but he omits Salmon's caveat that, "'tis said [it] has not been executed for many years." Carey also includes Salmon's description of the crucifixion of Christian slaves in Algiers but fails to include the caveat that this behavior was provoked by "reports that were spread of some of their Christian neighbors having been equally cruel to the Turks they had taken."[14] Carey also deviates from Salmon by appending an extra paragraph detailing the brutal punishments given to Islamic men and women for various crimes—including the severing of thieves' hands and the drowning of adulteresses.[15] The general tendency of these deletions and additions is to make the Algerians seem even more savage toward each other and toward the Christian slaves.

Other additions and deletions were aimed at making the account more relevant to Americans. For example, while Seally described a daring 1635 raid on Algiers by a tiny band of Frenchmen as a "ridiculous undertaking," Carey omits the derogatory adjective. He also omits Seally's comments that the Frenchmen "had the good fortune" to capture several Algerian ships as well as his comment that they "madly encountered" several others.[16] Clearly, Carey was attempting to make the raid less the unlikely accomplishment of a bunch of lucky lunatics and more of a feat that might potentially be imitated by other small but intrepid navies, such as that of the United States. At the end of this narrative, Seally notes that piracies on "Europeans" continued until 1652. Carey refers instead to attacks on "Christendom," no doubt so that Americans (Christian but not European) could more readily deduce the parallels between themselves and the daring (*not* lunatic) Frenchmen.

Carey also occasionally inserts comments on explicitly American issues. In recognition of travel writers' frequent treatment of America as a strange and "savage" land, at one point he interrupts a description of Algerian mores to reflect, "Perhaps an African critic would turn from our description of his country with as much disdain as a citizen of the United States feels in attempting to peruse a frothy volume respecting North America fabricated by some of the professional book-builders of Paris or London." In a rather ironic footnote, considering his own methods, Carey offers several examples of European travel writers who never left home or plagiarized extensively from others when writing about America. Finally, Carey inserts a long paragraph comparing the Algerian slave trade to the American trade in Africans, which he damns as a European introduction to the New World.[17] In all these passages Americans are implicitly or explicitly passive victims, while others, European or savage, act upon them.

The importance of this emphasis becomes apparent as Carey shifts from travel literature to captivity narrative. In his final and only original chapter, he discusses America's recent conflict with Algiers. Here he focuses almost exclusively on what he perceives as the government's shameful passivity in hesitating to create a navy. Blaming England for the truce which allowed Algiers to capture the American ships, he heartily approves of recent congressional efforts to build vessels that, should they ever meet the Algerians, "will fully avenge the injured honor of America."[18] This declaration is followed by thirty pages of appendices consisting of letters, newspaper articles, and poetry about the Algerian captures that together form a composite captivity narrative. The story of the initial capture, including the typical account of how the Algerians stripped the Americans of their clothing, is told in a letter from Captain William Penrose, who laments that "it is impossible to subsist long in this miserable situation." Details of the captives' hard labor performed with fifty-pound iron chains which "reache[d] from our legs to our hips" and the severity of the Algerian masters are provided by a letter from Captain John McShane. A letter from Captain O'Brien laments the lack of a navy to assist the captives. Correspondence between David Humphreys and the captives adds further pathetic touches regarding their suffering, all of which culminates in an anonymous account urging the reader to behold the captive "cruelly rent from the embraces of a beloved wife—from the arms of his infant—from every object beneath the circling rays of the sun, that could afford a gleam of momentary joy, and consigned to chains and misery!" Finally, the whole collection is capped off by a typically melodramatic Humphreys poem lamenting the captives' pathetic state. Here is pathos and sensibility in spades to reward the patient reader who has slogged through Carey's earlier, far more technical account of Algerian history, culture, and geography. This section of Carey's account also forces the American reader to imagine the possibility of being captured by savages rather than, as with so much European Orientalism, the possibility of conquest and empire.

Like Carey's book, the two other major accounts of Algiers published in the 1790s adopted the hybrid form of travel literature and captivity narrative, often borrowing words and passages from Carey and others. They also emphasized Algerian savagery in much the way American captivity narratives had emphasized the savagery of Native Americans. However, these accounts differed from Carey's and their English predecessors in that both were substantially written by or from the point of view of nonelites rather than by upper-class travelers (as in the case of Seally) or relatively elite armchair travelers (like Salmon or Carey). John Foss was a sailor aboard the *Polly*, one of eleven American ships captured by Algerians in 1793. *The Journal of the Captivity and Sufferings of John Foss* was the earliest eyewitness account of Algiers written by an American. James Wilson Stevens, the author of the decade's most comprehensive history of Algiers, was not a captive himself, but he garnered much of his information from his correspondence with Isaac Brooks, a common sailor aboard one of the captured ships. Brooks, according to Stevens, had been "reduced . . . nearly to a state of blindness by his ordeal."[19] Foss and Brooks are excellent examples of how the words and thoughts of plebeian individuals were finding their way into the growing and globalizing late-Enlightenment public sphere.

Foss's and Brooks's nonelite seafaring background helps to explain why they so often emphasized liberty in their accounts. Beyond the obvious deprivations of captivity, liberty was always an important issue for "Jack Tar," the common seaman, who became less than free the moment he stepped on board the little kingdom of the captain and who risked further loss of liberty at every turn, whether captivity, impressment, or prison ships.[20] This desire for liberty no doubt was heightened by the times; the first Algerian episode occurred less than a decade after the Declaration of Independence and during a period when defining the meaning of the inalienable right of liberty was a crucial issue for the United States. Foss's climactic section on his captivity in Algiers creates great pathos in the contrast between Algerian slavery and American liberty. He writes of the captives as "respectable citizen[s], and affectionate parent[s]" who "vindicated the cause of liberty, and adorned society by inflexible honor" in the Revolution, but who now "expected to end our days in the most laborious slavery." This gloomy future was somewhat ameliorated by the "humanity" of the "Republican government of the United States," which provided each of the captives with a monthly allowance to purchase clothing and other necessities. "Our relief," Foss writes, "was a matter of admiration to [the] merciless Barbarians [who] viewed the American character from this time in the most exalted light."[21] Perhaps Foss hoped this example of republican liberty might prove an inspiration to the Algerians. The "barbarians," however, were not the only ones who needed instruction on this count. Sadly, release from the dey hardly guaranteed Foss and his comrades their liberty. On his homeward voyage he was first captured by a British ship and briefly impressed, and later twice captured by Spanish privateers and once again briefly impressed. His liberty was only secure when, more than a year after his release, he set foot on American soil at Cape May, New Jersey.[22]

The portions of Stevens's account most likely influenced by sailor Brooks also reveal delight in liberty. The captives' sense of relief is palpable in a detailed section discussing their state of mind at the prospect of release. "They were haunted with the dismal apprehensions of servitude for life, and hope, the pleasing illusion that gilds the dark regions of adversity, seemed fled for ever," until their release appeared to be at hand. In detailed discussions of the captives' slavery, Brooks, through Stevens, concedes that many other captives were treated worse and that the Americans were among the favorites in Algiers. The rumors of the worst punishments—castration, tongues cut out of prisoners mouths, and even shaved heads—were false, Brooks asserts, and Americans generally bore their "sufferings" with dignity. Nonetheless, "frequent and severe punishments were inflicted upon them for the most trivial remissness, and a thousand inadvertencies, which are natural to those who have been accustomed to the enjoyment of their liberties."[23] Much as Frederick Douglass would argue years later about his own servitude, Brooks and Stevens's point is that the deprivation of liberty and the substitution of arbitrary punishment, however harsh, is the cardinal offense of slavery.

Both Stevens and Foss also focused on Algerian savagery, which, for them was in many ways the obverse of Americans' desire for liberty. In doing so, they borrowed heavily from earlier Orientalists. Despite Foss's insistence that his first-hand experience insured that "the facts herein stated will not be called in question," the bulk of his book was lifted from English accounts and Carey's book.[24] Rather than copy word for word, his usual method was to take general observations from Carey, probably some from other sources, and to intersperse examples purportedly from his own experience throughout. For example, in his section on punishment, he essentially copied Carey's discussion of the roasting alive of Christians, the "exquisite agonies" of the metal hooks, and the slave crucifixions. He also added details not found in Carey, such as passages on the beheading of Islamic women and Christian slaves.[25] After these general (yet vivid) descriptions, he added a series of specific anecdotes of harsh treatment of Christian slaves by Algerians that occurred in 1794–95, including two instances of slaves who were beheaded. Foss testified, "I was an eyewitness to these inhuman scenes, which will never be effected from my memory."[26]

Although Foss adds the theme of Algerians' supposedly inhuman savagery and cruelty to the standard travel literature accounts, he also seems marginally sympathetic to the North Africans when he writes, "Still, we may derive some useful lessons from these barbarians." Sounding a bit like the early European observers of American "noble savages," he grudgingly compliments Algerians on their economy and occasional kindness. A man that he met early in his captivity offered Foss an entire cake after seeing that he was willing to eat a small crumb off the pavement. This, writes Foss, "was the greatest deed of charity I ever knew from a Mahometan during my residence in this wretched place." In another instance, Foss recounts the strange behavior of the North Africans who, during a heavy rainstorm, stripped themselves naked and rolled their clothing into bundles while Foss sought shelter in vain. After the rain, the North Africans unbundled their clothing and dressed themselves under the watchful eye of a wet but thoughtful Foss. "I must confess," Foss wrote, "I thought them something in the right; for after the storm is over, be it ever so violent, they have dry clothes on their backs."[27]

Stevens's *An Historical and Geographical Account of Algiers* was far more comprehensive, detailed, and balanced than Foss's and Carey's work. It was also less popular, apparently going through only one printing.[28] In form, Stevens's account was much the same as the others, with long borrowed passages interspersed with original material. Stevens took portions of the travel literature sections from Carey, but he most likely copied other sections from British Orientalist literature. Stevens's account was also similar to his fellow Americans' in that much of what he added to the British Orientalist literature emphasized the Algerians' "deplorable barbarism." Some of Stevens's accounts of savage punishment are taken word for word from Carey, such as the roasting alive and crucifixion of Christian slaves. Other portions seem to paraphrase Carey, for example, the "exquisite torture" of those who were thrown over the walls and caught by the iron hooks. Still other more detailed passages appear to be taken from English Orientalist sources, such as a description of a Muslim transgressor being sawed in two, which also would be used by Foss when he published his account the following year.[29]

While neither Stevens nor Foss saw the Algerians as fully civilized, the former captive generally emphasized the natives' savagery more than the less passionate historian. Two examples of anecdotes told by both illustrate this divergence. The first involves a cruel Algerian overseer named Shereif who fell to his death quite suddenly one day in the spring of 1795. Both authors agreed that he was violent and savagely cruel and that he died while chasing a Christian slave. For Stevens his death was merely "accidental," while for Foss it was providential, the result of a "suffering Christian['s]" prayer that, "God grant [Shereif] may die the first time [he] offer[s] to abuse another man."[30] The second anecdote involved a Christian slave and Muslim woman alleged by the authorities to have violated Islamic law by consorting with each other. In Stevens's version the man was a Neapolitan tavern keeper caught with the Muslim woman by one of the dey's spies. In Foss's version he was an innocent slave who noticed the woman being taken away by an official and merely asked of what crime she was accused.[31] Both writers agreed that the Christian man (whether lover or innocent bystander) suffered harsh punishment, but the woman's fate was worse: death by drowning in a sack weighted down with a bombshell. When the woman's body somehow managed to slip out of the sack and float to the surface a day later, she was made a marabout or saint.[32] In the end, any subtle differences in the narratives are probably less important than the shared emphasis on Algerian savagery and the contrast to American liberty. Such a perspective was perhaps a natural result of the continuing American exposure to captivity by "savages" at home and abroad and of the influence of the captives themselves in writing these earliest examples of American Orientalism.

At the turn of the nineteenth century, Americans grew less fearful of savages at home and abroad as their nation grew more powerful and more able to protect its citizens. In North Africa the successful resolution of the *Philadelphia* crisis gave the new nation greater credibility abroad. At home, Americans celebrated the

Louisiana Purchase, approved by the Senate just eleven days before the capture of the *Philadelphia*. The purchase roughly doubled the size of the new nation and many hoped it would give access to the Pacific Ocean, thereby broadening the country's role in world trade.[33] Thus, the United States took simultaneous steps toward establishing a presence in the Pacific as well as the Mediterranean. There were other connections between the *Philadelphia* crisis and the Louisiana Purchase. Both stemmed initially from fears of weakness and captivity. With Napoleon Bonaparte in control of New Orleans, the United States feared the French might impede or capture the numerous vessels that used the Mississippi as a highway to connect the farms of the trans-Appalachian Northwest Territory to the Atlantic ports of the East.[34] Furthermore, Jefferson viewed the Louisiana Purchase as an answer to "savage" warfare with the Western Indians, which, as with the crisis of 1794, could include capture of American settlers by the "barbarians." The purchase was intended to protect Americans in two ways: by creating peaceful trading alliances with natives and by providing territory into which hostile or inconveniently situated Indians might be relocated, thereby making the Mississippi Valley safe for white Americans.[35]

The Louisiana Purchase and success in the Mediterranean ultimately helped to allay Americans' prevailing sense of weakness and victimization, but the United States was still not much of an empire at this point. On the day that Consul Lear arrived in Tripoli to negotiate the peace treaty, a new crisis over possession of Texas and West Florida was coming to a head in Madrid. The United States came close to declaring war against Spain, an aggressive posture that an earlier generation of American historians viewed as at least a partial result of the navy's success in North Africa. According to Henry Adams, "Even the blindest could see that one more step would bring the people to the point so much dreaded by Jefferson, of wishing to match their forty-fours against some enemy better worthy of their powers than the pirates of Tripoli."[36] In the end, the United States backed down, opting to buy West Florida rather than to risk war with Spain. As these cautious steps suggest, 1804 marked an intermediate stage in the new nation's position in the world. It was postcolonial yet pre-imperial. Having created a navy in response to Barbary captivity and purchased vast new lands in response to other threats, the United States was emerging from its subservient position within the British empire to become an independent actor of some consequence. It was not, however, ready or able to exert the kind of power that many European nations could, and it remained intimidated even by a collapsing (but well connected) imperial power like Spain.

This transition was reflected and to some extent crafted by the substantial

American Orientalist literature written in response to the Tripolitan crisis. As the new nation flexed its military muscles, it also began to shed its dependence on British literature. A new, more American approach placed less reliance on the words of British authors and less emphasis on the "savage cruelty" of the North Africans. As a result, the Tripolitans came off as more human, more nuanced, and less stereotypical "barbarians" than had the Algerians in the 1790s. Many factors undergirded this shift. Tripoli was not Algiers, and the bashaw did not have quite the same reputation for cruelty as the dey. The Americans writing in this period, all of whom were associated with the U.S. Navy or the diplomatic corps, were of a higher status than the common sailors in Algiers. More fundamentally, the new nation's growing power prompted its citizens to view the "savages" in America and Africa less as fearsome enemies who might easily capture and destroy them and more as the remnants of interesting but doomed races who might make good trading partners while they persisted. President Jefferson hoped to send a number of scientific expeditions, including the one ultimately led by Lewis and Clark, to map out the territory beyond the Mississippi and to explore potential for commerce with the natives. A number of proto-anthropologists, most notably Albert Gallatin, Jefferson's treasury secretary, began to study Indian languages and mounds out of scientific curiosity.[37] Similarly, Americans in North Africa now considered the locals with as much curiosity as terror. Less victims than explorers, the new cohort of Orientalists sought to understand how the United States might benefit from its contact with North Africans rather than merely document the "barbarians'" savagery and brutality.

While Carey, Foss, and Stevens wrote history interspersed with fiction, the first popular Orientalist work to capitalize on the Tripolitan crisis interspersed history into largely fictional accounts. *The History of the Captivity and Sufferings of Maria Martin,* exemplified the movement away from dependence on British literature and the declining importance of savagery. The first American edition was published during the Tripoli crisis as *The Affecting History of the Captivity and Sufferings of Mrs. Mary Velnet,* a fictional captivity narrative set quite topically in Tripoli and apparently stolen from an earlier British narrative of the same title.[38] Primarily a work of fiction focusing on the slavery and suffering of a young Italian lady at the hands of the "savage" Tripolitans, it went through two editions in the United States. The most vivid prose was reserved for the various tortures imposed on Mrs. Velnet, climaxing with a long and graphic description of her "exquisite pain" from a "torture machine" shaped something like a windmill with

Frontispiece and title page to *Captivity and Sufferings of Maria Martin* (1815 ed.). Courtesy the Western Reserve Historical Society, Cleveland, Ohio.

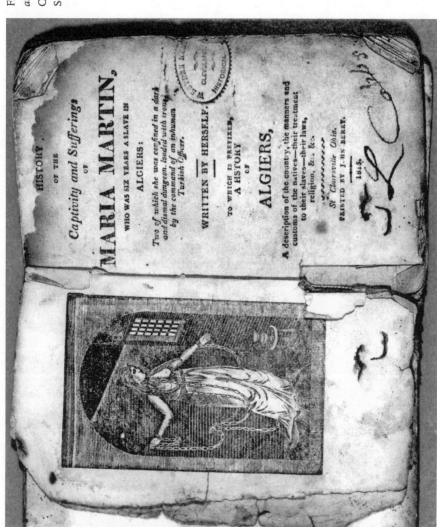

sharp metal spikes that rolled over the captive's naked body, piercing her "flesh to the bone" until her arms and legs were wrenched out of joint while the spikes continued "tearing and hacking" her flesh.[39] Needless to say, the Tripolitans in such an account were little more than caricatures, and the narrative was aimed more at entertainment than edification despite a short section offering a general description of Tripoli most likely copied from a travel narrative.[40]

American publishers were not satisfied for long with this warmed-over British narrative. They soon transformed the heroine from an Italian lady named Velnet into a woman named Maria Martin who, at first, was of indeterminate origins but in later editions became an Englishwoman. She must have been popular; her tale went through six editions between 1807 and 1812.[41] Nearly all of the torture that was so striking in Mrs. Velnet's story was absent from the 1807 edition, and the main form of Mrs. Martin's suffering was her confinement in a prison cell— perhaps a reflection of American Orientalists' preoccupation with liberty and its absence. In subsequent editions, some of the torture described in Mrs. Velnet's tale crept back into Mrs. Martin's story. The torture machine reappeared but in an abbreviated passage, and instead of Mrs. Martin suffering exquisite pain, an unnamed male captive who had attempted to escape was the victim.[42]

Still more striking was the change in the form of Mrs. Martin's narrative. While Mrs. Velnet's story almost entirely described her sufferings, the first half of Mrs. Martin's story consisted of passages from Carey's *History of Algiers* intended to instruct the reader on the story's setting, now transferred from Tripoli to Algiers.[43] Thus, while Mrs. Martin's story took a step away from the focus on savagery of the earlier American Orientalist literature, it now imitated its predecessors in their hybrid form and even in their frequent theft of Carey's words.[44] At first glance, the switch in locale from Tripoli to Algeria seems a strange choice. The Algerian crisis had been settled for nearly a decade before the first Algerian edition of Maria Martin came out in 1806. Why move the setting from a place that had recently been in the newspapers to one farther from the minds of Americans? A purely practical consideration may have been that changing the setting to Algeria allowed the publishers to bulk up the story by including passages from Carey's recently reprinted book. Deeper considerations, however, may also have been at play. In 1804, as Ms. Velnet faced the torture machine, Americans were still following the fate of the unfortunate captives from the *Philadelphia*. But by 1806, when Mrs. Martin sat in her cold prison cell, the *Philadelphia* prisoners and the navy had returned home triumphantly from the shores of Tripoli. Tripolitans, in short, had been tamed and no longer made credible "savage monsters," so Mrs. Martin's publishers were forced to change the story's setting due to the recent successes of the U.S. Navy.

The nonfiction accounts of North Africa published shortly after the War in Tripoli were written by participants. Compared to the participant-Orientalists from the Algerian crisis, these authors tended to be higher status and less fixated on native savagery. In his book, *American Captives in Tripoli,* the *Philadelphia*'s surgeon, Dr. Jonathan Cowdery described the despair of the *Philadelphia*'s capture and the improbable success of its burning, as well as the ultimate release of the captives and defeat of the bashaw. Everyone, it seemed, needed Cowdery's medical services, from the captive *Philadelphia*ns to the bashaw's own family, allowing him to see more of Tripolitan society than arguably any other American before him and to describe much of it in the first captivity narrative to emerge from the crisis in Tripoli. Readers would have known what to expect by this time: the typical instructive-entertaining, travel literature–captivity narrative hybrid that had proven so successful from Mathew Carey to Maria Martin. Indeed, Cowdery's editor described his work as "instructive and amusing," promising that later editions would contain "the particulars of the capture of the *Philadelphia* frigate;—a general description of *Tripoli*; with the adjacent country, its curiosities, etc., and a sketch of the customs and manners of its inhabitants;—to which will be added, the journal at full length, kept during his captivity, and an appendix containing the treaties and general relations between the United States and the Barbary powers."[45] Yet Cowdery's book, as published, contained none of that. The only instructive material directly pertaining to the manners of the Tripolitans came in a section of less than one page at the end of the volume under the heading "Further Particulars." The rest of the book consisted solely of a chronologically organized first-person account of Dr. Cowdery's adventures and impressions in Tripoli without any of the long instructive passages on history, geography, and manners that readers would have expected. As such, it was unique in American literature. It was also the first wholly original piece of nonfiction Orientalist literature produced in the United States with no reliance on British sources.

Cowdery's work departed from its predecessors in content, as well as form. Anyone hoping for another melodramatic account of suffering American captives and savage barbarians whose chief interest was imposing "exquisite pain" on Christians would have been disappointed. Certainly the title of the book, *American Captives in Tripoli,* would have encouraged such expectations. So would the editor's preface, which promises passages on "the capture and the treatment of our fellow citizens . . . and their release from the shackles of slavery." In the afterword, the editor writes of the "fraud, duplicity, and cruelty" of the North Africans, of their "natural ferocity" and "political depredations." At one point he calls Tripoli a "hideous monster," and he begs western nations to "strike off the chains from the bleeding arms of their citizens in captivity, and revenge the injuries of Christendom."[46] By contrast, Cowdery's actual journal contains virtually none of this sort of language. It hardly discusses the American captives at all, instead providing a balanced and rather favorable portrayal of a Tripoli far from the mindless, inhuman savagery of Maria Martin's or even John Foss's Algiers.

All captivity narratives have as a dramatic high point the capture of their heroes. In the Algerian literature, readers typically were made to feel the initial terror of the sailors, to imagine the barbarous violence of the Algerians, and to experience the shame and dehumanization of the captives who were stripped of their clothing and possessions. Foss described these pirates as "a parcel of ravenous wolves."[47] Cowdery, too, began his narrative with his capture by violent North Africans—but in his case the Tripolitans "fell to cutting and slashing their own men who were stripping the Americans and plundering the ship." He experienced virtually no violence to his person, saved his clothing, and lost only a bit of money. He was helped by a Tripolitan officer who held him by the hand, promised his friendship, and helped Cowdery off the *Philadelphia* into a lifeboat. This officer would not let the doctor take his trunk (which the Tripolitans pledged would be returned to him) or his manservant, and he stole some money from Cowdery's pockets, but, nevertheless, Cowdery's experience was hardly as shocking or disturbing as the usual capture story.[48]

Earlier captives generally had nothing but contempt for North African rulers and their legal systems. Foss described the dey of Algiers as a man of "a very malicious disposition" who "often (when he is in a rage) commands deeds of inhumanity to be committed."[49] Stevens described how the dey's attendants walked ahead of him and beat anyone who got in his way.[50] All of the earlier Orientalists dwelt in great detail on the punishments administered by his government. Cowdery, on the other hand, seems quite taken by Tripoli's ruling bashaw. He describes a "good looking man, aged about 35" who makes a "handsome appearance" at their first meeting. Elsewhere, Cowdery sees him as polite, even apologetic for a religious leader's rudeness.[51] Far from terrifying others, the bashaw himself seems somewhat terrified of bomb attacks on Tripoli, during which he hides in a bombproof cellar. He apparently suffers from epilepsy, and one of his fits terrifies the common people, whom Cowdery considers superstitious.[52] Cowdery rarely shows anyone being brutally punished in Tripoli. On the one occasion when the bashaw sentences a man to death, it is a North African who murdered an Englishman. The good doctor writes only that it was determined that the murderer "ought to suffer death," without giving any details of the execution.[53] Earlier Orientalists doubtless would have dedicated at least a paragraph or two to the man's "exquisite suffering" as he faced death.

Earlier captives also typically devoted many sentences to descriptions of their confinement in tiny, damp, primitive cells at night and their endurance of cruel taskmasters, heavy lifting, and horrific punishments during the day. None of that is present in Cowdery's account. He spent little more than a day or two in anything that could be considered a prison, and the only work he did was in his capacity as a doctor. Most of all, earlier captives complained constantly about the lack of food or, in those rare instances when they ate regularly, about the unpalatability of the Mediterranean diet of bread and oil. By contrast, Cowdery's Tripoli is a gourmand's delight. Our hero frequently reports on his visits to the city's many gardens and the wonders he finds, such as pomegranates, dates, oranges, apricots, date tree sap (which "tasted like mead"), lemons, squash, cucumbers, figs, watermelon, muskmelon, apples, peaches, plums, and more. Even on a bad day, his life is a perpetual feast compared to other accounts of scanty meals of bread and water. For example, on December 20, 1803, he writes, "The market was so poor that we could get nothing for dinner, but a shoulder of poor dromedary."[54] Such a meal might have fed John Foss for a week!

Cowdery's relatively sunny depiction of North Africa was not merely due to his personal idiosyncrasies, nor to his location in Tripoli. At the same time that the doctor was penning his journal, Tobias Lear, the new American consul in Algiers and a former aide to George Washington, was writing a similar account. In his unpublished journal, Lear echoed Cowdery's praise of North African agriculture, noting that "fruits of the tropical and temperate climate [are] abundant and very fine [and] the grapes exceeded by none in the world." He also commented on the abundance of wild fowl and high quality of the livestock. The land, he wrote, was extraordinarily rich but frequently "badly cultivated." He did not attribute this situation to an intrinsic lack of agricultural knowledge but rather to the custom of confiscation of produce by Turkish soldiers and others, which provided little incentive for farmers to increase their yield. Still, despite these difficulties, the Algerians managed to produce surpluses of wheat and barley to be sold at market.[55]

Lear and Cowdery's emphasis on agriculture was more significant than it might appear today when industrial technology is the preeminent sign of advanced cultures. Historically, agriculture has been the measure of civilization. Although North America has frequently been seen as an agricultural cornucopia, many observers feared that American farmers in the early nineteenth century were abusing the land by using outdated practices. These concerns prompted a scientific agricultural movement in which gentlemen around the nation—many of whom were also involved in new industrial projects—joined together in agricultural societies to spread information and technology that they hoped would convince common farmers to save their fields by adopting a more scientific approach to their work.[56] Well-connected gentlemen such as Lear and Cowdery would have been closely acquainted with this movement. Understood in this context, Lear's and Cowdery's encomiums to North African agriculture take on greater significance and certainly differ from the earlier denunciations of Algiers as uncivilized and savage. Rather, these accounts make North Africans appear technologically advanced and suggest that they may have lessons to teach American farmers as well as products to sell to American merchants.

Cowdery's shipmates, who wrote their own captivity narratives in the form of letters to friends and colleagues, also placed less emphasis on Barbary savagery than had their predecessors in Algiers. These captives expected their letters to be widely read, published in newspapers, and disseminated to a curious and worried public. Despite the relative brevity of the twenty-month *Philadelphia* crisis, more than twenty letters from captives, nearly all officers, appeared in American newspapers, and many others were probably circulated from person to person in manuscript form.[57] While the captives did not hesitate to report on deplorable conditions and injustices, they did so in a matter-of-fact way, rarely dwelling on their deep suffering or making efforts to forge emotional contacts with their readers. Most of the complaints revolved around confinement, loss of clothing, and the brief movement of the officers from the American house into the prison. One writer lamented that the British consul had not yet rescued him from imprisonment as promised. Most were surprisingly admiring of their captors. Shortly after the capture, William Knight, the ship's sailing master, described the bashaw only as "a very handsome man" and asserted "we are [treated] well[,] much better than I expected." A letter written in November of 1805 by a *Philadelphian* reported that "our unfortunate countrymen in captivity are in good health and spirits, and are treated with more humanity than they were before the bombardments by our squadron under the command of Commodore Preble." A midshipman wrote, "It's true we have been treated with more lenity than we had reason to expect from a Barbary Prince." Nonetheless, by November the crew's inactivity was starting to make him anxious: "How much better would it have been for us to have been put to hard labour, as our crew [was,] then we could feel the fresh air, which is so essential to human nature."[58] A few men expressed more alarm. One wrote, "Though we struggle to support with fortitude the horrors of our situation, yet human nature is scarcely equal to the conflict." An officer wrote of the crew's situation: "I confess I never saw anything that wounded my feelings equal to the sight of those poor fellows."[59] Still, compared to the letters written from Algiers, these were quite calm and generally employed the language of expertise far more frequently than they tried to touch the readers' sensibilities.

The one account written by a nonofficer, William Ray's *The Horrors of Slavery*, was, like Cowdery's work, original, chronologically oriented, and almost entirely independent of British Orientalism.[60] Ray's interpretations of events in Tripoli, however, differed sharply from Cowdery's and other officers'. In its unremitting focus upon liberty and savage tyranny, Ray's account is reminiscent of the earlier accounts of more plebeian captives such as John Foss and Isaac Brooks. Deistic, fiercely egalitarian, and suspicious of all authority because of its tendency toward arbitrary power, Ray embodied working-class Republicanism of the type described by Sean Wilentz, and his account clearly reflects these concerns.[61] His perspective might best be described as "Republican working class Orientalism" to distinguish it from the more genteel Orientalism of armchair travelers, naval officers, and diplomats.

Ray's dogged obsession with liberty and its opposite, tyranny, set him apart even from other nonelite observers like Foss and Brooks. For Ray the "horrors of slavery" began long before he and his fellow tars set foot in Tripoli. As a young man of modest means, he was constrained by "the tyranny of passions / and versatility of fashions," as well as by the fluctuations of fortunes and "creditors' voracious jaws." Soon he faced the prospect that he "should, or might be, forthwith arrested / and creditors with right invested / to seize his property while any, And when he'd not another penny / To take his body sick or well, / and drag it to a *worse* than hell." While he managed to avoid debtors' prison by enlisting in the marines, even in America he was unable to ignore the stain of slavery. A self-professed disciple of "the peerless Jefferson," he could not abide the hypocritical tyranny of Southern planters:

> Are you republicans?—Away!
> 'Tis blasphemy the word to say—
> You talk of freedom? Out, for shame!
> Your lips contaminate the name.[62]

Ray even decried the tyranny of parental oppression in a long digression, and he condemned the use of spirituous beverages in the navy because it made the sailors slaves to their passions.[63]

As soon as Ray stepped on board the *Philadelphia*, the pace of tyranny quick-ened. He ironically noted that his voyage began on July 4, the "glorious anniver-sary of American independence." On board the *Philadelphia*, however, there was no independence to be found. Sailors were tormented by midshipmen ("puny brats of despotism") and senior officers alike. Ray jumps ahead of the story to recount how, shortly after the captives had been freed, one of them had the te-merity to blacken the deck with his dirty feet, for which he was soundly whipped by the deck officer. According to Ray, "That a man, but just escaped from the sanguinary clutches of Tripolitan barbarians, weak, pallid, and broken with toil, chains, and hunger, should so soon be treated worse than by those savages . . . was enough to awaken the spirit of indignation in the bosom of a sainted an-chorite." For Ray it is clear that savagery is the handmaiden of tyranny: "Are the officers of our navy legally invested with such absolute power?—or, is such power as unlawfully assumed as it is arbitrarily exercised?"[64] His implied question is: "Who is the real savage?" In short, do not the ship's officers and the bashaw all exercise "arbitrary power"? By the time the *Philadelphia* finally runs aground in Tripoli—roughly seventy pages into the book—the Tripolitans' savagery and the bashaw's despotism seem a departure only in degree from what Ray had already experienced. Ray's Tripoli is a far more violent and disturbing place than Cowdery's. Men are frequently bastinadoed. Twice he reports on malefactors who have limbs amputated in punishment. One "wretch" had his left hand and right foot amputated and the stumps "dipped in boiling pitch" until he breathed his last "in the most exquisite agonies." Another man's head was chopped off and carried on a pole throughout the town. While these instances are quite similar to some of the punishments extensively described by earlier English and American writers, they serve a different purpose in Ray's book. Rather than exemplifying the contrast between Eastern savagery and Western civilization, they underscore the constant threat to liberty from arbitrary tyrants, whether they be bashaws or midshipmen.

Certainly, Ray seems more viscerally angry at his American superiors than at the Tripolitans. His anger no doubt reflects the importance of class, or at least rank, in Ray's worldview. Dr. Cowdery, an officer who in his journal has set him-self as the authority on Tripoli, gets the lion's share of Ray's ire. He takes pains to contradict Cowdery's account on many points, nearly always on the grounds that as an officer the doctor has no understanding of or compassion for what the crew experienced. From the initial capture in Tripoli harbor, Ray finds Cowdery's account lacking. While Cowdery claims the raiding Tripolitans fought among each other, with some having their hands amputated and others being killed, Ray tersely notes, "I never saw any hands amputated, nor do I believe there were any lives lost; for myself and a hundred others were in the ship much longer than the Doctor, and none of us saw or heard of the carnage amongst themselves." He also doubts Cowdery's claim that the doctor single-handedly fought off one of the attackers, noting sarcastically that it was "certainly the most heroic action that has ever been read of any of the Philadelphia's officers." While Cowdery lost virtually none of his clothing or personal possessions and was "treated to a supper, . . . lodged in this comfortable mansion, and had mats to sleep on," Ray did not fare as well. He accuses Cowdery of failing to "think proper to descend to the task of relating how the crew were provided for, or whether they were but half alive or all dead." Ray tells a much more traditional story of the capture, echoing the Algerian captives' accounts of their experiences. He relates that the crew members were stripped of all, or nearly all, their clothing, thrown into the sea, and, after they struggled to land, marched through town and spat on by soldiers.[65]

While Cowdery generally admired the bashaw, Ray saw him as majestic but "tawdry." Cowdery generally saw Tripoli as a cornucopia; Ray ate the paltry portions of bread and oil traditionally granted captives and averred that Tripoli's market made "a wretched appearance." Reacting to Cowdery's description of having to eat a camel's shoulder for dinner, he writes, "What the Doctor here complains of in such dolorous language, would have been a feast and produced strains of joy with us." While the doctor usually lived in comfort in the "American House," he and the officers were occasionally brought to the crew's prison to threaten them or to confine them during attacks on Tripoli. Cowdery's description of one of these episodes enraged Ray: "Poor Doctor! In this whining tale there are several misrepresentations. That the officers were in the prison amongst us, contaminating fellows, is true; but the Doctor and his fellow officers, though nobody doubts their feeling very big, must be gigantic monsters indeed, if they had hardly room enough to stand in a cell at least twenty five feet high, and which contained every night nearly three hundred men, who were chiefly absent the whole day."[66]

While the doctor visited with the bashaw's family and treated their medical problems, Ray and his fellows were beaten by Muslim and renegade Christian taskmasters and forced to perform tasks such as carrying heavy barrels of gunpowder while walking on tender feet. "What would the querimoneous Doctor think, if he had been doomed to such hardships," Ray wonders. Finally, Ray also criticizes the doctor for allegedly preferring to treat the wealthy people of Tripoli to assisting sick members of the crew. When John Hilliard, a popular crew member, died of the flux, the doctor was visiting the bashaw's son, thereby, according to Ray, depriving Hilliard of proper medical care. "The company of a 'prince,' in a flower-garden, was much more pleasing to the Doctor, than the company of a languishing sailor, in a dreary cell," Ray concludes.[67]

Ray's distrust of authority and love of liberty is also evident in his treatment of the *Philadelphia*'s other officers. He is particularly harsh toward Lieutenant David Porter, who had caused the young navy a great deal of consternation earlier when he stabbed a man to death in Baltimore. Ray blames Porter's careless navigation for the *Philadelphia*'s grounding, but perhaps more seriously from Ray's perspective, he alleges that Porter ordered some marines flogged merely for a reply to him that was "not quite so obsequious and parasitical as to please the ear of consummate arrogance." When the men failed to remove their hats while begging mercy, Porter ordered them flogged again. "Suppose," Ray wonders, "an officer had cooly and deliberately stabbed a man in Baltimore, and had to fly from the pursuit of justice, and dare not return to America for fear of the halter, could anything better be expected from such an officer, than that he would treat his men with the cup of torture?"[68] Ray also heaped criticism on Captain Bainbridge who "was thought, by many of our sailors to be a good officer" but who trusted his subordinates too much. Ray implicitly placed much blame on Bainbridge for the *Philadelphia*'s fate. He writes that the bashaw's commodore once asked the crew "whether we thought our captain a coward or a traitor?" When they replied, "Neither," the commodore said that had Bainbridge not been such a coward and surrendered so quickly, he could easily have gotten the ship free and escaped as soon as the wind shifted. Ray, usually so outspoken, did not contradict the commodore at the time or in his narrative.[69] Perhaps more damningly, Ray also accused Bainbridge of ignoring the needs of the captive crew members in order to protect himself from criticism. Bainbridge, according to Ray, refused to obtain government funds to help feed the crew. In losing the *Philadelphia*, "he had committed a most flagrant blunder, and to parry off the shafts of obloquy would hold up the idea of . . . frugality in his expenditures."[70]

Rank was important to Dr. Cowdery as well, but his conception was essentially the opposite of Ray's—which is no doubt one reason why the doctor so irritated the marine. Cowdery's perception of Tripoli was shaped by a view similar to what David Canadine has labeled "ornamentalism." Rather than the classic notion of Orientalism as a devaluing of the savage "other," ornamentalism suggests feelings of class unity among elite westerners and elite easterners, albeit usually with the "Orientals" as subservient. In this conception, nonelites, both eastern and western, are seen as inferior to the leaders of whatever nationality.[71] As a source of cross-cultural elite solidarity, it is the converse of Marx's call for the "workers of the world" to unite. After 1804, working-class Orientalism was declining, and ornamentalism was ascending due to the higher-class status of Americans in North Africa. With the involvement of the navy, many Americans in North Africa were now high-ranking officers, and, of course, every one of the *Philadelphia's* crew was a member either of the navy or marines, which probably put them a notch or two higher on the status ladder than the common merchant marines who had been captives in Algiers. Furthermore, the growth of the diplomatic corps brought with it more elite professional observers like Tobias Lear. Much the same thing was occurring in the Western frontier. As Lewis and Clark made their way across the mountains, these elite government officials brought a different and potentially more imperial perspective than the trappers and traders who had preceded them.

Despite their differences, Ray and the ornamentalists together marked something of a new phase in American Orientalism. Unlike their predecessors, none of these observers viewed all North Africans as savages, and, as a result, these writers were able to portray their captors as more fully human rather than as mere caricatures of the savage other. In the past, American Orientalists had augmented the existing British emphasis on savagery; this cohort muted it. Analyzing the meaning of this new direction is a complicated project. British writers themselves had begun to mute the savagery theme by the end of the eighteenth century, in large part due to the declining power of the North Africans, so the American writers may have just been following the British lead.[72] However, the earliest American Orientalists had actually augmented the importance of savagery when they stole from their British counterparts, and the new Orientalists seemed generally disinclined to rely on British sources. Thus, the post-1804 American rejection of the savage barbarian trope seems particularly notable. In rejecting the earlier caricatures of North Africans, the new American Orientalists rejected not only dependency on British authors but also the old mentality of weakness and victimization embodied by Carey and Foss. Americans who were unafraid of the North Africans represented a nation more confident in its ability to protect its citizens.

The new Orientalism also reflects the declining significance of the captivity narrative for American Orientalism. Just as Lewis and Clark were meeting western natives from a position of some power, Americans in North Africa now were secure enough to relax their concerns about capture by the local natives. American ornamentalists saw the North African rulers, who were frequently of Turkish descent and had lighter complexions, as less savage than the subjected native North Africans.[73] These writers still occasionally continued to compare North African natives to Native Americans, but unlike earlier Orientalists, the intent was usually to emphasize North Africans' weakness or superstition rather than their fearsomeness. Lear compared native farm laborers to "our southern Indians," based on their hairy appearance and tawny complexions. Far from threatening, these natives "are in a state of abject submission to the Turks." Eaton saw similarities between the "savage arabs" and the "savages of America," except that the Arabs were "less enterpizing, and [had] nothing of that wild magnanimity which invigorates the free born sons of our forests." Cowdery never mentions Native Americans in his journal, but his editor notes in an appendix that Tripolitan marriages are proclaimed by old women running through the streets "making a most hideous yelling, and frequently clapping their hands to their mouths, similar to the American Indians in their *pow wows*."[74] However savage these North Africans might have been, they hardly appear threatening in this treatment.

Rather than viewing Native Americans and native North Africans as formidable but "savage" enemies, Americans were now coming to see them as backward, inferior races offering little resistance to American advancement. In the case of Native Americans, this attitudinal adjustment was part and parcel of a more aggressive territorial expansionism that would soon become Manifest Destiny. For the time being, however, American Orientalists rarely engaged in such dreams. If anything, most probably envisioned an empire of trade rather than something on the British model of overseas territorial conquest and administration. As sailors, naval officers, diplomats, and overseas merchants, American Orientalists wanted free trade unhampered by captivity and other "savage" depredations. If Tripoli looked like a wealthy and surprisingly sophisticated place—well, all the better to profit from its trade once the troubling problem of captivity was resolved. Ray probably had these ideas in mind when he wrote:

Where late yell'd the savage, and wolves howl'd for prey,
Gay Villages rise and the arts flourish round us;
And science forth beams like the dawning of day,
Nor earth holds our commerce, nor oceans can bound us;
Lo! India's vast shore!
Our seamen explore!
See Lybia's wild deserts an Eaton march o'er!
To prove Nature's equal eternal degree—
Heav'n ne'er formed us slaves—man was born to live free.[75]

In this Jeffersonian vision, industrious American yeomen were busy civilizing the trans-Appalachian frontier with their new settlements while American sailors tamed Asia and Africa through commerce. To Ray's vision, Jefferson himself would add the dream of the far West as an avenue to the Pacific and commercial intercourse with the Far East. These visions of commercial dominance were made possible by the changing perceptions of the world prompted by American Orientalists and proto-anthropologists like Albert Gallatin and Meriwether Lewis, as well as by changing perceptions of American strength prompted by military success in North Africa and the West. They offer the first suggestion of a "new empire" that would come to fruition later in the century, when a vastly enlarged United States would establish an empire of trade in the Pacific.[76]

CHAPTER NINE

Beyond Captivity

The Wars of 1812

On June 1, 1812, President James Madison asked Congress to declare war against Great Britain for committing "a series of acts hostile to the United States as an independent and neutral nation." The United States, he concluded, must oppose "force to force in defense of their national rights." Thus began the War of 1812, frequently referred to as a second war for American independence.[1] Although Madison's declaration and the ongoing conflict between the United States and Britain over neutral shipping rights might appear to have little relation to captivity generally or Barbary specifically, both played their parts in the coming of the War of 1812. In turn, the war itself prompted a final Barbary captivity crisis and a second Barbary war that could not be resolved until the United States and Great Britain reached a peace settlement in 1815. Just as the War of 1812 prompted Americans to revisit and ultimately resolve longstanding issues in the Anglo-American relationship, this second war of 1812 did the same for the American–North African relationship, offering a chance to assert U.S. strength and competence and to exhibit America's readiness to tame "barbarians" in the old world as well as the new. Finally, after this other war of 1812 was resolved, Americans could proclaim themselves fully independent of Britain and Barbary.

The causes of the war with Britain have long puzzled historians. They have debated whether events in the West—Indian aggression supposedly incited by the British—or events in the Atlantic—British maritime depredations—were more important. They have also wondered about the trigger for the war: If naval and Indian depredations were continuing issues, what had changed by 1812? Answers to these questions become more apparent if one takes a larger view of the conflict, going back at least eighteen years to 1794, when the new nation faced a similar set of circumstances. Americans had suffered from Indian attacks on the western frontier, which the public blamed on the inflammatory rhetoric of a British official.[2] At the same time, the British had captured a number of American ships in the West Indies and continued to impress American sailors, while, in the Mediterranean, Algerians had captured eleven American ships, provoking the second phase of the Algerian crisis.

In 1794 Americans viewed all of these events as part of the same fabric. The warp and woof were captivity and British culpability, with the latter emphasized more by Republicans than Federalists. The conspiratorial mind-set was perhaps most evident at a series of Republican influenced public meetings held in early 1794.[3] Philadelphians condemned Britain for insulting American dignity by, among other things, "foment[ing] and maintain[ing] a savage war upon the frontiers of the United States . . . insidiously let[ting] loose the barbarians of Africa to plunder and enslave the citizens of the United States, . . . arrogantly attempt[ing] to prescribe boundaries to the American commerce . . . [and] basely authoriz[ing] piratical depredations to be committed by her own subjects on the ships and citizens of the United States."[4] The last point, referring to British capture of American ships and impressment of sailors, was critical. The notion of captivity was what linked all these injustices. The British and the Algerian pirates captured ships and sailors. With some cause, many Americans viewed the British as responsible for recent Indian attacks in the Northwest.[5] Tying together the Algerian captures and West Indian captures, a group of Baltimore sailors declared, "It appears to be believed by all, that the same nation which insults us in the West Indies, has been instrumental in letting loose those barbarians." Although many called for war, conflict with Britain at a time when the United States had no navy would have been disastrous. Instead, Americans relied on diplomacy, which resulted in Jay's Treaty of 1795.[6] Tellingly, early reports of that treaty erroneously suggested that it would lead to the release of the Algerian captives.[7]

Despite Jay's efforts, impressment remained a hot-button issue, becoming far more significant as the United States found itself a vulnerable neutral carrier during the Napoleonic Wars. Britain impressed roughly nine thousand American seamen between 1793 and 1812, and France captured a smaller number.[8] One writer, at least, blamed European jealousy of American commerce for both impressment and Barbary piracy, accusing the European powers of "being accessories to these piracies on the property and persons of our citizens." A Philadelphia writer, reporting on Congress's efforts to check impressment during the Tripoli crisis, reminded his readers of another group of mariners "whose cruel bond-age was incurred in protecting the commerce of the United States, and whose continuance in chains reproaches every man of the American nation," thereby rhetorically yoking together impressed sailors and the captives in Tripoli as fellow slaves. At about the same time, a Charlestonian wrote of "the transatlantic people" taking the weakness of America's navy as an excuse to "profit and pillage" American commerce. "A handful of pirates," he explained, "takes American vessels, imprisons American citizens, keeps them in chains and demands a contribution," thus linking Barbary piracy to the pillaging by other "transatlantic" people, presumably including the British navy.[9] A song supposedly sung aboard a British prison ship by impressed American sailors made the analogy more explicit:

> One hope, yet to thy bosom clung,
> The Captain mercy might impart;
> Vain was that hope, which bade thee look,
> For mercy in a *Pirate*'s heart.[10]

Anyone remembering the crisis of 1794 would find such connections between British impressment and Barbary piracy natural and familiar.

These themes intensified in the crisis immediately preceding the War of 1812. As in 1794, the United States appeared to face British-backed depredations on the frontier and at sea. The fundamental maritime issue was the stubborn persistence of impressment and a series of troubling incidents, including the *Chesapeake-Leopard* affair of 1807 and the *President–Little Belt* affair of 1811. A series of American policies from the Embargo of 1808 to Macon's Bill Number 2 of 1810 and the delicate negotiations with France and Britain are all well known. In the West, Americans faced a new surge of Indian hostility, culminating with the Battle of Tippecanoe in 1811. While the United States appears in retrospect to bear much of the blame for these hostilities, at the time many Americans believed British agents instigated them. William Findley of Pennsylvania assured his colleagues in the House of Representatives that "we all know" British agents were responsible, and Felix Grundy of Tennessee blamed Britain for "intriguing with the savage tribes." There is little evidence that this was true, and almost up to 1812 official British policy was to pacify the natives.[11] Nevertheless, the wide belief in British instigation of "savages" persisted.

Although Barbary captivity was not a cause of the crisis of 1811, it played a role in the public debate. Representative Daniel Sheffey of Virginia opposed war

with England as impractical and discounted the rhetoric about national independence. "You have been in the habit of paying tribute (considered as a bane
of dependence) to the Dey of Algiers and other Barbary powers for the express
purpose of securing the property of your merchants from capture, and your citizens from slavery," he noted. Therefore, war with even more powerful European
powers appeared to be extremely imprudent. However, his colleague Israel Pick-
ens of North Carolina did not view the Barbary example as applicable to relations
with Britain. Drawing from the language of the honor culture, he noted, "Honor
is a rule between equals only." Referring to Algiers, he continued, "If we have
found it expedient to purchase terms from a power but little removed above our
Western savages, will it therefore follow that such terms are admissible between
two civilized and independent states?"[12] The principles of honor demanded war
against England but not necessarily against "savage" North Africans or Native
Americans. More importantly, the idea of piracy continued to help Americans
see a unifying pattern to Western and maritime depredations. Adam Boyd of
New Jersey simply called Britain "a nation of pirates," while Henry Clay referred
to Britain's "piratical depredations committed upon . . . the ocean." Richard M.
Johnson of Kentucky called on Britain to "renounce the piratical system of paper blockade, to liberate our captured seamen on board her ships of war . . .
[and] to treat us as an independent people." In addition, Britain must be expelled
from North America for setting the Indians on frontier settlers.[13] In other words,
the British were allegedly just as savage and lawless as the Native Americans
or North Africans and, therefore, just as deserving of punishment, a belief that
many Americans had held since at least 1794. Thanks to that conviction and to
the earlier Barbary crises, the United States now had a small but working navy,
making military actions against Britain seem more possible than in 1794, if still
a bit quixotic.[14]

While Congress debated the war, the theme of Barbary piracy and captivity circulated through the popular culture in James Ellison's play, *The American Captive*.
Ostensibly a typical Orientalist fiction, the drama took place during the Tripolitan
War, as its subtitle, "Siege of Tripoli" suggests. It tells the story of a group of captive Americans and their leader, Anderson, loosely based on William Eaton. The
savage, tyrannical bashaw has exiled his own brother, the rightful ruler. Anderson
is able to get support from Immolina, the rightful bashaw's daughter; escape captivity; join up with Immolina's exiled father; gather an army; and, finally, invade
Tripoli and free the captives. Like many similar plays and novels, *The American
Captive* takes a strong antislavery stance.[15] Immolina asks, "By what authority
. . . does this country, or any other country on the globe, subject any portion of

the human species to slavery?" When Anderson, a Yankee, denies that the United States has slaves, a North African responds, "Go where the Senegal winds its course, and ask the wretched mothers for their husbands and their sons! What will be their answer? *Doom'd to slavery, and in thy boasted country too!*"[16]

In its subtext, however, *The American Captive* tells more about Anglo-American relations in 1812 than it does about American slavery or the siege of Tripoli. The author makes frequent allusions to the American Revolution. Anderson is said to be noble because he is the son of a Revolutionary soldier. He prays to be infused with "that heroic courage, that energy of soul, which so distinguished the father of my country," and as the American troops arrive, the band plays "Washington's March."[17] Ellison often refers to a second sort of war for independence: the fight against imported goods, which took on added political significance after the Embargo of 1808. In the play's prologue, he complains:

'Tis foreign genius charms the present age,
Hence foreign genius must supply the stage.
Our homebred authors must suspend their fight
And hidden lie in dark oblivion's night.

This theme reemerges in the epilogue, which concludes, "You've had this night presented to your view / an humble plant—in native *soil* it *grew.*"[18] Theater goers would have been familiar with such language from their exposure to promanufacturing propaganda that attacked dependence on British imports—both of manufactured products and intellectual goods—and sought to encourage economic independence through domestic production.[19]

The dramatic climax of the play emphasizes themes of republican liberty and tyranny. Immolina, imprisoned by the usurper, is saved at the last minute from execution by the "inhuman barbarous monsters" who hold her captive. Anderson marches into Tripoli at the head of an army and declares to the bashaw that at last, "A slave has power to strike a Tyrant dead." Jack, a common sailor, reaches into the Revolutionary heritage when he proclaims, "Columbians, still let this your glorious motto be, 'Liberty or Death.'" Anderson, too, refers to the Revolution in his final oration:

'Tis all I ask—that still my country reigns
To place her sons above ignoble chains . . .
Columbia's hardy sons by birthright free,
She would protect or cease herself to be.
For this in arms she dared Britannia's might,
And roused her dearest blood to brave the fight.

Ellison followed this rousing finale with a short epilogue emphasizing maritime rights. As theater goers walked home with these words echoing in their minds, they would no doubt also have thought about the ongoing congressional debates, in which the war hawks were condemning British depredations, and of their newspapers, which were filled with discussions of maritime rights. Given this context, Ellison's play was more likely to elicit condemnations of British "pirates" than Tripolitans, which no doubt was the author's hope.[20]

Five months later, President Madison delivered his war address. In his first four points he emphasized British maritime depredations, noting that "our commerce has been plundered in every sea." This point echoed Ellison's bashaw, who delivered a long speech on rapaciousness in which he concluded, "Plunder, alone, can prop our sinking realm." Madison also employed the language of sensibility to describe sailors impressed by Britain, remarking that they had been "torn from their country and everything dear to them . . . dragged on board ships of war of a foreign nation and exposed, under the most distant and deadly clime." He accused Britain of "hover[ing] over and harrass[ing] our entering and departing commerce" and instituting "the most lawless proceedings in our very harbors." Finally, he accused them of spurring on "the warfare just renewed by the savages on one of our extensive frontiers," warfare "distinguished by features particularly shocking to humanity."[21] In 1811, as in 1794, British "pirates" and their savage clients were once again in league as they attempted to capture Americans and, metaphorically, to reenslave the nation. After some military success in the two wars of 1812, however, a more self-confident American public would finally begin to move beyond these now familiar tropes of captivity and piracy.

While the idea of captivity helped focus American anger against Britain, the war itself produced the final captivity crisis in Barbary. On July 17, 1812, a month and a half after Madison's war address, the dey of Algiers suddenly refused America's tribute and declared war against the United States, meaning he now intended to capture its ships. Despite having accepted partial payments in the past, he now categorically refused a shipload of naval and military stores because it did not entirely fulfill the United States' obligation. He threatened to enslave consul Tobias Lear and all American citizens in Algiers and to declare war against the United States if the entire payment owed him was not made immediately. Describing himself as in a "state of embarrassment," Lear did his best to negotiate for more time. In the end, the dey forced him to pay $37,750 in order to insure his family's safe departure and that of about twenty other American citizens, all of whom quickly fled North Africa aboard the American ship *Allegheny*.[22] This pathetic episode did little to boost national self-confidence.

For some time after the Americans' expulsion, the crisis followed a course similar to previous captures. Before departing from Algiers, Lear asked John Norderling of Sweden, to act as de facto American consul to assist American merchants or other Americans "unhappily brought in by the cruizers of the regency" as slaves. As soon as he left Algiers, Lear began efforts to spread word of the danger to American marines. He hailed a British ship bound to Malta, asking the captain to inform the American consul on the Mediterranean island that "there was no doubt but the Algerine cruizers would capture any American vessels they might meet." Following David Humphreys's precedent, he began to draft a circular letter apprizing the American consuls in the Mediterranean of his expulsion and warning of the dey's hostility. As Humphreys had in 1793, he requested that they warn all American mariners and forward the information by ship to "all ports and places in [the Mediterranean] . . . where it is likely an American vessel may be found." When the *Allegheny* was boarded by the British brig *Goshawk*, which was headed toward Spain, Lear gave its captain copies of the letter to distribute to the American consuls. Lear's reliance on British ships and the *Goshawk*'s friendly disposition toward him would seem to undercut later stories about British complicity in the dey's actions. Lear continued to distribute copies of his letter until he reached Gibraltar, where British officials informed him of the start of the War of 1812, confiscated his vessel, and imprisoned the *Allegheny*'s crew.[23]

By mid-August these efforts appeared to have succeeded. Lear reported to Secretary of State James Monroe, "I entertain strong hopes that the Algerines will be disappointed in their expectation of having a large number of our vessels, which must have been the motives for their extraordinary conduct towards us." Eight days later, events occurred that would dash his optimism. Apprised of Lear's warning, the American merchant brig *Edwin*, of Salem, Massachusetts, left Malta for Gibraltar on August 5 in a convoy, a measure frequently taken to protect ships from capture. Unfortunately, according to Captain George Smith, she fell away from the group and was unable to catch up. On the twenty-fifth, an Algerian frigate captured the *Edwin*, enslaved its crew, and stole its cargo. Because of the wartime conditions, news of the capture did not reach Lear until more than two months later, when he received a letter from John Norderling informing him of the *Edwin*'s fate. Lear put a good face on the situation, noting that it was "fortunate that the Algerines have captured but one vessel, and that they will find no more" due to Lear's efforts and wartime shipping disruptions.[24]

Nevertheless, the capture provided serious problems for a republic already at war with a far superior power.

The *Edwin*'s crew faced more pressing difficulties. Like earlier captives, one of their first priorities was to inform others of their plight. Almost immediately after arriving in Algiers, Captain Smith begged for paper and quickly scratched out notes to his contacts in Gibraltar and Malta describing his situation and asking for loans to pay the Algerians for his redemption. At about the same time, his first mate, Francis Garcia, sent a similar letter to his wife in Massachusetts. Many other letters from the *Edwin* crew arrived at the same time, according to newspaper reports.[25] The details related in these accounts were nearly identical to those of earlier captures. Smith and Garcia reported that the Algerians stripped them of their clothing and put them to work as slaves "without distinction of persons." Garcia wrote that the sight of Captain Smith, "unused to heavy labor," carrying a weighty load on his back along with the others "double[d] the misery" of his captivity. Initially, the officers as well as the crew were forced to sleep together in a "dismal cell." The crew slept on the "rocks and mire," but the captain and mate received slightly better accommodations. Smith, a man of some property, entertained hopes that he might be able to redeem himself if the United States did not go to war with Britain. For the time being, at least, he nevertheless signed his name "George C. Smith a slave in Algiers," and he considered his impressed seafaring brothers lucky that, unlike him, they had avoided "the most horrid place in the world." Garcia held out little hope for himself. He wrote his wife, "As for my ever seeing you again, it will be in that eternal world where sorrow, I hope, will be quite banished from my mind."[26]

Due to the outbreak of the War of 1812, the captives' ability to communicate with their countrymen was far more limited than had been the case for their predecessors. In Gibraltar, Lear did not hear of their capture until November 3, more than two months after the event. Word dribbled into the American press two months later, but the first definitive news of the capture did not reach the leading Republican newspaper until Garcia's letter was published in March, nearly seven months after the capture.[27] By contrast, it had taken just over two months for notification of the 1793 captures to reach home.[28] As a result of poor communications and the larger problems of the war, the captives' plight received little publicity in the United States compared to earlier Barbary crises and there were no fundraising drives at home. However, Americans in Cadiz, Gibraltar, and Lisbon contributed a few thousand dollars for the captives at benefits, quite probably inspired by Smith's letters to his Mediterranean contacts.[29]

The capture of the *Edwin* led Americans, particularly Republicans, to add Barbary captivity to the list of British depredations. Just a month after first word of the capture reached America, a newspaper writer reported on the fate of American "ghosts." Some had been "mangled by the tomahawk and scalping knife, some, broken hearted by slavery [i.e., impressment] in ships and some [were in] chains in the suburbs of Algiers." Calling himself the "Ghost of Montgomery"—the first hero of the American Revolution—the writer called for revenge against England for creating these new apparitions. In a later article, he explicitly compared the Algerian captives to the sailors impressed by the British, arguing that even the fate of the *Edwin*'s crew was preferable to that of the seamen enslaved by Britain (a line of reasoning with which Captain Smith emphatically disagreed). Other authors continued to suggest that British hands were behind Indian depredations on the frontier as well. One writer characterized their activities as "systematized hostility" carried out from independence through 1812.[30]

Others, most notably Tobias Lear, linked Britain directly to the *Edwin*'s capture. Lear's official report was rather circumspect on this point, suggesting only that renewed British enmity toward the United States made American ships an attractive target for the dey, who would also realize that so long as war with Britain continued, American ships would not be able to "revenge the insult and injury." He speculated that the dey would also expect British gratitude if he captured American ships, but Lear did not go so far as to state explicitly that Britain was behind the captures. In response to criticism of these vague insinuations, he soon stated unequivocally, "I had reason to think the conduct of the Dey of Algiers toward the United States was instigated by the British."[31] Somewhat later, a Philadelphian who claimed to have lived in Algiers made similar charges. Writing about the "tributary system of the Barbary Powers," he complained that it did not "comport with the honor or dignity of an enlightened and independent nation" to submit to the "lawless and piratical banditti" who had captured the *Edwin*. However, the situation was complicated because the Barbary Powers were "all more or less under the immediate guidance" of Britain, "in a great measure account[ing] for the late rupture on the part of the Algerines against the United States, which was most probably directed by G[reat] Britain, and assisted by her allies at the court of Algiers."[32]

Although many subsequent historians have echoed these charges of British culpability, the record does not support them. The central piece of evidence then and later is a letter from the English prince regent to the dey reaffirming the two nations' friendship and begging the dey "not to permit those who are enemies of Great Britain to lessen the harmony now existing between the two nations," giving the dey implicit approval to attack ships belonging to England's enemies at sea.[33] However, the dey's break with the United States occurred well before the letter was written and just before he could have received news of Madison's declaration of war, at a time when America was not yet clearly an "enemy" of Great Britain. Furthermore, British sympathy and friendship to Lear and the *Alleghany* after they were expelled from Algiers suggests that word of the Anglo-American war had not yet reached British naval officers in Barbary at the time of the capture, although it is clear that officials in Gibraltar had been alerted by the time Lear arrived there. To say that the British were conspiring with the Algerians to prompt the dey's actions, therefore, seems a bit of an exaggeration. More probably, the dey, sensing American vulnerability, expecting no friction from his British friends, and perhaps anticipating an Anglo-American war, opportunistically sought to profit from America's difficulties in the summer of 1812. At any rate, the declaration of war worked to the dey's detriment, as the British naval threat now prevented American merchant ships from entering the Mediterranean.

In Algiers, conditions for the captives improved to varying degrees. By October, Norderling, the Swedish consul, managed to convince the Algerians to let Captain Smith out of the common cell with the other captives and into his own house. Garcia was soon able to move in with the British vice-consul, and James Pollard, an American captured on a Spanish ship, was also released to Norderling's care.[34] Over the next two years all reports agreed that these three were well treated. An American agent who visited in early 1814 reported that Pollard and Smith were considered prisoners on parole who were virtually as free as the foreign consuls, "enjoying always an ample participation of all genteel amusements of the place; and drawing, whenever they think fit, upon the trustee of the funds subscribed by their countrymen . . . without any other check than their own discretion." Similarly, Garcia was "exempt from all labor" and enjoyed "perfect freedom of exercise in the city and neighborhood." As usual, the common sailors fared worse. They were "continually subject to rigorous labor" and scanty provisions, but they were allowed a small allowance from government funds and the money raised by their countrymen around the Mediterranean. Additionally, Lear sent each of them a set of winter clothes, a jacket, and a blanket shortly after their capture.[35]

Despite these improvements, the captives and their countrymen realized that the war with Britain might delay their redemption indefinitely. While the war prevented American ships from sailing near the Mediterranean, the disappointing scarcity of American captives made the dey all the more determined to gain top dollar for those few he had. Thus Smith's earlier hope that he might redeem himself at a relatively reasonable price of $1,600 was thwarted. Smith, however, expressed no bitterness about the war. He wrote that it was "just" and expressed the hope that when it was over Britain's "pride" would be humbled, her "monopolizing system done away with," and she would finally "respect the nations." Like many of his countrymen, he understood "Great Britain and her infernal agents" to be responsible for Indian use of "the scalping knife" against "our peaceful citizens." Linking Indian depredations to impressment, he added, "I rejoice at the stand my country has made for my seafaring brethren—this comes home to my bosom." Unlike some others, he did not suppose that British agents also lay behind his own capture.[36]

The Madison administration did not forget the captives. As the news from the war with Britain continued in its discouraging vein, the Algerian crisis was a secondary but disturbing issue. Before the *Edwin* debacle, Mordecai M. Noah had been chosen America's new consul to Tunis, the first Jew to hold such a position. As news of the events in Barbary reached Washington, Secretary of State James Monroe hoped that Noah might be able to resolve the crisis quietly and quickly, perhaps by forging connections with the powerful Jewish merchants in North Africa. In his instructions to Noah, Monroe wrote about the importance of public opinion. The *Edwin*ites' captivity, he explained, had "excited the warmest sympathy of their friends, and indeed of the people generally of this country." This observation seems a bit of a stretch considering that the capture received far less publicity than earlier crises and was overshadowed by the war. Monroe no doubt sensed that should the war end with the United States defeated and its navy shattered, as seemed probable, the *Edwin* capture would loom large, indeed. Not only would it be a continuing humanitarian crisis, but also it would effectively prevent the United States from trading in the Mediterranean. Noah seems to have understood this point; he afterwards explained that Monroe hoped to be able to redeem the prisoners cheaply in light of most Americans' opinion that the previous decades' large expenditures on "tribute" to Algiers were "discreditable to their character as an independent nation, and would be found hereafter injurious to their commercial interest."[37]

Once he arrived in Spain, Noah began searching for an intermediary to deal with the dey. He settled on Richard R. Keene, an American-born merchant who was then a Spanish citizen. Noah promised him a reward for each American captive freed and instructed him to act as though he were on a private mission. This instruction reflected Monroe's concern that the dey would raise the price of the captives if he knew the government sought to redeem them, much as Jefferson before him had sought to keep quiet American interest in redeeming the earlier captives.[38] In Algiers, Keene, posing as a representative of the American merchants in Cadiz, found that the dey's asking price for his American slaves was far above the $3,000 per person Monroe was willing to pay. In response to Keene's inquiries, the dey declared that his policy would be "to increase, not to diminish the number of my American slaves" and that he would not release them for a million dollars. On the brink of defeat, Keene caught a lucky break when a series of complicated events pushed the British consul, Hugh McDonald, to pressure the dey to release two of the American captives. As a result, the dey freed the two men least valuable to him: William Turner of Salem, an eighteen-year-old basket maker, and John Clark, of New York, a "bungling carpenter." At about the same time, a British ship arrived with four prisoners claiming to be Americans from Louisiana. Keene redeemed them, too, presumably out of concern that they would eventually be enslaved by the Algerians, as had others in similar situations, and, of course, to gain more of a reward from Noah.[39]

From Noah's perspective, Keene had managed to salvage the mission, turning it into at least a partial success. The administration did not see it that way. While Monroe's hope had been to end the crisis quietly and to negate the Algerian threat, Noah did neither. His efforts cost the United States nearly $25,000, and, the administration suggested, Keene and Noah's lack of discretion had alerted the dey to the Americans' interest in purchasing the captives' freedom, thereby increasing their price. Monroe was probably unfair to Noah in making this last accusation. Even before Keene arrived, the dey apparently recognized that America's likely defeat in the War of 1812 would make it impossible for the captives to be freed militarily and therefore would increase their value. As one of the leading Jewish Algerian merchants explained to Keene, the dey expected the American navy to be destroyed in the war, so that afterwards, in order to attack Algiers "they would have to incur expenses in preparing an adequate force to make that attack, to an amount much greater" than that which the dey requested to free the captives and make peace.[40] Therefore, Algiers had little incentive to free the captives or make peace at the time of Keene's mission.

By 1815, with the war over and the American navy miraculously intact, the Noah-Keene mission threatened to prove a real embarrassment. American officials had attempted to buy off the dey, and they had failed at it. Furthermore, by purchasing the freedom of four French-speaking sailors who may not even have been American, they had essentially created four new American "slaves," and wasted funds on what might easily have been ignored as France's problem. This humiliating episode no doubt was an underlying reason for Noah's recall in 1815, which Monroe attributed to concerns that Noah's religion would produce an "unfavorable effect" on Muslim North Africans, a strange justification considering that Noah's religion had originally been seen as an advantage in negotiating with North Africa's Jewish merchants.[41]

In a democracy, however, it can be difficult to bury embarrassing facts, and some aspects of Keene's mission were bound to leak out to the public, if only because of the expenses incurred. Therefore, as the administration began to prepare for war with Algiers, they selectively released some details to Congress and the public. Americans soon learned of the dey's refusal to "sell his American slaves" even for $2 million, and his intention to charge the American government $2 million "for the privilege of passing the streights of Gibraltar." They also learned that an American agent had been sent secretly to negotiate with the dey but had not succeeded, and that at some point two Americans had been freed "under circumstances not indicating any change of hostile attitude on the part of the Dey." The report did not, however, connect Keene's mission to the release of the two Americans, nor did it mention the alleged Louisianans at all.[42] Clearly, the administration was making an attempt at damage control by hiding from the public the details most embarrassing to Monroe—the payments made to free the two *Edwin*ites and the four captives who were not yet slaves and may not even have been Americans. At the same time, by highlighting the dey's insolence toward the United States, the report's publication served to whip up public anger against the dey rather than the administration.

The chief exhibit in the war furor of 1815, however, was the captives, who had more or less slipped out of public view during the near-catastrophic British invasion of 1814. As the war with Britain ended and Congress began to discuss fighting Algiers, the public was reminded of the captives' plight. A Portsmouth, New Hampshire, writer reminded his readers that during the British war "the crew of one unfortunate ship have been languishing in slavery nearly three years" and urged his countrymen to redeem the "forlorn captives" through a public subscription fund. The newspaper's editors praised those humanitarian sentiments but urged war rather than "paying tribute." Another writer hoped that "not one moment should be lost in equipping our navy to attack the pirate" to force the dey to "give up our captive countrymen and relinquish his annual tribute."[43] The captives themselves participated in this publicity drive by sending a good deal of information back home to assist with the war preparations, reporting on the size and positions of the Algerian fleet, on a coup d'etat, and on the new dey's apparent willingness to negotiate with the United States should the fleet arrive.[44]

The sense of relief at fighting an uncomplicated war with clear goals against a weaker enemy after the difficult, complicated, and ultimately useless war against Britain was palpable. Hezekiah Niles called the new war, "among the most popular that one people ever declared against another." Indeed, Federalists as well as Republicans appeared to support it, with the exception of a writer in one Federalist newspaper who tartly observed, "A brilliant war in the Mediterranean, may help forward the next election—and that will be worth all it may cost, either in lives or money." Others of a less ironical bent anticipated only glory in the war. "We could not wish a finer school for our navy," wrote one. "It is fortunate that the pirates have afforded us a fair opportunity for scourging them for their first offences against us," wrote another. As Niles explained, comparing this war to the one just completed, "We have no *Algerine* merchants settled in [our] cities, and controlling our monied institutions"—that is, nothing like the alleged British sympathizers (largely Federalists) in the war against Britain. Consequently, "We see [the Algerians'] outrages in the real deformity that belongs to them, and [we are] united to punish, to end them."[45] Who could possibly be against freeing white slaves and punishing pirates?

However, it is clear that, for Republicans at least, the war was not only about the captives or the dey. Many also saw it as an exclamation point punctuating the struggle against England. The Republican *Aurora* expected John Bull to be disturbed by the sight of the American fleet in the Mediterranean, "for the Algerines are the allies and mere instruments of England." Niles compared the *Edwin's* capture to British impressment, recalling an incident in which a British captain in the East Indies impressed the entire crew of an American ship to fight the Dutch, promising that he would soon free them. "To be sure *he* did not," Niles concluded, "but the Dey of Algiers might be more just." After all, he observed, England captured ten thousand American citizens while the dey captured "but one vessel." The *Savannah Republican* speculated that the British might influence the Ottoman empire to send its navy to defend Algiers. The Republican *National Intelligencer* reprinted portions of an infamous essay by Lord Sheffield, praising the Algerians as useful in subduing American commerce in the Mediterranean since the United States "cannot pretend to a navy" and therefore could not protect free trade. An American commentator chortled, "His Lordship is still living— what does he think 'of a free trade,' about the Barbary powers, and an American navy now?"[46]

In the weeks and months leading up to the war, the American press published a number of descriptions of Barbary, much as it had in earlier crises. This sort of popular Orientalism was a way to inform the public about Algiers as well as to justify or critique the war. Previous crises, as we have seen, provoked a great deal of discussion about Barbary captivity and Barbary geography. In 1815 newspapers published a few articles in this vein. The *National Intelligencer*, for example, reprinted a long account of an Englishman's captivity in Algiers. Strangely enough, editors do not appear to have reprinted the many accounts of American captivity in Barbary that had been written during the preceding decades. James Cathcart did propose to sell a book dealing in part with his own experiences, but it appears never to have been published, perhaps due to lack of interest.[47] The one American Orientalist in whom the press seemed interested was William Eaton, who, not coincidentally, always took a very aggressive stance toward the North Africans. One excerpt reprinted from his biography recalled his meeting with the dey of Algiers, whom he portrayed as a "huge shaggy beast sitting on his rump." As Eaton approached, the dey "reached out his forepaw, as if to receive something to eat." The author wondered, "Can any man believe that this elevated brute has seven kings of Europe, two republics, and a continent tributary to him ...?"[48] Similarly, the account of the British captive concluded by decrying that the Christian nations made continual wars among themselves, thereby "allow[ing] these infidels, who are the perpetual enemies of the civilized world, to trample on every right and the law of nations."[49] Overall, the tone was less weak and despairing than it was contemptuous of the "savages" and righteously indignant at their behavior.

Instead of seeing themselves as hapless victims, Americans now saw themselves as righteous heroes willing to act bravely against savages in Africa and America, in contrast to decadent Europeans. Describing the United States as a "rising republic" and contrasting it to the European states, one author predicted that "a prouder destiny awaits us—. . . to lead the van in the emancipation of the whole civilized world, from a servitude so degrading." Similarly, Niles speculated, "Perhaps, it is reserved for the United States, a new people, yet in the 'gristle of manhood,' to relieve *Christendom* of its shackles, and afford an example of punishment that shall command the barbarians to respect the rights of mankind."[50] Word that Sir Sidney Smith of the Congress of Vienna was considering a European solution to Barbary piracy prompted an American to predict, "It is within the scope of our conjecture, that Com. Decatur will have *civilized* these piratical powers long before the British naval hero shall be able to procure [European] consent to effect his great object."[51] Americans now viewed themselves as experts at civilizing savages of all sorts. As one American wrote, "We felicitate ourselves in the hope, that it is reserved for this continent, so recently wild and haunted only by prowling savages, to discipline those ferocious barbarians to justice and to relieve the civilized world from disgraceful servitude and tribute."[52]

For once the United States military met all expectations. Under Stephen Decatur and William Bainbridge, it quickly captured two Algerian war ships, blockaded the port of Algiers, and forced the dey to agree to a treaty dictated by the Americans. In language similar to the Tripoli treaty of 1806, this agreement stated that mariners caught by the Algerians could no longer be enslaved but must instead by treated as prisoners of war and exchanged rank for rank with prisoners captured by the United States within a year.[53] In this way, and with the continued threat provided by a vigorous navy, the United States expected to end the system of Barbary slavery once and for all. Decatur also sailed into Tunis and Tripoli to force their rulers to make similar agreements. He insisted that the bashaw of Tripoli release ten European captives—eight Italians and two Danes. An American in Tripoli observed, "How delightful it was to see the stars and stripes holding forth the hand of retributive justice to the barbarians, and rescuing the unfortunate, even of distant but friendly European nations, from slavery."[54]

As a result, at least one newspaper writer now viewed Decatur not only as the hero of Tripoli but also as the "champion of Christendom." "He demanded from these barbarians," the writer explained, "a release from slavery 'of all Christian prisoners,' and obtained it. This is a glory which never encircled the brow of a Roman pontiff; nor blazed from an imperial diadem." Others wrote of the greater respect the United States now received from England, Spain, and even Ireland. If the outcome of the war with Britain had been a bit murky, this war offered nothing but glory. The United States' honor was restored and its independence— from Barbary, from Europe, from England—underscored.[55] Tributary to no one, Americans could now see themselves as superior to all. The honor was magnified further by the fact that, in some respects, the United States' actions did not seem to have been dictated by mere self-interest. Freeing European captives did little to help Americans directly, and considering the relatively low value of America's Mediterranean trade, it would probably have been cheaper to pay tribute than to pay for the war. Nevertheless, as Niles explained, "The word is—MILLIONS IN DEFENSE, BUT NOT A CENT FOR TRIBUTE—further, at least, than that degrading stipend which the vile politics of king-governed *Europe* has given [Barbary] a sort of right to demand and receive, from *sovereign* nations."[56] Having redeemed itself through war, the new nation also resolved to redeem George Smith, Francis Garcia, and the other men whose capture had prompted and justified that war. Stephen Decatur insisted that they be freed as soon as the treaty was signed and sent them home aboard the USS *Epervier*. Unfortunately, there would be no family reunions or joyful celebrations at their return. After passing Gibraltar in July, the *Epervier* and its passengers disappeared somewhere in the Atlantic, never to be heard from again.[57]

Captain Smith, his men, indeed the entire episode, nearly vanished without a trace. Previous Barbary crises had produced a number of captivity narratives and a great deal of Orientalist literature, but not this one. The men's untimely deaths, of course, made it impossible for them to produce firsthand accounts, but their disappearance from public view also was a result of declining interest in traditional Barbary captivity narratives. The dearth of new Barbary accounts was not due to any lack of interest in captivity narratives generally. Between 1814 and 1818 American presses published two captivity narratives of seamen impressed by the British, one of a seaman in a British prison, four of Americans captured by Indians, and one of a mariner trapped on a desert island.[58] These accounts reflect the anxieties associated with the alleged British depredations leading up to the War of 1812, as well as continuing interest in captivity. The relative decline of Barbary captivity within this flourishing genre suggests that capture by North Africans was becoming less of a perceived danger for Americans.

American publishers did reprint two older captivity narratives in an effort to capitalize on public interest in Algiers. Considering the English origins of these republished accounts, Barbary captivity appears to have become more of an interesting and disturbing fate that befell others rather than a clear and present danger. The first republished account was a British narrative written by Joseph Pitts and first published in 1704. The American publishers excerpted portions on Algiers from Pitts's much longer manuscript, which originally provided an extensive travel narrative of the Islamic world. They also updated the story, setting it in 1778, a century after Joseph Pitts was actually captured. More importantly, the publishers appended to the book a short, recent narrative of a British subject captured by Algerians in 1815 that had also appeared in American newspapers that year.[59] The other reprint was that old fictional favorite, *The Captivity and Sufferings of Maria Martin*. At least one version now emphasized Martin's Englishness, unlike some earlier editions that had made her identity more ambiguous, allowing readers to imagine she might be American. This story was twice republished in exactly the same language as earlier editions, without any updates to reflect recent events, and included the long description of Algiers copied from Mathew Carey's book. One can only wonder whether American readers read Mrs. Martin's story differently than they had before in light of their recent successes in Algiers. Certainly, the American edition of the Pitts narrative suggests that its publisher anticipated readers would connect that captivity narrative to recent events, since the appended 1815 narrative calls for the "Christian nations" to extirpate the pirates, something the Americans believed they were accomplishing.[60]

The only new American Barbary captivity narrative published after the war was the fictional *An Affecting Narrative of the Captivity and Sufferings of Thomas Nicholson*, which went through three printings between 1816 and 1818. This short account followed *Maria Martin*'s example in its title, its hero's term of captivity, and its structure. As with *Martin*, the first part was a fictional account of the hero's capture, his six years of confinement, and his escape in 1814 or 1815. The narrative contained typical passages describing the terror of the Algerians' attack, the degradation and humiliation of the prisoners, various grotesque punishments, and Algerian savagery. The author treated these events as though they actually occurred to Nicholson, and readers may well have believed they were reading a true account, but there is no evidence that an American by the name of Nicholson was ever a captive in Algiers during this period. Like Martin's narrative, Nicholson's also contains a short description of Algiers touching on geography, cultural mores, and history, which contained details readily available from previous works. In a nod to recent events, it closed with a brief description of "Commodore Decatur's late expedition," at least part of which was taken word for word from earlier newspaper accounts lauding Decatur for giving the "Barbarians" an "'electric shock' as was never before discharged from a Christian battery."[61]

While old-fashioned Barbary captivity narratives were losing popularity, a new genre of Saharan shipwreck narratives suddenly rose to prominence after 1815. These stories bore some resemblance to earlier Barbary narratives, but the protagonists were not captured by Barbary corsairs nor treated as slaves to be redeemed for the profit of a bashaw or dey. Instead, they were victims of shipwrecks off West Africa who were captured in the Sahara by nomadic Arabs. Their sufferings occurred in their travels through the desert. For them, the Barbary Coast city of Mogadore represented civilization and freedom, as all were ransomed there from the savage Arabs by friendly European consuls. The most famous example of this new genre was James Riley's *Sufferings in Africa* (1817), which told the dramatic story of the shipwreck of the American brig *Commerce*, the travails of some of its crew through their captivity in the desert, and their arrival to and eventual freedom in Mogadore. The story bore some similarities to classic Barbary narratives: Riley and his men were stripped by their captors, they endured harsh "sufferings," and Riley provided a travel narrative of the Sahara in a tone vacillating between condescension and admiration. Much the same can be said of the other famous shipwreck narrative of this era, *The Narrative of Robert Adams, A Barbary Captive* (1817). Despite its title, Adams's book was more of a travel account / captivity narrative of sub-Saharan Africa, most notably (and controversially) purportedly offering the first modern description of Timbuktu. A portion also covers his trials and tribulations in Morocco. Apparently an African American from New York state, Adams's identity and the truthfulness of his story were frequently debated then and continue to be to this day. Two other shipwreck narratives by Judah Paddock (1817) and Archibald Robbins (1818) were also published during this period.[62]

The move south from the Barbary coast to the Sahara and sub-Saharan regions of Africa tended to deemphasize American weakness, since the captives in this new genre were victims of their own poor seafaring or of nature rather than of the inability of the new nation to protect its sailors. Furthermore, unlike their predecessors, they had no difficulties obtaining freedom once they reached the Barbary Coast. Like their predecessors, however, their stories continued to raise questions about American Orientalism and imperialism, and, most importantly, the role of slavery in the new nation.[63]

The only really new American Orientalist nonfiction published in direct response to the Algerian War was Mordecai Noah's *Travels in England, France, Spain, and the Barbary States*. Noah, the consul to Tunis who launched the mission to free the *Edwin* captives, mixed an account of his official activities with a travel narrative. For example, his description of England segues into a discussion of Anglo-American relations, his description of Cadiz blurs into analysis of the *Edwin* capture, and standard descriptions of the geography of the Barbary states are interrupted by accounts of American military exploits during the War in Tripoli and the Algerian War. Much of these portions covered events already discussed in an earlier defense of his actions as consul, which he had published in 1816 after he was fired from his position and the government refused to pay many of the expenses incurred during his mission. Clearly, part of Noah's purpose in writing *Travels* was to defend his actions further.[64] His travel account of Barbary reflects another of his concerns, however—the region's Roman antiquities. Noah writes, "I had long expressed a desire to visit the country of Dido and Hannibal; to trace if possible the field of Zama, or seek out the ruins of Utica; but travelers in those regions, now inhabited by Barbarians, must be strongly protected." To provide one example, he offers a long description of the Algerian town of Constantine, which "was the *Cirta* of the ancients, and was one of the most important and splendid cities of Numidia, the ruins of which, in ample quantities, are still to be seen." Noah is struck by the contrast between the "wonderful battles fought by the ancients" in North Africa and the modern "Musselmen" who are "wholly ignorant of the military art," refusing even to "receive instructions from a civilized person."[65] Thus, while earlier accounts stressed the North Africans' fearsome savagery, Noah's emphasis on their decline makes them seem far less threatening and more easily disciplined or even conquered. Tellingly, he compares North African and American natives, finding the "Musselman's" haphazard knowledge of medicine to be "in the same manner as it is practiced by [American] savages."[66]

Because much of Noah's *Travels* attempts to justify his handling of the *Edwin* disaster, the American captives and the problem of captivity play a part in his account. Unlike many previous American Orientalists, however, he writes little about the captives' plight, nor does he do much to intertwine the captives' experience with his account of North Africa. The portions of the *Travels* dealing with the history and geography of Barbary never once mention the *Edwin* and contain only short references to earlier American captives. The only mention of captivity in his discussion of the first Algerian crisis is a single, bland sentence: "A dispute with Algiers, threw some American seamen in their power, who were made captives, and subjected to the well known rigors of the country." In his discussion of the roots of the 1815 Algerian war, Noah eschews mentioning the *Edwin* but includes a vivid account of an attempt to capture a different American ship. The crew, "horror struck at the idea of slavery, and indignant at the piratical course pursued by Algiers," successfully fought off the attackers, throwing the entire crew of the Algerian cruiser into the sea.[67]

While providing few details about the specific experiences of the American captives, Noah does offer a generalized captivity narrative as part of his description of Barbary slavery. He attempts to make the reader feel the terror of the "peaceful mariner," whose ship suddenly is boarded by North Africans "with sword in hand and shrieking imprecations, their sunburnt and black complexions rendered savage by their eyes of fire." He provides standard accounts of captives' arrival in Algiers, their despair at being separated from their families, and their confinement in crowded, unwholesome prisons. Unlike his predecessors, however, Noah has little interest in depicting American weakness. Rather than hapless Americans, most of the captives Noah describes are Europeans, and often wealthy ones, such as the wife of a rich Neapolitan merchant and her "two beautiful daughters in tears and despair" who have "just left their seminaries of learning in France."[68]

While old-fashioned Barbary captivity narratives waned in popularity, naval histories captured the public imagination after the wars of 1812. They chronicled American naval successes against Britain but also devoted significant discussion to the Barbary wars. They did not, however, have much to say about Barbary captivity. The two most ambitious examples were published in 1816. Horace Kimball's *The Naval Temple* provides a comprehensive history of the navy from the Revolutionary War to the War in Algiers. Barbary themes are prominent from the frontispiece, which depicts the American navy returning in triumph from Algiers, through sections covering the first Algerian crisis, the War in Tripoli, and the 1815 Algerian war. The American captives, however, are barely discussed. Kimball does not mention the more than one hundred Americans imprisoned during the first Algerian crisis, referring only to the "depredations committed on our commerce in the Mediterranean." In twenty-three pages covering the War in Tripoli, the capture of the *Philadelphia*'s crew receives only one terse sentence indicating that "the Tripolitans made prisoners of the officers and men in number three hundred." They are briefly mentioned only twice in the rest of the narrative. Similarly, Kimball's coverage of the Algerian war says little about the captives. He attributes the war's causes to "the hostile conduct of Algiers," never mentioning the captives but for an elliptical reference to the Americans' demand to "release all the prisoners" in the final treaty. He never mentions the *Edwin* by name, nor does he recount the story of its capture or the sad fate of its crew in Algiers or afterwards.[69]

The second book, *The Naval Monument*, is narrower in scope, focusing primarily on the War of 1812 and the War in Algiers, with most of its material culled from *Niles' Weekly Register*. In the preface, however, the anonymous author offers a brief review of America's earlier naval history, in which the War in Tripoli is featured but the American captives never mentioned. The treatment of the War in Algiers is little more than a long string of copied documents, mostly official letters from naval officers. The *Edwin* prisoners do not appear until the ninth of ten pages when Decatur threatens to capture more Algerians should the dey send "the prisoners off." The only other reference comes on the next page, when Decatur reports that after three hours the negotiators returned "with the treaty signed, as we had concluded it, and the prisoners."[70]

The public was now relatively uninterested in the captives, but they could not get enough of naval heroes. The *Analectic Magazine*, which became the *Analectic Magazine and Naval Chronicle*, filled a good portion of its pages with biographies of heroes such as David Porter and accounts of recent naval battles, including the war in Algiers. The *Port-Folio Magazine* ran a long biography of Captain William Henry Allen. The *Analectic Magazine* constantly praised Decatur, reprinting many of his letters. The editors were particularly impressed by his gallant gesture of freeing the ten Italian and Danish captives from Tripoli. "The days of chivalry, though past in the old, seem yet to subsist in the new world, which still furnishes gallant spirits who go forth, to assert not only the freedom of their countrymen, but also that of strangers," they wrote. Their account of the Algerian War, written essentially in the same words as the *Naval Monument*, however, barely mentioned the American prisoners at all.[71] The only genre in which the American captives were frequently remembered was in rhyme, where poets presumably looked to them to add pathos, and in sailors' songs. For example, in the naval song, "William's Welcome Home from Algiers," the hero "from slavery comes to greet thee," and in another song the sailors are reminded that "Your captive brethren in Algiers, / To you address their sighs and tears" before being instructed to "Go tell the Dey, within his walls, / You tribute pay in cannon balls."[72] Apparently, memory of the captives was preserved by the common sailors who could easily have shared their fate, but the public at large was more interested in captains than mariners.

The focus on naval heroes modulated the tone of public discourse from weakness and despair toward triumph and glory. For the time being, however, the glory was derived not from conquest but from republican exceptionalism. The American navy may not have been bigger or more powerful than Britain's, as even the *Naval Monument* had to concede, but its men were supposed to be at least as brave and more skilled. More importantly, they were more humane, as Decatur's selfless acts in Tripoli showed. As the *Naval Monument* concluded, "Peace, they have wrested from Algiers, and what is more, our sons, and the sons of other countries, have these men restored from captivity and slavery." As the *Analectic Magazine* described it, "Both our pride and humanity are solaced with the conviction that our ships of war, ennobled as they are by many other attributes, have, by the late treaty with Algiers, become *sanctuaries* not like the Catholic and Mahometan churches, for robbers and assassins, but for the oppressed Christian slaves of all nations."[73]

This new attitude can be understood as a developing sense of American mission abroad. The exceptional new republic was now showing decadent Europe how to maintain freedom and quash savagery in the Mediterranean. As Mordecai Noah explained, "The feelings of our citizens were in unison with these sentiments; we had terminated the war with Britain honourably and gloriously for our country, now let us redress our wrongs, said they, and the wrongs which liberty has sustained in the Mediterranean."[74] This sense of mission was not necessarily antithetical to desire for territorial expansion. Noah ended by declaring, "Let our flag be proudly and triumphantly displayed on the shores of Numidia, and near the mouldering ruins of the great republic of antiquity." The idea of the United States as a new Rome, bringing civilization to the Barbarians, would, in the next generation, morph into Manifest Destiny, but for the time being the vision was one of "sailors rights and free trade"—the ability to trade safely with all the world without the threat of piratical depredations or captivity.[75] A navy, as its proponents had long argued, existed to protect commerce. Or, at least, it protected commerce of a certain type; Barbary's despised commerce in human "slaves" would no longer be accepted.

All of this naval enthusiasm culminated in the extensive Naval Expansion Act of 1816. This was the first naval buildup under peacetime conditions. Previously naval construction had only been spurred by the crises in Barbary or conflict with France or England. The idea was, as the secretary of the navy suggested, to protect American commerce. As one more poetical senator wrote, it would "secure for the nation that safety at home, and that respect from abroad, the foundation for which was so amply laid by the heroic exploits of our navy during the last war." Newly elected president James Monroe tied the navy's protection of commerce to the support of national "rights" and national "character" and to "saving the property of . . . [American] citizens from spoilation" from pirates in the Mediterranean and in the West Indies, where the threat was growing. The navy would also be employed to combat a different type of captivity, interdicting ships violating the American ban on the slave trade, which had been enacted in 1808. Ten years later, in 1818, Congress declared the slave trade equivalent to piracy.[76] Amid this naval triumphalism and sense of a mission to protect commercial and individual liberty, the American captives whose plight had prompted the bulk of naval buildup and operations over the previous three decades were largely ignored or forgotten. They had been a useful means of uniting the nation and rallying it to greater naval activity, but they also had been an embarrassment and a symbol of weakness and dependence. In the end, there was no place left for them in the consciousness of the rising new republic.

Captivity and Globalization

Perhaps it is enough to conclude that events in North Africa had an extraordinary impact on the inhabitants of the new American republic, and globalization or the increasing contact between world cultures was an important phenomenon then as well as now. Such a conclusion certainly offers a corrective to modern-day commentators who discuss globalization as though it were a recent development. Merely to assert that this phenomenon has a long history here and elsewhere, however, does not take us far enough. Historians need to begin to construct a history of globalization that will consider how and when it emerged, how it changed and evolved over time, what impact it had on individuals and societies at different times, and how it may evolve in the future. Creating such a history is, for the time being at least, far beyond the capacity of a single individual, nor can it be deduced from any one set of events. Nevertheless, the story of America's interaction with Barbary piracy can, perhaps, contribute a bit to this larger story.

The first thing to consider is the significance of captivity itself. With rare exceptions, captivity is no longer an issue in modern globalization, but it was central to early-modern globalization when face-to-face contacts, rather than long-range communications, were essential to cultural interaction and when the store of cross-cultural knowledge was frequently meager. Thus scholars have increasingly become interested in the European propensity to kidnap natives in order to learn more about their cultures (particularly their languages) as well as to indoctrinate them into European culture (particularly Christianity). These practices were crucial to establishing communication between Europeans and members of other cultures, as in the famous example of the former captive known as Squanto who was able to greet the newly arrived Pilgrims in their own language, which he had learned to speak in England. Natives were also frequently captors, kidnapping Europeans from similar motives. As the colonial era continued, Europeans, natives, and Africans all became victims of captivity and, as such, they broadened the various cultures' knowledge of each other. Americans' captivity in North Africa was a continuation and the culmination of this trend. As the large body of Orientalist literature prompted by Barbary slavery testifies, Americans learned a great deal about North Africa during these years, and, presumably, North Africans learned much about the new nation arising in the West. However, the North African crisis pretty much marked the end of captivity as an important factor in globalization.[1] There were occasional captivity crises well into the twentieth century (the Iranian hostage crisis of the late 1970s is a notable modern example), but, with the rise of the nation state and international law, they were increasingly rare. With the development of new transportation and communications technologies, cultures have become able to learn about each other quite easily without exchanging captives.

One remarkable aspect of captivity as a form of cultural interaction is that it was frequently the province of nonelites. Modern-day social historians treasure captivity narratives as one of the few early-modern genres providing a voice to women, common mariners, and enslaved people. As this book has shown, nonelites were influential in writing and disseminating early American Orientalist literature, and ordinary seamen held as captives in North Africa, such as Richard O'Brien, became influential publicists and, in a sense, the new nation's first area studies experts. So long as captivity remained an important aspect of early national Americans' contact with other cultures, ordinary people unlucky enough to find themselves captured by "savages" played important roles in shaping the emerging public sphere and in influencing public opinion.

Why did accounts of captivity loom so large, filling long newspaper columns and keeping book publishers busy well into the early national era? By the late eighteenth century, the odds of capture were quite low, particularly for anyone who was not a sailor. Captivity generally, and Barbary captivity particularly, disturbed early national Americans not so much because of the statistical risk or the pain it caused individuals (although that was a concern), but because of what it revealed about the new nation as a whole. As an actual occurrence, it was no doubt troubling, but as a metaphor for dependence and subservience, captivity was devastating, and that is why it generated so much interest. On the most fundamental level, captivity forced Americans to confront the troubling suspicion that despite their recent declaration to the contrary, they were not yet fully independent—not from the dangers of the larger world, not from the claims of

North African deys and bashaws, and possibly not even from the British government that many suspected stood behind the North Africans and other so-called savages.

Some Americans also saw Barbary captivity as analogous to the dependent servitude of hundreds of thousands of Africans in America. This was an analogy that the Barbary captives themselves did not make and, given the racial climate of the era, probably would not have endorsed. Nevertheless, the prevalence of discussions about Algerian captivity in the public sphere allowed antislavery activists to make such analogies and to condemn the hypocrisy of an American savagery as brutal as that practiced by "savage" North Africans. Such arguments no doubt made many Americans uneasy even if they did not entirely convince. The captives and their countrymen and women were more convinced by a second analogy linking African savagery to Native American savagery, which persisted from the beginning to the end of America's encounter with North Africa. This analogy must have also helped to fix in the public mind the increasingly common association between dark skin and inferiority that would become particularly notable in the heightened racism of the late antebellum period, when racial inferiority would be connected to pro-slavery arguments, Indian removal, and Manifest Destiny.

Finally, the metaphor of captivity was powerful in the conflict between America's first political parties. Neither party could afford to be blamed for American weakness and the submissiveness that captivity implied. Federalists accused Republicans of starving the new nation's military with their excessive frugality and at times suggested that their connections to slavery at home inured them to the horrors of slavery in North Africa. Republicans, for their part, accused Federalists of excessive bellicosity and of overfondness for the British, who were allegedly behind North African captivity, Indian attacks on the frontier, and impressment at sea. In a nation where suffrage was coming to be equated with manhood, both parties were compelled to defend the nation's manly honor by supporting naval buildups to counter the North Africans and other "pirates."

The creation of the navy and the persistent concerns about national emasculation, dishonor, and weakness ultimately contributed to the diminished importance of captivity and the emergence of a new phase in America's relationship to the world. The *Philadelphia* capture would never have occurred had the new nation not committed itself to a navy after the 1793 Algerian captures. But the naval buildup also made it possible, perhaps inevitable, for the United States to react with force to the early-nineteenth-century captivity crises. Propelled by ideas of national honor and masculinity, tired of submission and victimization, and stimulated by new strength on the North American continent following the Louisiana Purchase, Americans now wished to see themselves as heroic figures in the mold of Stephen Decatur rather than as hapless victims of pirates.

After 1815, captives and captivity no longer played a central role in defining the new nation's interaction with the world or the public's understanding of globalization. The influence of captives began to decline in the transmission of information between North Africa and North America, while diplomats and naval officers became ascendant. These new men tended to view Arabs and native North Africans much as they viewed Native Americans, as declining races who had become, or were on their way to becoming, ignorant savages. At the same time, they took an ornamentalist view of the rulers (usually lighter-skinned Turks) as reasonably intelligent, civilized, and nearly equal to white Americans. On the whole, they saw North Africa and North Africans as more likely to become potential trading allies or, perhaps, even clients, rather than fearsome potential captors. This shift resulted from and further reinforced Americans' new sense of power and competence abroad. But captivity persisted as a powerful metaphor. Commenting on the American invasion of the Philippines some eighty-five years later, Mark Twain wrote, "There must be two Americas: one that sets the captives free, and one that takes a once-captive's new freedom away from him."[2] This trope of America liberating the captive nations would become common during the cold war, and even now Americans and others continue to argue about whether their policies are aimed at liberating or enslaving such metaphorical captives.

Lists of Letters from Captives

TABLE A.I
Letters Sent by Richard O'Brien

Date	Recipient	Source
Aug. 24, 1785	Thomas Jefferson	CFP/*PTJ*
Aug. 26, 1785	Lisbon merchants	*EG*, Feb. 17, 1786
Aug. 27, 1785	General warning	*SG*, Nov. 28, 1786
Aug. 28, 1785	Congress	PCC
Oct. 19, 1785	Matthew Irwin	PCC
Nov. 3, 1785	Thomas Jefferson	*PTJ*
Dec. 9, 1785	Thomas Jefferson	*PTJ*
Jan. 16, 1786	Dohrman	*EG*, June 16, 1786
Jan. 18, 1786	Thomas Jefferson	*PTJ*
Jan. 26, 1786	Dohrman	*MG*, June 8, 1786
June 8, 1786	Thomas Jefferson	*PTJ*
July 11, 1786	William Carmichael	SDAD
July 12, 1786	Thomas Jefferson	*PTJ*
Sept. 13, 1786	William Carmichael	SDAD
Apr. 28, 1787	Thomas Jefferson	SDAD
Sept. 25, 1787	Thomas Jefferson	*PTJ*
Oct. 25, 1787	Thomas Jefferson	*PTJ*
Sept. 22, 1788	G. Washington (petition)	Ser. 4, GWP
Dec. 20, 1788	Matthew Irwin	PCC
Feb. 19, 1790	William Carmichael	Diary
Mar. 30, 1790	Marquis de Lafayette	Diary
Apr. 8, 1790	State of Pennsylvania	Diary
Apr. 30 1790	William Carmichael	Diary
May 15, 1790	William Carmichael	Diary
May 15, 1790	William Short	Diary
May 17, 1790	William Carmichael	Diary
May 17, 1790	William Short	Diary
July 5, 1790	Colonel Gram	Diary
July 7, 1790	Abigiah Gram	Diary
July 12, 1790	Thomas Jefferson	Diary
July 16, 1790	Thomas Jefferson	Diary
July 1790	Washington	Diary
Aug. 1790	"Several . . . to America"	Diary
Aug. 17, 1790	Charles Colville	Diary
Aug. 28, 1790	William Short	Diary
Sept. 1, 1790	William Carmichael	Diary
Sept. 6, 1790	Lord [Fife]	Diary
Sept. 9, 1790	William Carmichael	Diary
Sept. 25, 1790	William Short	Diary
Oct. 24, 1790	William Short	Diary
Oct. 29, 1790	William Carmichael	Diary
Oct. 29, 1790	William Short	Diary
Oct. 29, 1790	Mr.& Mrs. R. Montgomery	Diary

continued

TABLE A.I *continued*

Date	Recipient	Source
Nov. 3, 1790	Robert Montgomery	Diary
Jan. 17, 1791	William Carmichael	Diary
Feb. 25/26, 1791	George Washington	Diary
Feb. 25, 1791	William Carmichael	Diary
Feb. 25, 1791	Congress	Diary
Mar. 5, 1791	Robert Montgomery	Diary
Mar. 13, 1791	Mrs. O'Brien	Diary
Mar. 13, 1791	Mrs. O'Brien	Diary
Mar. 14, 1791	James Simpson	Diary
Apr. 28, 1791	William Carmichael	Diary
July 17, 1791	Congress	SDAD
Sept. 27, 1791	Thomas Jefferson	*Barbary,* 1:38
Dec. 31, 1791 (3)	Thomas Jefferson	SDGD
Jan. 8, 1792	Thomas Barclay (from "captives")	*PTJ*
Mar. 29, 1792	George Washington House & Senate (petition)	Ser. 4, GWP
Sept. 17, 1792	James Simpson	SDCD
Feb. 6, 1793	David Humphreys	SDAD
Feb. 12, 1793 (2)	Bulkeleys	Ser. 4, GWP
Mar. 20, 1793	Unknown	Ser. 4, GWP
Mar. 26, 1793	David Humphreys	Ser. 4, GWP
May 1793	David Humphreys	Ser. 4, GWP
Sept. 13, 1793 (multiple)	William Carmichael	CFP
Nov. 5, 1793	James Simpson	SDGD
Nov. 12, 1793	George Washington	*ASPFR,* 1:417-18
Nov. 12, 1793	David Humphreys	SDDP
Nov. 16, 1793	Robert Montgomery	SDDP
Nov. 28, 1793	James Simpson	Carey, 84
Dec. 6, 1793	David Humphreys	SDDP
Dec. 29, 1793	David Humphreys	SDDP
Dec. 29, 1796	House & Senate (petition)	Carey
Jan. 6, 1794	David Humphreys	SDDP
Jan. 9, 1794	David Humphreys	SDDP
Feb. 1794	James Simpson	SDGD
April 1794	James Simpson	SDGD
April 12-26, 1794	David Humphreys	SDDP
April 1794	David Humphreys	SDDP
June 18, 1794	David Humphreys	SDDP
Aug. 13, 1794	David Humphreys	SDDP
Aug. 21, 1794	David Humphreys	SDDP
Sept. 24, 1794	James Simpson	SDGD
Oct. 1794	David Humphreys	SDDP
Nov. 9, 1794	David Humphreys	SDAD
Feb. 4, 1795	David Humphreys	SDDS
Oct. 12, 1795	David Humphreys	SDDP
Oct. 12, 1795	John Adams	*MG,* Jan. 14, 1796

Note: In some cases this table includes references to letters that no longer exist. Carey, Matthew Carey, *A Short History of Algiers,* 3d ed. (New York: Duyckinck, 1805); *CH, Charleston Columbian Herald;* Diary, Richard O'Bryen Diary, AM 109, Historical Society of Pennsylvania, Philadelphia; *EG, Charleston Evening Gazette; MG, Maryland Gazette; PG, Pennsylvania Gazette; SG, Salem Gazette.* For full citation information for *ASPFR, Barbary,* CFP, *GWP,* PCC, *PTJ,* SDAD, SDCD, SDDP, SDDS, SDGD, please see the abbreviation list on page 219.

TABLE A.2
Letters Sent by Captives Other Than Richard O'Brien

Date	Author	Recipient	Source
Apr. 15, 1786	Isaac Stephens	John Adams	*PTJ*
Feb. 22, 1787	Hanna Stephens	Congress	PCC
May 9, 1787	Mr. Stewart	?	*PG*, May 9, 1787
Feb. 9, 1788	Stephens	Congress	PCC
Sept. 13, 1789	Stephens	his brother	*MG*, Feb. 4, 1790
Sept. 23, 1789	Stephens	Congress	PCC
Nov. 6, 1790	Angel D'Andries	Nathaniel Moody	*MG*, July 21 1790
1792	John Robinson	?	*PG*, Apr. 11, 1792
Nov. 3, 1793	Samuel Calder	Dominick Terry	*Barbary*, 1:54
Nov. 4, 1793	Capt. Penrose	ship's owners	Carey, 77
Nov. 13, 1793	John McShane	David Humphreys	SDDP
Nov. 13, 1793	John McShane	William Bell	Carey, 82
Dec. 1, 1793	Moses Morse	Dominick Terry	*Barbary*, 1:87
Dec. 4, 1793	Samuel Calder	David Pearce	SDAD
Dec. 18, 1793	Michael Smith	brother-in-law	*BG*, May 26, 1794
Dec. 1793	Multiple signors	U.S. House of Rep.	*ASPFR*
Jan. 7, 1794	James Taylor	Gibbs, Channing, & Engs	SDAD
Mar. 26, 1794	Mary Morris	Edmund Randolph	SDAD
Apr. 10, 1794	Capt. Furnass	David Humphreys	SDDP
Apr. 12, 1794	Capt. Newman	David Humphreys	SDDP
1794	John Burnham	?	*BG*, Dec. 1, 1794
Dec. 18, 1794	Burnham	Edmund Randolph	*Barbary*, 1:88
July 10, 1795	James Cathcart	Humphreys	SDAD
before Aug. 1, 1795	various captives	their families	*BG*, Aug. 3, 1795
Sept. 8, 1795	Samuel Calder	David Pierce	*BG*, Nov. 30, 1795
Sept. 9, 1785	William Penrose	a friend	*MG*, Jan. 14, 1796
Apr. 6, 1796	James Taylor	Newport resident	*CH*, July 28, 1796
May 4, 1796	Stephens	Boston gentleman	*CH*, Oct. 17, 1796

Note: BG, *Boston Gazette;* Carey, Matthew Carey, *A Short History of Algiers*, 3d ed. (New York: Duyckinck, 1805); CH, *Charleston Columbian Herald;* MG, *Maryland Gazette;* PG, *Pennsylvania Gazette.* For full citation information for *ASPFR, Barbary,* PCC, *PTJ,* SDAD, SDDP, please see the abbreviation list on page 219.

Abbreviations

Annals	*Annals of the Congress of the United States, 1789–1824.* 42 vols. Washington, DC, 1834–56.
ASPFR	*American State Papers: 1, Foreign Relations.*
Barbary	Dudley W. Knox et al., eds. *Naval Documents Related to the United States Wars with the Barbary Powers.* 6 vols. Washington, DC: Government Printing Office, 1939–44.
CFP	Cathcart Family Papers, New York Public Library.
GWP	George Washington Papers at the Library of Congress, 1741–99. Library of Congress, Washington, D.C.
	Series 2. Letterbooks.
	Series 4. General Correspondence, 1697–1799.
NASPMA	Benjamin Franklin Cooling, ed., *The New American State Papers, Military Affairs.* 19 vols. Wilmington, DE: Scholarly Resources, 1979.
NASPNA	K. Jack Bauer, ed. *The New American State Papers, Naval Affairs.* 10 vol. Wilmington, DE: Scholarly Resources, 1981.
PCC	Papers of the Continental Congress and Domestic Letters of the Department of State. M40. National Archives, Washington, D.C.
PTJ	Julian P. Boyd et. al., ed. *The Papers of Thomas Jefferson.* Princeton: Princeton University Press, 1950–.
SD	General Records of the Department of State. RG 59. National Archives, College Park, Maryland.
SDAD	State Department Consular Despatches. Algiers. M23.
SDCD	State Department Consular Despatches. Cadiz. T186.
SDDP	State Department Diplomatic Despatches. Dispatches from U.S. Ministers to Portugal. M43.
SDDS	State Department Diplomatic Despatches. Dispatches from U.S. Ministers to Spain. M31.
SDGD	State Department Consular Despatches. Gibraltar. T206.
SDGW	State Department Miscellaneous Records. Copybooks of George Washingtion's Correspondence with Secretaries of State, 1789–1796. M570.

SDLD   State Department Consular Despatches. Lisbon. T180.

SDMD   State Department Consular Despatches. Malaga. T217.

Preface

1. Michael Warner, *The Letters of the Republic: Publication and the Public Sphere in Eighteenth-Century America* (Cambridge: Harvard University Press, 1990); David Waldstreicher, *In the Midst of Perpetual Fetes: The Making of American Nationalism, 1776–1829* (Chapel Hill: University of North Carolina Press, 1997); David Shields, *Civil Tongues and Polite Letters in British America* (Chapel Hill: University of North Carolina Press, 1997); Mary P. Ryan, "Gender and Public Access: Women's Politics in Nineteenth-Century America," in Craig Calhoun, ed., *Habermas and the Public Sphere* (Cambridge: MIT Press, 1992), 259–88; Albrecht Koschnik, "The Democratic Societies of Philadelphia and the Limits of the American Public Sphere, circa 1793–1795," *William and Mary Quarterly*, 3d ser., 58 (July 2001): 615–36; John L. Brooke, "Ancient Lodges and Self-created Societies: Voluntary Association and the Public Sphere in the Early Republic," in Ronald Hoffman and Peter J. Albert, eds., *Launching the "Extended Republic": The Federalist Era* (Charlottesville: University Press of Virginia, 1996), 273–377; Lawrence A. Peskin, "From Protection to Encouragement: Manufacturing and Mercantilism in New York City's Public Sphere, 1783–1795," *Journal of the Early Republic* 18 (Winter 1998): 589–615.

2. Benedict Anderson, *Imagined Communities: Reflections on the Origin and Spread of Nationalism* (London: Verso, 1983).

Introduction

1. For an example of a recent captivity narrative, see Gracia Burnham, *In the Presence of My Enemies* (n.p.: Living Books, 2004).

2. Sven Beckert, "Emancipation and Empire: Reconstructing the Worldwide Web of Cotton Production in the Age of the American Civil War," *American Historical Review* (Dec. 2004): 1405–38; Thomas Bender, *A Nation among Nations: America's Place in World History* (New York: Hill and Wang, 2006); Edward Davies, *The United States in World History* (London: Routledge, 2006); Carl Guarneri, *America in the World: United States History in Global Context* (New York: McGraw Hill, 2007).

3. Charles Hansford Adams, ed., *The Narrative of Robert Adams, A Barbary Captive* (New York: Cambridge University Press, 2005); Robert J. Allison, *Stephen Decatur: American Naval Hero, 1779–1820* (Amherst: University of Massachusetts Press, 2005); Robert J. Allison, *The Crescent Obscured: The United States and the Muslim World, 1776–1815* (New York: Oxford University Press, 1995); Paul Baepler, ed., *White Slaves, African Masters: An Anthology of American Barbary Captivity Narratives* (Chicago: University of Chicago Press, 1999); Frank Lambert, *The Barbary Wars: American Independence in the Atlantic World* (New York: Hill and Wang, 2005); Frederick C. Leiner, *The End of Barbary Terror: America's 1815 War against the Pirates of North Africa* (New York: Oxford University Press, 2006); Timothy Marr, *The Cultural Roots of American Islamicism* (New York: Cambridge University Press, 2006); Michael B. Oren, *Power, Faith and Fantasy: America in the Middle East, 1776 to the*

Present (New York: Norton, 2007); Richard B. Parker, *Uncle Sam in Barbary: A Diplomatic History* (Gainesville: University of Florida Press, 2004); Malini J. Schueller, *U.S. Orientalisms: Race, Nation, and Gender in Literature, 1790–1890* (Ann Arbor: University of Michigan Press, 1998); Fuad Sha'ban, *Islam and Arabs in Early American Thought: Roots of Orientalism in America* (Chapel Hill: University of North Carolina Press, 1991); Joseph Wheelan, *Jefferson's War: America's First War on Terror, 1801–1805* (New York: Carroll and Graf, 2003); Richard Zacks, *The Pirate Coast: Thomas Jefferson, the First Marines, and the Secret Mission of 1805* (New York: Hyperion, 2005).

Chapter 1. Captivity and Communications

1. Ray W. Irwin, *The Diplomatic Relations of the United States with the Barbary Powers* (New York: Russell and Russell, 1931), 21–36.

2. *Salem Gazette*, Oct. 25, 1785, p. 3.

3. Ibid.

4. *Boston Gazette*, Oct. 31, 1785, p. 2; *Maryland Gazette*, Nov. 17, 1785, p. 1; *Charleston Columbian Herald*, Nov. 24, 1785, p. 2. The amount of time between ports (eighteen days from Salem to Annapolis and seven days from Annapolis to Charleston) suggests that a single copy of the Cadiz letter made its way down the coast rather than multiple copies being sent out simultaneously. For travel times in 1800, see Alfred D. Chandler, "The Information Age in Historical Perspective," in Chandler and James W. Cortada, eds., *A Nation Transformed by Information* (New York: Oxford University Press, 2000), 9.

5. *Boston Gazette*, Oct. 31, 1785, p. 4; *Salem Gazette*, Nov. 8, 1785, p. 3.

6. *PTJ*, 8:440, 464–65, 512, 521, 525, 542–44, 555; *PCC*, reel 104, 24:567; *Maryland Gazette*, Nov. 17, 1785, p. 1. This item, reprinting McComb's letter, was taken from the Philadelphia press. It must have appeared there around November 15.

7. *PTJ*, 27:196–97; James Simpson to Jefferson, Oct. 8, 1793, SDGD (paraphrased in *PTJ*, 27:224).

8. David Humphreys, "To all governors . . . ," Oct. 8, 1793, SDCD; *PTJ*, 27:196–97; Humphreys to Edward Church, Oct. 8, 1793, SDLD; Michael Murphy to Secretary of State, Oct. 11, 1793, SDMD.

9. Michael Murphy to Secretary of State, Oct. 11, 1793, SDMD; Samuel Calder to Mr. David Pearce Jr., SDAD, Dec. 4, 1793.

10. *Boston Gazette*, Jan. 6, 1794, p. 3.

11. Humphreys to Sec. State, Oct. 10 and 13, 1793, SDDP.

12. Humphreys to Edward Church, Oct. 8, 1793, SDDP; *PTJ*, 27:222–23.

13. *Pennsylvania Gazette*, Dec. 11, 1793; *Maryland Gazette*, Dec. 19, 1793, p. 2.

14. *PTJ*, 27:230–33.

15. Peter Walsh to Thomas Jefferson, Oct. 16 and 17, 1793 (2 letters), SDCD.

16. *Pennsylvania Gazette*, Dec. 11 and 24, 1793; *Boston Gazette*, Dec. 16, 1793, p. 3; *Maryland Gazette*, Dec. 19, 1793, p. 3.

17. Richard R. John, *Spreading the News: The American Postal System from Franklin to Morse* (Cambridge, MA: Harvard University Press, 1995), 25–63.

18. I have been inspired to use this metaphor by Robert Darnton, "An Early Informa-

tion Society: News and the Media in Eighteenth-Century Paris," *American Historical Review* 105 (Feb. 2000): 1–35.

19. Richard D. Brown, *Knowledge is Power: The Diffusion of Information in Early America, 1700–1865* (New York: Oxford University Press, 1989), 113–31; Frank Luther Mott, *American Journalism: A History of Newspapers in the United States Through 250 Years, 1690 to 1940* (New York: Macmillan, 1941), 51–52.

20. R. A. Houston, *Scottish Literacy and the Scottish Identity: Illiteracy and Society in Scotland and Northern England, 1600–1800* (New York: Cambridge University Press, 1985), 194–200; Brown, *Knowledge is Power*, 113–14.

21. *Pennsylvania Gazette*, June 11, 1794; *Charleston Columbian Herald*, Aug. 30, 1787, p. 2.

22. *Maryland Gazette*, Feb. 6, 1794, p. 2; *Charleston Evening Gazette*, Apr. 7, 1787, p. 3. For a similar report, see also *Columbian Herald*, Jan. 22, 1794, p. 2.

23. *Boston Gazette*, May 1, 1786, p. 3.

24. *PTJ*, 10:653–54. Jefferson also looked into the case of a Captain Greene, whose father, for unknown reasons, believed he might be among the captives in Algiers.

25. *Columbian Herald*, Aug. 4, 1788, p. 3. Other similar narratives were delivered in Danbury, Connecticut, by a freeman named Johnson (*Maryland Gazette*, Apr. 22, 1790, pp. 2–3); in Newburyport, Massachusetts, by a Mr. Stewart (*Pennsylvania Gazette*, May 9, 1787); and in Frederick, Maryland, by an unknown man (*Pennsylvania Gazette*, Oct. 8, 1788).

26. Washington to Thomas Barclay, Aug. 31, 1788; Washington to Thomas Thomson, Sept. 18, 1788; Washington to Barclay, Sept. 18, 1788, ser. 2, GWP; Henry P. Johnston, ed., *The Correspondence and Public Papers of John Jay* (New York: Lenox Hill, 1970), 3:383–84.

27. Brown, *Knowledge is Power*, 114–16.

28. *Boston Gazette*, Dec. 16, 1793, p. 3. On the public nature of such letters, see Brown, *Knowledge is Power*, 31–32.

29. For examples of oral reports of letter contents, see *Boston Gazette*, Nov. 23, 1789, p. 3 ("the emperor of Morocco lately sent a vessel to Madeira, with information to Mr. Clark"); and *Boston Gazette*, June 27, 1793 ("Captain Hoover saw a letter from the American consul at Malaga."). Letters passing on news received orally were ubiquitous.

30. Samuel Langhorne Clemens, *The Adventures of Huckleberry Finn* (New York: W. W. Norton, 1961), 158–59.

31. Reprinted in *Maryland Gazette*, June 19, 1794, p. 3; *Columbian Herald*, Apr. 16, 1794, p. 3. For other Bulkeley letters, see *Boston Gazette*, Oct. 17, 1796, p. 3; *Maryland Gazette*, Jan. 30, 1794, p. 2. On the Bulkeleys' Philadelphia connections, see Thomas M. Doerflinger, *A Vigorous Spirit of Enterprise: Merchants and Economic Development in Revolutionary Philadelphia* (Chapel Hill: University of North Carolina Press, 1986), 62.

32. *Boston Gazette*, Oct. 31, 1785, p. 4.

33. For example, see *Charleston Columbian Herald*, Nov. 21, 1785, p. 2; and *Maryland Gazette*, Nov. 17, 1785, p. 2.

34. *PTJ*, 8:559.

35. Jefferson to O'Brien, Nov. 4, 1784, CFP; Samuel Calder to Mr. David Pearce Jr., Dec. 4, 1793, SDAD.

36. *Boston Gazette*, Nov. 16, 1789, p. 2.

37. *PTJ*, 9:645–46, 10:535–36. On the operations of the early State Department, see Leonard D. White, *The Federalists: A Study in Administrative History, 1789–1801* (1948; reprint, Toronto: Free Press, 1968), 128–44.

38. *Boston Gazette*, Sept. 25, 1786, p. 2. The newspaper report does not identify Randall, but the wording is identical to his report dated May 14, 1786, in *PTJ*, 9:535.

39. *Boston Gazette*, Jan. 4, 1796, p. 3; *Maryland Gazette*, Mar. 24, 1796, p. 1. For an early and inaccurate rumor of the completion of the treaty, see *Boston Gazette*, Mar. 16, 1795, p. 2. For an account of the negotiations, see Irwin, *Diplomatic Relations*, 69–81. For a warning to the public from Secretary of State Timothy Pickering that the treaty was not yet in operation, see *Pennsylvania Gazette*, June 15, 1796.

40. Simpson to Secretary of State, Jan. 20, 1794, SDGD.

41. H. G. Barnby, *The Prisoners of Algiers* (New York: Oxford University Press, 1966), 100; Irwin, *Diplomatic Relations*, 26–27; *PTJ*, 11:376; Simpson to Secretary of State, Oct. 20, 1794, SDGD.

42. Based on 285 items gathered from thorough readings of the *Boston Gazette*, the *Maryland Gazette*, and the *Charleston Evening Gazette/Columbian Herald*, as well as a keyword search of the online version of the *Pennsylvania Gazette* for the period between the first captures in 1785 and ultimate release in 1797. The datelines for 1785–87 break down as follows: All U.S. cities 55%, London 37%, West Indies 3%, Europe 4%, Africa 1%. For 1794–97, datelines appeared as follows: All U.S. cities 95%, London 4%, West Indies 0%, Europe 0%, Africa 1%.

43. *Boston Gazette*, Apr. 30, 1787, p. 3; *Columbian Herald*, May 21, 1787, p. 2.

44. Marcus Rediker, *Between the Devil and the Deep Blue Sea* (New York: Cambridge University Press, 1987), 203.

45. See Michael Warner, *The Letters of the Republic: Publication and the Public Sphere in Eighteenth-Century America* (Cambridge: Harvard University Press, 1990), 30–33, for a particularly cogent explanation.

Chapter 2. The Captives Write Home

1. I have found at least sixteen. For a complete list of all published and unpublished letters sent by the captives, see the appendix.

2. Hester Blum, "Pirated Tars, Piratical Texts: Barbary Captivity and American Sea Narratives," *Early American Studies* 2 (Fall 2003): 133–58.

3. Roy Harvey Pearce, "The Significance of the Captivity Narrative," *American Literature* 19 (Mar. 1947): 1–20. On captivity narratives, see, too, Richard VanDerBeets, ed., *Held Captive by Indians* (Knoxville: University of Tennessee Press, 1994), xix–xxxix.

4. Pearce, "Significance," 13.

5. Maureen Harkin, "Mackenzie's Man of Feeling: Embalming Sensibility," *ELH* 61 (1994): 318–20. On sensibility, see John Mullen, *Sentiment and Sociability: The Language of Feeling in the Eighteenth Century* (Oxford: Clarendon Press, 1988); Julie Ellison, "Race and Sensibility in the Early Republic: Ann Eliza Bleecker and Sarah Wentworth Morton,"

American Literature 65 (1993): 445–94; Northrop Frye, "Towards Refining an Age of Sensibility," *ELH* 23 (1956): 144–52. For an example of a sailor purchasing such literature, see Blum, "Pirated Tars," 31.

6. VanDerBeets, *Held Captive*, 320.

7. For more discussion of these narratives, see chap. 8.

8. Ray W. Irwin, *The Diplomatic Relations of the United States with the Barbary Powers* (New York: Russell and Russell, 1931), 89. O'Brien would serve as the first consul. See chap. 7.

9. Kirsten D. Sword, "Wayward Wives, Runaway Slaves and the Limits of Patriarchal Authority in Early America" (Ph.D. diss., Harvard University, 2002); Mary Beth Sievens, *Stray Wives: Marital Conflict in Early National New England* (New York: New York University Press, 2005); Christopher Castiglia, *Bound and Determined: Captivity, Culture-Crossing, and White Womanhood from Mary Rowlandson to Patty Hearst* (Chicago: University of Chicago Press, 1996).

10. For a somewhat imaginative account, see H. G. Barnby, *The Prisoners of Algiers* (New York: Oxford University Press, 1966), 26–57. See also Robert J. Allison, *The Crescent Obscured: The United States and the Muslim World, 1776–1815* (New York: Oxford University Press, 1995), 113, and Paul Baepler, ed., *White Slaves, African Masters: An Anthology of American Barbary Captivity Narratives* (Chicago: University of Chicago Press, 1999), 109–11. The date of their arrival was certainly before August 12, as Cathcart reports being settled in at Algiers by then; see Baepler, *White Slaves*, 113.

11. Mentioned in a letter from Jefferson to O'Brien; the letter from the captains was subsequently lost. Jefferson to O'Brien, Paris, Nov. 4, 1785, box 1, CFP.

12. Richard B. Parker, *Uncle Sam in Barbary: A Diplomatic History* (Gainesville: University of Florida Press, 2004), 60–63, and 220–22, has uncovered new evidence that eleven American captives, including Cathcart, claimed British citizenship and petitioned the king for assistance. The truth of their claims is impossible to verify, and the situation is further complicated by the lack of a clear definition of American citizenship during the Confederation period.

13. *Salem Gazette*, Nov. 28, 1785, p. 3; *Charleston Evening Gazette*, Feb. 17, 1786; PCC, 6:117, reel 55, and 17:377, reel 100.

14. *Evening Gazette*, Feb. 17, 1786.

15. On O'Brien's Revolutionary service, see *Appleton's Cyclopaedia of American Biography* (New York: D. Appleton and Co., 1898), 4:551, and PTJ, 12:184. I assume O'Brien was lead writer because his name came first in the signatures and the others afterward in alphabetical order, and because the letter's style matches his later efforts.

16. Isaac Stephens to John Adams, Apr. 15, 1786, PTJ, 9:565; O'Brien to the Dohrmans, Jan. 16, 1786, in *Evening Gazette*, May 16, 1786, p. 3; "Intelligence from Algiers," *Maryland Gazette*, June 7, 1786, p. 2 (also contains information reported by an American sailor named John Lagerholm and a Captain Richard Norrie who saw the captives on or before Jan. 6, 1786).

17. O'Brien to Jefferson, July 12, 1786, PTJ, 10:131–32; O'Brien to William Carmichael, Sept. 12, 1786, SDAD. O'Brien continued to believe that Lamb and the dey had made an agreement and that "the terms were recorded on the books of the [Algerian] Regency" as late as 1792. See *Barbary*, 1:35–36.

18. O'Brien to Jefferson, Apr. 28, 1787, SDAD (also paraphrased in *PTJ*, 11:321–22); *Barbary*, 1:35–36; Barnby, *Prisoners*, 87.

19. PCC, 7:287–88, reel 56.

20. Ibid., 2:319–22, reel 72.

21. O'Brien to William Carmichael, Sept. 13, 1786, SDAD; O'Brien to Jefferson, Apr. 28 and Sept. 25, 1787, SDAD; Jefferson to Jay, Dec. 31, 1786, *PTJ*, 10:649–50.

22. O'Brien to Jefferson, Sept. 25, 1787, *PTJ*, 12:180–84.

23. I am counting letters, fragments of letters, and references to letters in other documents.

24. O'Brien to Matthew and Thomas Irwin, Dec. 20, 1788, PCC, p. 181, reel 73.

25. "Richard O'Bryen Diary," AM 109, Historical Society of Pennsylvania, Philadelphia. For full details, see appendix.

26. David Humphreys to George Washington, Apr. 4, 1793, ser. 4, GWP; O'Brien to David Humphreys, Mar. 26, 1793, SDAD; Carmichael to O'Brien, Sept. 13, 1793, CFP.

27. "Richard O'Bryen Diary," June 21, 1790; Mar. 11, 1791. The letters from O'Brien's mother were nearly two years in transit.

28. William Carmichael to O'Brien, Aug. 26–Sept. 2, 1788, CFP; Algerine Captives to Washington, Sept. 22, 1788, ser. 4, GWP.

29. *Maryland Gazette*, Feb. 4, 1790, p. 3; PCC, 21:577–78. reel 102.

30. "The Diplomatic Journal and Letter Book of James Leander Cathcart, 1788–1796," *Proceedings of the American Antiquarian Society* 64 (Oct. 1954): 320, 326.

31. *Barbary*, 1: 28–30. Apparently four died of the plague while one died of smallpox and one of consumption; cf. *PTJ*, 12:549–51.

32. O'Brien to Washington, Jan. 8, 1792, ser. 4, GWP.

33. "Richard O'Bryen Diary," cover page.

34. O'Brien to Cathcart, 1793, CFP; O'Brien to Humphreys, Mar. 26, 1793, ser. 4, GWP.

35. *Barbary*, 1:28–30; Barnby, *Prisoners*, 98–100; Irwin, *Diplomatic Relations*, 43–46. *PTJ*, 11:99–102; 12:150–52, 173, 313.

36. The three privately ransomed captives were John Robertson, Charles Caldwell, and George Smith. On Caldwell and Robertson, see *Pennsylvania Gazette*, Apr. 1, 1792, and *PTJ*, 27:822–24. On Smith, see O'Brien to Cathcart, Mar. 6, [1783], CFP; and O'Brien to David Humphreys, Mar. 26, 1793, SDAD.

37. *Barbary*, 1:29. For a much earlier expression of this fear, see O'Brien to Matt. and Thoms. Irwin, Dec. 20, 1788, PCC, p. 181, reel 73.

38. Accounts of the exact number vary. Frank Lambert, *The Barbary Wars: American Independence in the Atlantic World* (New York: Hill and Wang, 2005), 75, reports 105 captives, which accords with a list in SDGD and O'Brien to Humphreys, Nov. 12, 1793, SDDP. Parker, relying on different sources, including a later account by James Foss, reports 108. Perhaps these discrepancies reflect confusion over who should be considered American. (Some foreign nationals sailed on American ships.)

39. Samuel Calder to the House of Dominick Terry and Co., Nov. 3, 1793, *Barbary*, 1:54; John McShane to David Humphreys, Nov. 13, 1793, SDDP; Moses Morse to House of Dominick Terry, Dec. 1, 1793, *Barbary*, 1:87; Calder to David Pearce Jr., Dec. 4, 1793, SDAD;

James Taylor to Gibbs and Channing, Jan. 7 [1794], SDAD; William Penrose to his owners in Mathew Carey, *A Short History of Algiers* (New York: Evert Duyckinck, 1805), 77–78; McShane to William Bell in Carey, *A Short History,* 82–84.

40. *ASPFR,* 1:417–18, 421–22; O'Brien to Humphreys, Nov. 12, 1793, SDDP; O'Brien to Robert Montgomery, Nov. 16, 1793, SDDP; James Simpson to Secretary of State, Nov. 25, 1793, SDGD.

41. Samuel Calder to David Pearce Jr., Dec. 4, 1793, SDAD.

42. O'Brien to Humphreys, Dec. 6, 1793, SDDP.

43. *ASPFR,* 1:417–18; "Extracts of Captain O'Brien's fragments of letters of the 29th of Dec. [1793] and 6th of January [1794]," SDDP.

44. O'Brien to Humphreys, Nov. 12, 1793, SDDP; O'Brien to James Simpson, Nov. 28, 1793, in Carey, *A Short History,* 84–87; O'Brien to Humphreys, Dec. 6, 1793, SDDP; "Extracts of Captain O'Brien's fragments of letters of the 29th of Dec. [1793] and 6th of January [1794]," SDDP; Humphreys to Secretary of State, May 18, 1794, SDDP; *ASPFR,* 1:418. The various positions on the navy are discussed in greater detail in chap. 6.

45. O'Brien to Humphreys, Jan. 9, 1794, SDDP.

46. "Extract of a letter from Capt. Furnass dated Algiers April 10, 1794"; "Extract of a letter from Capt. Newman dated Algiers 12 April, 1794"; "Extract of a letter from Capt. O'Brien to D. Humphreys dated Algiers June the 18th, 1794"; "A list of deaths among the American captives at Algiers from the 1st day of January to the 1st day of August, 1794"; SDDP.

47. James Taylor to Messrs. Gibbs and Channing, Jan. 7 [1794], SDAD; "Extract of a letter from Capt. Newman dated Algiers 12 April 1794," SDDP.

48. "Extract of a letter from Capt. Newman"; Carey, *A Short History,* 83.

49. "Extract of a letter from Capt. Newman"; *Boston Gazette,* May 26, 1794, p. 3, and Aug. 3, 1795, p. 3.

50. *Boston Gazette,* Dec. 1, 1794, pp. 1–2 (originally printed in the *New York Minerva,* also found in the *Charleston Columbian Herald,* Nov. 26, 1794, p. 2); Burnham to Edmund Randolph, Dec. 18, 1794, SDAD.

51. *Boston Gazette,* Dec. 1, 1794, pp. 1–2.

52. Edward M. Cifelli, *David Humphreys* (Boston: G. K. Hall, 1982), 49–50; Humphreys to Washington, Nov. 1, 1785, ser. 4, GWP. The relevant portion of the poem was reprinted in Carey, *A Short History,* 98–106.

53. Cifelli's study of David Humphreys, particularly pp. 92–101, helped me reach these conclusions. The quotation is from p. 96.

54. Carey, *A Short History,* 98, 106.

55. Cifelli, *David Humphreys,* 50; John Jay to Humphreys, May 19, 1786, the Papers of John Jay (ID #89861), available at www.columbia.edu/cu/web/digital/Jay.

56. Cifelli, *David Humphreys,* 50; Humphreys to Thomas Jefferson, June 5, 1786, *PTJ,* 9:608–9.

57. David Humphreys, *A Poem on Industry. Addressed to the Citizens of the United States of America* (Philadelphia: M. Carey, 1794), 19–20.

58. Cifelli, *David Humphreys,* 80–87; Humphreys to Washington, Jan. 23, Feb. 8, and Mar. 24, 1793, ser. 4, GWP.

59. Humphreys to Washington, Apr. 14, 1793, and enclosure of May 5, 1793, ser. 4, GWP. The enclosure is the Mar. 16 letter from O'Brien. Although the original recipient is not named, I assume from internal evidence (a reference to another letter dated Feb. 12 and the fact that Humphreys sent it to Washington, that it, too, was originally addressed to the Bulkeleys.

60. O'Brien to Humphreys, Nov. 12, 1793, SDDP.

61. Ibid.

62. Humphreys to Captain O'Brien, Captain Stephens et. al. and Humphreys to the "Mariners, citizens of the United States of America, now prisoners at Algiers," Nov. 30, 1793, SDDP.

63. O'Brien to Humphreys, Dec. 6, 1793, SDDP.

64. Humphreys to O'Brien, Jan. 1, 1794, Ibid.

65. Jefferson to O'Brien, Sept. 29, 1785, *PTJ*, 8:567–68; Jefferson to O'Brien, Nov. 4, 1785, CFP.

66. David Humphreys, "Instructions to Robert Montgomery, Esq., Consul of the United States of America at Alicant," n.d.; Humphreys to O'Brien and other Captains, Jan. 12, 1794; Humphreys to Montgomery, Jan. 12, 1794; Humphreys to Secretary of State, Feb. 12, 1794; Humphreys to O'Brien, Feb. 17, 1794; Humphreys to O'Brien, Mar. 3, 1794; Humphreys to Secretary of State, May 13, 1794; Humphreys to O'Brien, May 18, 1794; Humphreys to Secretary of State, June 11, 1794; Humphreys to Secretary of State, July 19, 1794; Humphreys to Capt. William Furnass, Aug. 11, 1794; Humphreys to Captain Newman, Aug. 11, 1794; Humphreys to O'Brien, Aug. 11, 1794; SDDP; F. L. Humphreys, *Life and Times of David Humphreys,* 2 vols. (New York: G. P. Putnam's Sons, 1917), 2:203. F. L. Humphreys was David Humphreys's nephew.

67. "A List of Deaths among the American Captives," SDDP.

68. "Extracts from Captain O'Brien's letter dated August 13, 1794," SDDP.

69. Humphreys to Secretary of State, Sept. 17, 1794, and Humphreys to P. E. Skjoldebrand, Nov. 9, 1794, SDDP; Harold C. Syrett, ed., *The Papers of Alexander Hamilton* (New York: Columbia, 1969), 16:459–60, 574–75, 17:278–81.

70. Humphreys to Secretary of State, Sept. 18 and Nov. 10, 1794; Humphreys to P. E. Skjoldebrand, Nov. 9, 1794; Humphreys to Secretary of State, Nov. 29, 1794, SDDP.

71. F. L. Humphreys, *Life and Times,* 2:230; "The Diplomatic Journal and Letter Book of James Leander Cathcart," 330–31; Humphreys, *The Miscellaneous Works of David Humphreys* (New York: T. and J. Swords, 1804; reprint, 1918), 70.

72. Humphreys to Secretary of State, Jan. 28, 1795, SDDS; Cifelli, *David Humphreys,* 88–90.

Chapter 3. Publicity and Secrecy

1. James Cathcart [possibly to O'Brien], Oct. 12, 1794, CFP. Richard O'Brien for the perusal of David Humphreys, n.d.; Cunningham and Nisbitt to Capts. McShane and O'Brien, June 11, 1794; Cathcart to O'Brien, Nov. 1, 1794, SDAD.

2. On the Marseilles chamber, see H. G. Barnby, *The Prisoners of Algiers* (New York: Oxford University Press, 1966), 156–57.

3. Cornelius Walford, "Kings' Briefs: Their Purposes and History," *Transactions of the Royal Historical Society* 10 (1882): 1–74; Lilian G. Ping, "Raising Funds for Good Causes During the Reformation," *Hibbert Journal* 35 (1936): 53–66; Mark Harris, "Inky Blots and Rotten Parchment Bonds: London Charity Briefs and the Guildhall Library," *Historical Research* 66 (1993): 98–110.

4. Stephen Chissold, *The Barbary Slaves* (Totowa, NJ: Rowman and Littlefield, 1979), 13–15, 102–29; Maria Antonia Garcés, *Cervantes in Algiers: A Captive's Tale* (Nashville: Vanderbilt University Press, 2002).

5. Walford, "Kings' Briefs," 15–19, 21–24. On the colonies, see Matthew Mulcahy, *Hurricanes and Society in the British Greater Caribbean, 1624–1783* (Baltimore: Johns Hopkins University Press, 2006), 141–89.

6. Walford, "Kings' Briefs," 46.

7. Quoted in Mulcahy, *Hurricanes*, 148. On More, see Susan Pederson, "Hannah More Meets Simple Simon: Tracts, Chapbooks, and Popular Culture in Late Eighteenth-Century England," *Journal of British Studies* 25 (1986): 84–113.

8. *PTJ*, 12:173, 313, 474; "Report of the Secretary of State in Relation to American Prisoners at Algiers," Dec. 30, 1790, in *Barbary*, 1:18–22.

9. *PTJ*, 12:313, 474; Henry P. Johnston, ed., *The Correspondence and Public Papers of John Jay*, 4 vols. (1890; reprint, New York: Lenox Hill, 1970), 3:358–59.

10. *PTJ*, 11:35–36, 99–102, 12:150–52; *Barbary*, 1:20.

11. Tench Coxe to John Jay, May 7, 1788, Pennsylvania Abolition Society Manuscript Collection, Library of Congress; Jay to Coxe, May 18, 1788, *Correspondence and Public Papers of John Jay*, 3:333–34; *Boston Gazette*, May 12, 1788, p. 4. Original emphasis.

12. Detailed in chap. 5.

13. *Pennsylvania Gazette*, Mar. 26, 1794, p. 1. Also printed in *Charleston Columbian Herald*, Apr. 16, 1794, p. 4.

14. William Allibone and others to Edmund Randolph, Apr. 7, 1794, SDAD.

15. Harold C. Syrett, ed., *The Papers of Alexander Hamilton* (New York: Columbia University Press, 1969), 16:497–98.

16. Richard Buel Jr., *Securing the Revolution: Ideology in American Politics, 1789–1815* (Ithaca: Cornell University Press, 1972), 97–112, 129–35; George Washington, *Writings* (New York: Library of America, 1997), 886–87, 888. Quotes from Buel, *Securing the Revolution*, 99.

17. Jurgen Habermas, *The Structural Transformation of the Public Sphere* (Cambridge: MIT Press, 1992), 27–43, and following.

18. *Charleston Columbian Herald*, June 25, 1794, p. 4.

19. "Benevolence" to Washington, Apr. 4, 1794, SDAD.

20. On the public/private distinction, see Humphreys to O'Brien, May 18, 1794, SDDP.

21. Frank Landon Humphreys, *Life and Times of David Humphreys*, 2 vols. (New York: G. P. Putnam's Sons, 1917), 2:218–19; *Pennsylvania Gazette*, May 28, 1794; Perez Morton to [?], May 18, 1794, SDAD; Mathew Carey, *A Short History of Algiers* (New York: Evert Duyckinck, 1805), 97–98.

22. On the captives' influence over Humphreys, see chap. 2.

23. Humphreys to Secretary of State, June 11 and Sept. 18, 1794, SDDP. "A Plan for Redeeming the American Citizens now in Captivity at Algiers," SDAD.

24. J. Blackden to the president, Sept. 13, 1794; Benjamin Lincoln to Secretary of State, Sept. 19, 1794, SDAD. On Lincoln's career, see Leonard D. White, *The Federalists: A Study in Administrative History, 1789–1801* (New York: Free Press, 1965), 304–5.

25. Syrett, *Papers of Alexander Hamilton,* 16:497–98.

26. "Extract of Captain O'Brien's Letter, continued from the 5th to 12th of April, 1794"; Humphreys to Secretary of State, Sept. 3, 1794; SDDP. Burnham left Lisbon in September and arrived in America before December 1.

27. *Boston Gazette,* Dec. 1, 1794, pp. 1–2.

28. *Boston Gazette,* Dec. 8, 1794, p. 4; *Pennsylvania Gazette,* Nov. 5, 1794.

29. On the circumstances surrounding this trip, see chap. 2.

30. Humphreys to Secretary of State, Jan. 28, 1795, SDDS; Barnby, *Prisoners,* 118.

31. I have based analysis of the petition on the copy printed in the *Amherst* (New Hampshire) *Journal,* Feb. 6, 1795, p. 3. For Washington's proclamation, see James D. Richardson, *Messages and Papers of the Presidents, 1789–1897* (Washington, DC: Government Printing Office, 1896), 1:179–80.

32. Humphreys to Washington, Nov. 23, 1793, ser. 4, GWP.

33. On the nature and devolution of these connections, see Jonathan D. Sassi, "The First Party Competition and Southern New England's Public Christianity," *Journal of the Early Republic* 21 (2001): 261–99.

34. *Amherst Journal,* Mar. 6, 1795, p. 2.

35. *Amherst Journal,* Mar. 6, 1795, p. 2; *Boston Gazette,* Mar. 2, 1795, p. 2.

36. *Gazette of the United States,* Feb. 10, 1795, p. 3; *Federal Intelligencer,* Feb. 16, 1795, p. 2.

37. *Federal Intelligencer,* Feb. 16, 1795, p. 3; Feb. 18, 1795, p. 4; Feb. 21, 1795, p. 3.

38. Randolph to George Washington, Feb. 11, 1795, Washington's Correspondence with Secretaries of State, 1789–1796, SDGW, and p. 118, ser. 2, GWP.

39. On the public-private distinction, see Humphreys to O'Brien, May 18, 1794, and Aug. 11, 1794, SDAD. Humphreys first proposed the lottery idea to Randolph on June 11, 1794. Newspaper publishers in America received copies in September, indicating that Humphreys must have sent copies to them in June without waiting for Randolph's response to the proposal.

40. J. Blackden to George Washington, Sept. 13, 1794, SDAD.

41. *Federal Intelligencer,* Feb. 26, 1795, p. 3; Feb. 24, 1795, p. 3.

42. *U.S. Statutes at Large* 1 (1794): 345; Syrett, *Papers of Alexander Hamilton,* 16:440, 459–60. Randolph informed Humphreys of the appropriation in his letter of July 19, 1794, which Humphreys received before departing Algiers. See *Barbary,* 1:77–78, and Humphreys to Randolph, Sept. 18, 1794, SDAD.

43. Syrett, *Papers of Alexander Hamilton,* 16:46–58; Ray W. Irwin, *The Diplomatic Relations of the United States with the Barbary Powers* (New York: Russell and Russell, 1931), 74–75. On the funding bill, see also Forrest McDonald, *Alexander Hamilton* (New York: Norton, 1979), 303–5.

44. Detlev F. Vagts, "The Logan Act: Paper Tiger or Sleeping Giant," *American Journal of International Law* 60 (April 1966): 268–302; Buel, *Securing the Revolution,* 113–35.

45. John C. Miller, *Crisis in Freedom: The Alien and Sedition Acts* (Boston: Little Brown and Co., 1952); Vagts, "The Logan Act"; Frederick B. Tolles, "Unofficial Ambassador: George Logan's Mission to France, 1798," *William and Mary Quarterly*, 3d ser., 7 (Jan. 1950): 3–25.

46. While this may be seen as part of the American "paranoid style," it is also important to note that paranoids may have real enemies, as can be seen in James Wilkinson's negotiations with Spain. For an interesting recent discussion of Wilkinson and filibustering, see Roger C. Kennedy, *Burr, Hamilton, and Jefferson* (New York: Oxford University Press, 1999), 127–46.

47. For an interesting but dated cold war–era analysis of this phenomenon, see Gabriel A. Almond, *The American People and Foreign Policy* (New York: Frederick A. Praeger, 1965).

48. Barnby, *Prisoners*, 230–301; *Boston Gazette*, Feb. 20, 1797, p. 2; *Maryland Gazette*, Feb. 16, 1797, p. 3.

49. *Maryland Gazette*, Feb. 16, 1797, p. 3; *Boston Gazette*, Feb. 27, 1797, p. 3; Perez Morton to [?], May 18, 1794, SDAD.

Chapter 4. Slavery at Home and Abroad

1. Olaudah Equiano, *The Interesting Narrative of the Life of Olaudah Equiano*, ed. Robert J. Allison (New York: Bedford Books, 1995); Marion Wilson Starling, *The Slave Narrative: Its Place in American History* (1981; reprint, Washington, D.C.: Howard University Press, 1988), 66–77. Equiano's African origins have recently been questioned, see Vincent Caretta, *Equiano the African: Biography of a Self-Made Man* (Athens: University of Georgia Press, 2005).

2. Equiano, *Interesting Narrative*, 53–54.

3. Mathew Carey, *A Short History of Algiers, With a Concise View of the Origin of the Rupture between Algiers and the United States*, 3d ed. (New York: Duyckinck, 1805), 31; Royall Tyler, *The Algerine Captive* (London, 1802; reprint, Gainesville, FL: Scholars' Facsimiles and Reprints, 1967), 2:50.

4. Linda Colley, *Captives: Britain, Empire and the World, 1600–1850* (New York: Anchor, 2004), 1–20, and throughout.

5. Laurence Sterne, *A Sentimental Journey and Other Writings* (1768; reprint, New York: Oxford University Press, 2003), 60.

6. John Foss, *Journal of the Captivity and Sufferings of John Foss*, 2d ed. (Newburyport, MA: 1798). This narrative is excerpted in Paul Baepler, ed., *White Slaves, African Masters: An Anthology of American Barbary Captivity Narratives* (Chicago: University of Chicago Press, 1999), 73–102.

7. For an example, compare Foss, *Journal*, 32–33, to Carey, *A Short History*, 30. For more on this topic, see chap. 8.

8. Foss, *Journal*, 52–53.

9. It is particularly similar to an episode in chapter 10 of Frederick Douglass's narrative. See *Narrative of the Life of Frederick Douglass, an American Slave*, ed. David W. Blight (New York: Bedford, 2003). Douglass also is critical of the savagery of Christians.

10. Foss cites Sterne's "bitter draught" quote in a different context on p. 137 of *Journal*.

11. Foss, *Journal,* 120, 121–22, 141–42.

12. *Boston Gazette,* Dec. 1, 1794, pp. 1–2 (originally printed in the *New York Minerva*) and *Charleston Columbian Herald,* Nov. 26, 1794, p. 2. For more on Burnham and his account, see chap. 3.

13. John Burnham, "The Curses of Slavery: Treatment of the American Prisoners at Algiers," *Rural Magazine: or Vermont Repository,* Mar. 1795, pp. 118–22.

14. "Treatment of the African Slaves in America," *Rural Magazine; or, Vermont Repository,* Mar. 1795, pp. 122–24.

15. Isaac Stephens to Congress, Feb. 9, 1788, PCC, 2:319–22, reel 72.

16. Anonymous, *The American in Algiers, or the Patriot of Seventy-Six in Captivity. A Poem, In Two Cantos* (New York: J. Buel, 1797).

17. Ibid., 9, 15.

18. Ibid., 27–33. Quotes from 31, 32.

19. Ibid., 32.

20. Carey, *A Short History.* For a more detailed discussion of plagiarism, see chap. 8.

21. Carey, *A Short History,* 32–33.

22. James Wilson Stevens, *An Historical and Geographical Account of Algiers Comprehending A Novel and Interesting Detail of Events Relative to the American Captives* (Philadelphia: Hogan and McElroy, 1797).

23. Ibid., 72.

24. Ibid., 77.

25. Ibid., 234–35.

26. Ibid., 235.

27. "Copy of a letter from an English slave-driver at Algiers to his Friend in England," *New York Magazine* 2 (Oct. 1791): 584. Also printed in the *Salem Gazette,* Feb. 10, 1795.

28. Isaac Bickerstaff [Benjamin West], *An Astronomical Diary, Kalendar, or Almanack, for the year of our Lord, 1791* (Hartford, CT: Nathaniel Patten, 1791). No page numbers.

29. John Vandike, *Narrative of the Captivity of John Vandike, who was Taken by the Algerines in 1791* (1794; reprint, Leominster, MA: Chapman Whitcomb, 1801).

30. Ibid., 6.

31. Susanna Rowson, "Slaves in Algiers: Or a Struggle for Freedom" (Philadelphia: Wrigley and Berriman, 1794), i. The play appears to have been first performed in Philadelphia in June 1794. See the notice in the *Charleston Evening Gazette,* Aug. 4, 1794, p. 4.

32. Ibid., 70.

33. Caleb Bingham, ed., *The Columbian Orator* (1797; reprint, Boston, 1819), 101. On Everett's authorship, see Marta Rojas, "'Insults Unpunished': Barbary Captives, American Slaves, and the Negotiation of Liberty," *Early American Studies* 1 (Fall 2003): 167.

34. Frederick Douglass, *Autobiographies* (New York: Library of America, 1994), 305–6.

35. Bingham, *Columbian Orator,* 105.

36. Ibid., 111–12.

37. Ibid., 112, 115.

38. Ibid., 117.

39. On Tyler, see Ada Lou Carson and Herbert L. Carson, *Royall Tyler* (Boston: Twayne, 1979), and G. Thomas Tanselle, *Royall Tyler* (Cambridge: Harvard University Press, 1967).

40. Tyler, *The Algerine Captive*, 1:136–37, 171–80.

41. Ibid., 1:169–70, 188–89.

42. Ibid., 2:49–50; Bingham, *Columbian Orator*, 115.

43. Winthrop Jordan, *White over Black* (Baltimore: Penguin, 1968), 485.

44. On the abolitionist societies, see Gary B. Nash, *Forging Freedom: The Formation of Philadelphia's Black Community, 1720–1840* (Cambridge: Harvard University Press, 1988), 100–116, and throughout; Shane White, *Somewhat More Independent: The End of Slavery in New York City, 1770–1810* (Athens: University of Georgia Press, 1991).

45. Nash, *Forging Freedom*, 103–6.

46. Pennsylvania Abolitionist Society minutes, Apr. 7, 1788, Library of Congress (microfilm).

47. I have found the ad in the *Pennsylvania Gazette*, Apr. 30, 1788, and *Boston Gazette*, May 12, 1788, p. 1; June 2, 1788, p. 1; and June 16, 1788, p. 4. It is quite possible that it ran in other newspapers, too.

48. Tench Coxe to John Jay, May 7, 1788, in Pennsylvania Abolition Society manuscript collection, Library of Congress (microfilm).

49. Henry P. Johnston, ed., *The Correspondence and Public Papers of John Jay*, 4 vols. (1890; reprint, New York: Lenox Hill, 1970), 333–34. On the Pennsylvania legislation, see Nash, *Forging Freedom*, 108.

50. See minutes for July 7, 1788, and Oct. 6, 1788, in Pennsylvania Abolition Society minutes, Library of Congress (microfilm).

51. H. W. Brands, *The First American* (New York: Anchor, 2000), 701–9; Nash, *Forging Freedom*, 105; John C. Van Horne, "Collective Benevolence and the Common Good in Franklin's Philanthropy," in J. A. Leo Lemay, ed., *Reappraising Benjamin Franklin* (Newark: University of Delaware Press, 1993), 436–37.

52. Quoted in James Parton, *Life and Times of Benjamin Franklin* (New York: Mason Brothers, 1864), 2:611–14.

53. *Maryland Gazette*, Nov. 11, 1790, p. 3. Bettye Gardner tentatively identifies "A Freeman" as Ezekial Cooper in "The Free Blacks of Baltimore" (Ph.D. diss., George Washington University, 1973).

54. This debate is summarized in T. Stephen Whitman, *The Price of Freedom: Slavery and Manumission in Baltimore and Early National Maryland* (Lexington: University Press of Kentucky, 1997), 142–43.

55. *Charleston Columbian Herald*, Aug. 12, 1790, p. 2.

56. Ibid.

57. Ibid., Aug. 14, 1790, p. 2.

58. Ibid., July 30, 1794, p. 4; Aug. 6, 1794, p. 4.

59. On the relative paucity of antislavery activity in South Carolina, see Rachel N. Klein, *Unification of a Slave State* (Chapel Hill: University of North Carolina Press, 1990), 272–76.

60. Robert J. Allison, *The Crescent Obscured: The United States and the Muslim World, 1776–1815* (New York: Oxford University Press, 1995), 224; R. Gerald McMurtry, "The Influence of Riley's Narrative Upon Abraham Lincoln," *Indiana Magazine of History* 30

(1934): 134; Charles H. Adams, ed., *The Narrative of Robert Adams: A Barbary Captive* (New York: Cambridge University Press, 2005), lii.

Chapter 5. Captive Nation: Algiers and Independence

1. *Boston Gazette,* May 1, 1786, p. 3; *Columbian Herald,* Mar. 5, 1787, p. 2; *Charleston Evening Gazette,* Dec. 15, 1785, p. 2.

2. Benedict Anderson, *Imagined Communities: Reflections on the Origin and Spread of Nationalism* (London: Verso, 1983) is the fountainhead of much of this historical stream. For more specific studies of the Anglo-American world, see David Waldstreicher, *In the Midst of Perpetual Fetes: The Making of American Nationalism, 1776–1820* (Chapel Hill: University of North Carolina Press, 1997); Sacvan Bercovitch, *The Rites of Assent: Transformations in the Symbolic Construction of America* (New York: Routledge, 1993); Jay Fliegelman, *Declaring Independence: Jefferson, Natural Language, and the Culture of Performance* (Stanford: Stanford University Press, 1993); Sean Wilentz, "Artisan Republican Festivals and the Rise of Class Conflict in New York City, 1788–1837" in Michael H. Frisch and Daniel J. Walkowitz, eds., *Working Class America* (Urbana: University of Illinois Press, 1983), 37–77; Susan G. Davis, *Parades and Power: Street Theatre in Nineteenth-Century Philadelphia* (Philadelphia: University of Pennsylvania Press, 1986); Mary Ryan, "The American Parade: Representations of the Nineteenth-Century Social Order," in Lynn Hunt, ed., *The New Cultural History* (Berkeley and Los Angeles: University of California Press, 1989), 131–53; Len Travers, *Celebrating the Fourth: Independence Day and the Rites of Nationalism in the Early Republic* (Amherst: University of Massachusetts Press, 1987); Albrecht Koschnik, "Political Conflict and Public Contest: Rituals of National Celebration in Philadelphia, 1788–1815," *Pennsylvania Magazine of History and Biography* 118 (1994): 209–48; Simon P. Newman, *Parades and the Politics of the Street: Festive Culture in the Early American Republic* (Philadelphia: University of Pennsylvania Press, 1997); Andrew W. Robertson, " 'Look on this Picture . . . And on This!' Nationalism, Localism, and Partisan Images of Otherness in the United States, 1787–1820," *American Historical Review* 106 (2001): 1263–80; Linda Colley, *Britons: Forging the Nation, 1707–1837* (New Haven: Yale University Press, 1992).

3. *PTJ,* 9:176–77 ("Les hostilités des corsaires Barbariques ont fait une grande sensation en Amerique").

4. *PTJ,* 8:559; 9:91–92, 211–12.

5. Robert A. Rutland, *The Papers of George Mason, 1725–1792* (Chapel Hill: University of North Carolina, 1970), 3:1201; Diary of William Faris, Dec. 20 and 24, 1793, MS 2160, Maryland State Archives, Annapolis; Charles Carroll to Joshua Johnson, Jan. 1794, Charles Carroll Letter-book, 1771–1833, Arents Collections, New York Public Library. I thank Jean Russo and Mary Jeske, respectively, for the last two sources.

6. Discussed in chap. 1. The three families were those of John Livingston, Dr. Spence, and Captain Greene.

7. Carl E. Prince et al., eds., *The Papers of William Livingston,* 5 vols. (New Brunswick: Rutgers University Press, 1979), 5:410–12.

8. *PTJ,* 8:585–586; *Evening Gazette,* Jan. 17, 1786, p. 2.

9. Robert J. Allison, *The Crescent Obscured: The United States and the Muslim World, 1776–1815* (New York: Oxford University Press, 1995), 3–7; *Boston Gazette,* Dec. 12, 1785, p. 3; *Pennsylvania Gazette,* Apr. 5, 1786.

10. *Evening Gazette,* Mar. 6, 1786, p. 2; *Boston Gazette,* May 1, 1786, p. 3.

11. PCC, 17:377, reel 100.

12. Merrill Jensen, *The New Nation* (New York: Vintage, 1965), 194–218; Lawrence A. Peskin, "From Protection to Encouragement: Manufacturing and Mercantilism in New York City's Public Sphere, 1783–1795," *Journal of the Early Republic* 18 (1998): 589–615.

13. *Evening Gazette,* May 6, 1786, p. 2; June 19, 1786, p. 2; *Columbian Herald,* Nov. 6, 1786, p. 2. See, too, *Pennsylvania Gazette,* May 11 and Nov. 30, 1785.

14. Jefferson to James Monroe, May 10, 1786, *PTJ,* 9:499–503.

15. *Columbian Herald,* Sept. 20, 1787, p. 2; *Boston Gazette,* Oct. 2, 1786, p. 2; *Columbian Herald,* July 1, 1786, p. 2.

16. *PTJ,* 9:176–77, 10:176–79, 385–86; *Pennsylvania Gazette,* Dec. 21, 1785.

17. *PTJ,* 10:176–79; *Pennsylvania Gazette,* Nov. 30, 1785.

18. Lawrence A. Peskin, "To 'Encourage and Protect' American Manufactures: The Intellectual Origins of Industrialization, 1763–1830" (Ph.D. diss., University of Maryland, 1998), 92–145.

19. *Boston Gazette,* May 29, 1786, p. 2; *Maryland Gazette,* Mar. 30, 1786, p. 2. See, also, *Columbian Herald,* Oct. 23, 1786, p. 2, and June 1, 1786, p. 3.

20. *Boston Gazette,* May 29, 1786, p. 3. The report actually stated that the ransom would cost £600 per master, £400 per mate, and £200 per crew member. Counting the two passengers as "mates," the figure comes to £6,200, or $27,528, when a Mexican dollar is valued at £4.55. This figure was the standard conversion rate throughout the eighteenth century, according to John J. McCusker, *Money and Exchange in Europe and America, 1600–1775* (Chapel Hill: University of North Carolina, 1978), 8.

21. *Boston Gazette,* Aug. 21, 1786, p. 3; *Maryland Gazette,* Aug. 3, 1786, p. 2. For other pessimistic reports, see *Boston Gazette,* July 24, 1786, p. 3; July 31, 1786, p. 2; Oct. 9, 1786, p. 3; *Columbian Herald,* Oct. 30, 1786, p. 2; Dec. 21, 1786, p. 2; *Maryland Gazette,* Aug. 1, 1786, p. 2; Oct. 5, 1786, p. 2; Dec. 7, 1786, p. 3.

22. PCC, p. 47, 483, reel 119; *PTJ,* 9:364–65, 549–53; Ray W. Irwin, *The Diplomatic Relations of the United States with the Barbary Powers* (New York: Russell and Russell, 1931), 37–40.

23. *PTJ,* 9:186–89, 525–36; PCC, p. 421, reel 115; *Pennsylvania Gazette,* Dec. 28, 1785.

24. *PTJ,* 9:383–84, 608–9; 10:68.

25. Ibid., 10:223–25, 479–80, 649–50; PCC, p. 154, 155, 159–62, reel 3; 8:357, reel 51.

26. *PTJ,* 10:223–25, 427–29; PCC, p. 532, reel 119.

27. *Evening Gazette,* Feb. 15, 1786, p. 2; June 19, 1786, p. 2; *Pennsylvania Gazette,* Apr. 19, 1786; *Maryland Gazette,* Aug. 10, 1786, p. 2–3.

28. *PTJ,* 10:223–25, 250–51, 630–31.

29. Henry P. Johnston, ed., *The Correspondence and Public Papers of John Jay,* 4 vols. (1890; reprint, New York: Burt Franklin, 1970), 3:196–99, 222–24.

30. Clinton Rossiter, ed., *The Federalist Papers* (New York: Mentor, 1961), 41–50. Quote from p. 45. Emphasis added.

31. Johnston, *Correspondence and Public Papers of John Jay*, 3:299–301.

32. *PTJ*, 8:195–96; *Pennsylvania Gazette*, June 18, 1793, pp. 2–3.

33. *Boston Gazette*, May 11, 1786, p. 3.

34. *Evening Gazette*, Feb. 17, 1786; *Salem Gazette*, Nov. 25, 1785, p. 3; PCC, 6:117, reel 55.

35. *Boston Gazette*, Mar. 5, 1787, p. 3; *Evening Gazette*, Dec. 23, 1785, p. 2; Adams to O'Brien, Oct. 6, 1785, CFP.

36. *Evening Gazette*, June 16, 1786, p. 3.

37. *PTJ*, 9:615–22; O'Brien to William Carmichael, Sept. 13, 1786, SDAD. For examples of Jefferson's distrust of the British press on this issue, see *PTJ*, 8:559, 585–87.

38. *PTJ*, 9:149–50, 238–39; 12:549–51; PCC, pp. 118–19, reel 4; *Maryland Gazette*, Mar. 27, 1788, p. 1.

39. *Boston Gazette*, June 25, 1787, p. 2; Aug. 27, 1787, p. 3; *Maryland Gazette*, Mar. 2, 1788, p. 1.

40. Irwin, *Diplomatic Relations*, 57–60; H. G. Barnby, *The Prisoners of Algiers* (New York: Oxford University Press), 104–11.

41. *Charleston Columbian Herald*, Jan. 22, 1794, p. 2; *Maryland Gazette*, Jan. 2, 1794, p. 1. Original emphasis. For similar reports, see *Boston Gazette*, Dec. 23, 1793, p. 3; Jan. 20, 1794, p. 3; *Maryland Gazette*, Dec. 26, 1793, p. 2; Jan. 9, 1794, p. 1; Feb. 27, 1794, p. 2.

42. *PTJ*, 27:199–200, 230–31.

43. Nathaniel Cutting to the Secretary of State, Lisbon, Feb. 1, 1794, SDAD.

44. Peter Walsh to Thomas Jefferson, Nov. 9, 1793; John Cooper to P. Walsh, May 10, 1793, SDCD Cadiz Series; James Simpson to Jefferson, Oct. 21 and 31, 1793, SDGD; Humphreys to Jefferson, Oct. 10, 1793; William Chapman to Humphreys, Oct. 9, 1793; Humphreys to Jefferson, Oct. 11 and 13, 1793, SDDP; Edmund Church to Jefferson, Nov. 9, 1793, SDLD.

45. Humphreys to Jefferson, Oct. 13, 1793, SDDP; *Annals*, House of Representatives, 3d Cong., 1st sess., 435–36.

46. *PTJ*, 27:469–71; *Boston Gazette*, Dec. 23, 1793, p. 3.

47. Foreign Office, General Correspondence, Algiers, F.O.3.7, Public Records Office, Kew Gardens, London; Stanley Elkins and Eric McKittrick, *The Age of Federalism* (New York: Oxford, 1993), 378.

48. Nathaniel Cutting to the Secretary of State, Lisbon, Feb. 1, 1794, SDAD.

49. *PTJ*, 27:596–97; Donald H. Stewart, *The Opposition Press of the Federalist Period* (Albany: State University of New York, 1969), 180–82.

50. Richard Hofstadter, *The Paranoid Style in American Politics and Other Essays* (New York: Vintage, 1967), 29.

51. The Federalists' reaction is discussed in chap. 3.

52. Elkins and McKittrick, *The Age of Federalism*, 375–85; Drew R. McCoy, *The Elusive Republic: Political Economy in Jeffersonian America* (New York: W. W. Norton, 1980), 162–65.

53. *Boston Gazette*, Jan. 27, 1794, p. 2; Feb. 10, 1794, p. 2; Feb. 17, 1794, p. 3.

54. *Boston Gazette*, Mar. 3, 1794, p. 2; Mar. 17, 1794, p. 2.

55. *New York Diary*, Feb. 25, 1794, p. 2; Feb. 26, 1794, p. 2; Feb. 27, 1794, p. 2; Mar. 4, 1794, p. 3; Mar. 6, 1794, p. 2; *Boston Gazette*, Mar 10, 1794, p. 4.

56. Elkins and McKittrick, *The Age of Federalism*, 388–94; *Columbian Herald*, Apr. 18, 1794, p. 2.

57. Elkins and McKittrick, *The Age of Federalism*, 389–94; Stewart, *The Opposition Press*, 185; Roland M. Baumann, "John Swanwick: Spokesman for 'Merchant Republicanism' in Philadelphia, 1790–1798," *Pennsylvania Magazine of History and Biography* (Apr. 1973), 160–61; *Pennsylvania Gazette*, Mar. 26, 1794, p. 1; *Boston Gazette*, May 19, 1794, p. 3; June 21, 1794, p. 2; *Columbian Herald*, June 9, 1794, p. 2.

58. *Columbian Herald*, Sept. 30, 1794, p. 2; *Maryland Gazette*, Sept. 18, 1794, p. 1; *Pennsylvania Gazette*, Sept. 10, 1794, and Feb. 11, 1795.

59. Richard Buel Jr., *Securing the Revolution* (Ithaca: Cornell University Press, 1972), 96; Philip S. Foner, ed., *The Democratic Republican Societies, 1790–1800* (Connecticut: Greenwood, 1976), 168.

60. David Waldstreicher suggests in *In the Midst of Perpetual Fetes* that early national identity was more a product of conflict than consensus.

Chapter 6. The Navy and the Call to Arms

1. Robert Middlekauff, *The Glorious Cause: The American Revolution, 1763–1789* (New York: Oxford University Press, 1982), 525–34; John C. Miller, *The Federalist Era, 1789–1801* (New York: Harper and Row, 1961), 150.

2. *PTJ*, 10:86, 123–26; Kenneth J. Hogan, *This People's Navy: The Making of American Sea Power* (New York: Free Press, 1991), 21–24. On the Lamb mission, see chap. 5 in this volume.

3. Marshall Smelser, *The Congress Founds the Navy, 1787–1798* (South Bend, IN: University of Notre Dame, 1959), 8–9; Clinton Rossiter, ed., *The Federalist Papers* (New York: Mentor, 1961), 86–87.

4. Craig L. Symonds, *Navalists and Antinavalists: The Naval Policy Debate in the United States, 1785–1827* (Newark: University of Delaware Press, 1980), 24–25; Smelser, *The Congress*, 8, 41–42.

5. H. Knox to G. Washington, Sept. 6, 1793, ser. 4, GWP; Smelser, *The Congress*, 48–49.

6. Edward Church to Jefferson, Sept. 22 and Oct. 8, 1793, in *PTJ*, 27:139–42, 220–22; Church to Jefferson, Oct. 30, 1793, SDLD; Michael Murphy to Jefferson, June 30, 1793, SDMD; Humphreys to Jefferson, Oct. 11, 1793, SDDP.

7. George Washington, "Fifth Annual Message to Congress," in *Writings* (New York: Library of America, 1997), 846–48.

8. Drew R. McCoy, "Republicanism and American Foreign Policy: James Madison and the Political Economy of Commercial Discrimination, 1789 to 1794," *William and Mary Quarterly*, 3d ser., 31 (1974): 633–46.

9. Murphy to Secretary of State, Dec. 4, 1793, SDMD; Cutting to Secretary of State, Feb. 10, 1794, SDAD; Murphy to Secretary of State, April 3, 1794, in *Barbary*, 1:71.

10. O'Brien to Humphreys, Oct. 1794, SDAD; Letter of "Cunningham and Nisbitt," June 11, 1794, SDAD. For more on this letter, see chap. 3.

11. Humphreys to Washington, Nov. 23, 1793, ser. 4 GWP. For a detailed discussion of this fast day, see chap. 3.

12. Smelser, *The Congress*, 51–52, 56–57.

13. *House Journal*, 3d Cong., 1st sess., 217; *ASPFR*, 1:413–23.

14. Smelser, *The Congress*, 49.

15. Humphreys to Washington, Nov. 23, 1793, ser. 4, GWP; Humphreys to Sec. State, Mar. 5, 1794, SDDP.

16. *Annals*, 3d Cong., 1st sess., 433–34, 487. Virginia's John Nicholas feared that the proposed naval squadron would prove too weak to take on the Algerians by themselves, for "a small number of sailors were sufficient to navigate one of their ships, and they had a militia to man them who were innumerable." Fellow Virginian William Giles expressed similar concerns.

17. Ibid., 439, 487. Speeches in the *Annals of Congress* are reported in the third person and presumably were often paraphrased rather than recorded verbatim. I have taken the liberty of treating them as first-person direct quotations to make them more immediate.

18. Ibid, 433.

19. Ibid., 436, 439, 451, 438.

20. Ibid., 493, 440, 436, 494.

21. William T. Hutchinson and William M. E. Rachal, ed., *Papers of James Madison*, 17 vols. (Charlottesville: University Press of Virginia, 1962–91), 15:222, 530–31; *Barbary*, 1: 60–61; *Annals*, 3d Cong., 1st sess., 449–50.

22. *Annals*, 3d Cong., 1st sess., 433, 437.

23. James Morton Smith, ed., *The Republic of Letters: The Correspondence between Thomas Jefferson and James Madison, 1776–1826*, 3 vols. (New York: Norton, 1995), 2:839; *Annals*, 3d Cong., 1st sess., 434, 439, 490.

24. *Annals*, 3d Cong., 1st sess., 435, 439–40.

25. *Barbary*, 1:69–70.

26. Ibid., 496, 439.

27. See chap. 5 for a discussion of this issue.

28. *Annals*, 3d Cong., 1st sess., 496.

29. Madison, "Political Observations" (April 20, 1795), in Hutchinson, *Papers of James Madison*, 15:530–532.

30. Based on the vote of March 10, 1794. Party identification was determined using the *Biographical Directory of the United States Congress* (Washington, DC: Government Printing Office, 2000).

31. Frank A. Cassell, *Merchant Congressman in the Young Republic: Samuel Smith of Maryland* (Madison: University of Wisconsin Press, 1971), 50–52.

32. Roland Baumann, "John Swanwick: Spokesman for 'Merchant Republicanism' in Philadelphia, 1790–1798," *Pennsylvania Magazine of History and Biography* 97 (1973): 159–62.

33. Jefferson to Madison, April 3, 1794, in Smith, *Republic of Letters*, 2:839; Report of the Secretary of War, April 15, 1794, ser. 4, GWP; Eugene S. Ferguson, *Truxton of the Constellation: The Life of Commodore Thomas Truxton, U.S. Navy, 1755–1822* (Baltimore: Johns

Hopkins Press, 1956), III–12. See also Robert G. Albion, "The First Days of the Navy Department," *Military Affairs* 12 (Spring 1948): 1–11.

34. Oddly, all reports from Algiers indicate roughly 180 guns while the congressional report has the figure at 280; see Oct. 8, 1794, SDCD.

35. *ASPFR*, 1:417–18; *Annals*, 3d Cong., 1st sess., 486–90; *Barbary*, 1:60.

36. *Maryland Gazette*, Mar. 13, 1794, p. 1.

37. *Annals*, 3d Cong., 1st sess., 440, 491.

38. Ibid., 495–98.

39. *NASPNA*, 1:5; Harold C. Syrett, ed., *The Papers of Alexander Hamilton* (New York: Columbia University Press, 1969), 16:395, 524–25, 527, 536, 565–66; 17:304–8, 429, 466–75.

40. *NASPNA*, 1:10–56; Syrett, *Papers of Alexander Hamilton*, 17:466–75.

41. *Boston Gazette*, Mar. 16, 1795, p. 2; Nov. 16, 1795, p. 3; Nov. 23, 1795, p. 3; *Maryland Gazette*, Mar. 12, 1795, p. 2; August 13, 1795, p. 2; Nov. 12, 1795, p. 2; *Columbian Herald*, Nov. 25, 1795, p. 2.

42. Ray W. Irwin, *The Diplomatic Relations of the United States with the Barbary Powers* (New York: Russell and Russell, 1931), 69–70; *Barbary*, 1:107–17.

43. *NASPNA*, 1:17–20; Maury Baker, "Cost Overrun, An Early Naval Precedent: Building the First U.S. Warships, 1794–98," *Maryland Historical Magazine* 72 (1977): 364–65.

44. *NASPNA*, 1:25.

45. *Annals*, 4th Cong., 1st sess., 233.

46. *Senate Journal*, 4th Cong., 1st sess., Mar. 22, 1796; Symonds, *Navalists*, 40.

47. For total costs, see Baker, "Cost Overrun," 371.

48. *Annals*, 4th Cong., 1st sess., 874, 885; *Barbary*, 1:151–53.

49. *Annals*, 4th Cong., 1st sess., 874, 882.

50. Ibid., 879.

51. Ibid., 869, 874, 876, 879, 882.

52. Ibid., 871, 878, 877.

53. See chap. 5.

54. *Annals*, 4th Cong., 1st sess., 884.

55. Ibid., 879, 878.

56. Ibid., 869, 873.

57. For a concise overview of the various twists and turns, see K. Jack Bauer, "Naval Shipbuilding Programs, 1794–1860," *Military Affairs* 29 (Spring 1965): 29–40.

58. Based on the votes of April 8, 1796, reported in *Annals*, 4th Cong., 1st sess., 886–87 and 891. Party affiliation was determined from the *Biographical Directory of the United States Congress*. Of the thirty-four congressmen who voted to continue six ships, twenty-seven (79%) were Federalists, five (15%) Democratic-Republicans, and two were of no identifiable party. Of the twenty-five who voted to continue only two ships, nineteen (76%) were Democratic-Republicans, four (16%) Federalists, and two were of no identifiable party.

59. *Annals*, 4th Cong., 1st sess., 1362, 1365, 1371, 2212.

60. *NASPMA*, 1:116–18.

61. *Annals*, 4th Cong., 1st sess., 1365–66.

62. See chap. 5.

63. *Annals*, 4th Cong., 1st sess., 1364, 1368–70. Italics added.

64. Irwin, *Diplomatic Relations*, 74–76; H. G. Barnby, *The Prisoners of Algiers* (New York: Oxford University Press, 1966), 286–89; *Boston Gazette*, Feb. 27, 1797, p. 3–4; *Charleston City Gazette and Daily Advertiser*, Feb. 18, 1797, p. 2.

65. *Annals*, 4th Cong., 2d sess., 2339–51.

66. *Annals*, 4th Cong., 2d sess., 2351–52. Party affiliation gathered from *Biographical Directory of the United States Congress*.

67. Richard Buel, *Securing the Revolution* (Ithaca: Cornell University Press, 1972), 144.

68. *Annals*, 5th Cong., 1st sess., 378, 382.

69. Stanley Elkins and Eric McKittrick, *The Age of Federalism* (New York: Oxford University Press, 1993), 555.

70. Smith, *Republic of Letters*, 2:982.

71. *Annals*, 5th Cong., 1st sess., 382–83.

72. *NASPNA*, 1:37–56; *Annals*, 5th Cong., 2d sess., 821–28.

73. *NASPMA*, 1:120–23; *Annals*, 5th Cong., 2d sess., 1267–70; Smelser, *The Congress*, 139–75; Symonds, *Navalists*, 66–80; Kenneth J. Hagan, *The People's Navy: The Making of American Sea Power* (New York: Free Press, 1991), 42–43.

Chapter 7. Masculinity and Servility in Tripoli

1. Robert J. Allison, *Stephen Decatur: American Naval Hero, 1799–1820* (Amherst: University of Massachusetts Press, 2005) 15; *Barbary*, 1:230–31. The practice of appointing former captives to such positions appears to have been a common one. Spain's Consul to Tripoli, for example, was also a former "slave" in Algiers. See *Barbary*, 1:206.

2. *Barbary*, 1:320–21, 358.

3. E. Anthony Rotundo, *American Manhood: Transformations in Masculinity from the Revolution to the Modern Era* (New York: Basic, 1993). See, also, the citations below.

4. Bertram Wyatt-Brown, *Southern Honor: Ethics and Behavior in the Old South* (New York: Oxford University Press, 1982); Joanne B Freeman, *Affairs of Honor: National Politics in the New Republic* (New Haven: Yale University Press, 2001).

5. Gary J. Kornblith, "Becoming Joseph T. Buckingham: The Struggle for Artisanal Independence in Early Nineteenth-Century Boston," in Howard B. Rock, Paul A. Gilje, and Robert Asher, eds., *American Artisans: Crafting Social Identity, 1750–1850* (Baltimore: Johns Hopkins University Press, 1995), 130; Toby L. Ditz, "Shipwrecked; or, Masculinity Imperiled: Mercantile Representations of Failure and the Gendered Self in Eighteenth-Century Philadelphia," *Journal of American History* 81 (June 1994): 51–80; Brian P. Luskey, "Jumping Counters in White Collars: Manliness, Respectability, and Work in the Antebellum City," *Journal of the Early Republic* 26 (Summer 2006): 173–219.

6. Paul A. Gilje, *Liberty on the Waterfront: American Maritime Culture in the Age of Revolution* (Philadelphia: University of Pennsylvania Press, 2004), 35–36, 83, 233; Myra C. Glenn, "Troubled Manhood in the Early Republic: The Life and Autobiography of Sailor Horace Lane," *Journal of the Early Republic* 26 (Spring 2006): 70–71.

7. Michelle Burnham, *Captivity and Sentiment: Cultural Exchange in American Litera-

ture, 1682–1861 (Hanover, NH: University Press of New England, 1997); Ann Fabian, *The Unvarnished Truth: Personal Narratives in Nineteenth-Century America* (Berkeley and Los Angeles: University of California Press, 2000); Richard VanDerBeets, ed., *Held Captive by Indians: Selected Narratives, 1642–1836* (Knoxville: University of Tennessee Press, 1994); Daniel E. Williams, ed., *Liberty's Captives: Narratives of Confinement in the Print Culture of the Early Republic* (Athens: University of Georgia Press, 2006).

8. See chap. 8 for a discussion of Velnet/Martin.

9. Susanna Rowson, *Slaves in Algiers* (Philadelphia: Wrigley and Berriman, 1794); James Ellison, *The American Captive* (Boston: Joshua Belcher, 1812).

10. Robert J. Allison, *The Crescent Obscured: The United States and the Muslim World, 1776–1815* (New York: Oxford University Press, 1995), 65.

11. Frank Lambert, *The Barbary Wars: American Independence in the Atlantic World* (New York: Hill and Wang, 2005), 125.

12. *Barbary*, 1:251, 276; 2:174. Isaac Stephens, former captain of the *Maria*, which had been captured in 1785 along with O'Brien's *Dauphin* also requested work aboard one of the new ships or at the Boston Naval Yard. Always something of a sad case, Stevens claimed to be in "a state of extreme poverty and distress" by 1802.

13. European nations also committed piracy upon the North Africans. See Jacques Heers, *The Barbary Corsairs: Warfare in the Mediterranean, 1480–1580* (London: Greenhill Books, 2001); and William Spencer, *Algiers in the Age of the Corsairs* (Norman: University of Oklahoma Press, 1976).

14. *Barbary*, 1:326–29, 357–58.

15. Richard Zacks, *The Pirate Coast: Thomas Jefferson, the First Marines, and the Secret Mission of 1805* (New York: Hyperion, 2005), 99; Richard B. Parker, *Uncle Sam in Barbary: A Diplomatic History* (Gainesville: University of Florida Press, 2004), 132; *Barbary*, 1:321.

16. Allison, *Crescent Obscured*, 175–77; Ray W. Irwin, *The Diplomatic Relations of the United States with the Barbary Powers* (New York: Russell and Russell, 1931), 94–95; Parker, *Uncle Sam in Barbary*, 126–27; *Barbary*, 1:380.

17. *Barbary*, 1:378–80, 384–85.

18. Ibid., 1:397–98.

19. Ibid., 1:403.

20. Ibid., 1:408–9.

21. Heather Nathans, "A Much Maligned People: Jews on and off the Stage in the Early American Republic," *Early American Studies* 2 (Fall 2004): 310–42; William Pencak, *Jews and Gentiles in Early America, 1654–1800* (Ann Arbor: University of Michigan Press, 2005).

22. *Barbary*, 1:578–79, 581–83; 2:166–70; Allison, *Crescent Obscured*, 174–75.

23. *Barbary*, 2:176–78, 214–15; Allison, *Crescent Obscured*, 123.

24. *Barbary*, 2:288–90.

25. Ibid., 2:196–97.

26. Ibid., 2:200–201, 223–25, 279–80.

27. Ibid., 2:224; Allison, *Crescent Obscured*, 174–75.

28. *Barbary*, 1:273–74; 2:111–12, 250–54, 288–90.

29. *Barbary*, 2:289, 301, 380.

30. Ibid., 2:380–81.

31. Ibid., 2:482–85, 487–88.

32. Ibid., 3:43, 47–48, 54–56, 61.

33. I base the 307 figure on the *Philadelphia* officers' report printed in the *Aurora*, Mar. 27, 1804, p. 2.

34. *Barbary*, 3:266–67, 272–73.

35. Ibid., 3:353–54.

36. Ibid., 3:403–4, 449; 4:8–9.

37. Tobias Lear, Copy of Letter to James Madison, No. 6. Algiers Jan. 1-Feb. 17, 1804. Including Diary or Journal of Occurrences at Algiers, pp. 34–36, Clements Library, University of Michigan, Ann Arbor.

38. For an excellent account, see Allison, *Stephen Decatur*, 47–54.

39. Allison, *Stephen Decatur*, 53.

40. *Barbary*, 3: 245–59, 380, 442, 455–56.

41. Ibid., 3: 272–73, 283–85.

42. Ibid., 4:65–66, 80, 141–42.

43. Zacks, *Pirate Coast*, 9.

44. *Barbary*, 5:2–3, 86–87.

45. Zacks, *Pirate Coast*, 94.

46. Ibid., 348–70.

47. For examples, see O'Brien to Washington, Jan. 8, 1792; O'Brien to Humphreys, Mar. 26, 1793, ser. 4, GWP.

48. See chap. 3.

49. For example, see *Barbary*, 3:432–34.

50. *Barbary*, 3:223–24, 312.

51. *Aurora*, Apr. 12, 1804, p. 2; *Boston Gazette*, Mar. 11, 1805, p. 2; Aug. 29, 1805, p. 1; *Barbary*, 5:124–25.

52. *Barbary*, 3:425; *Barbary*, 4:186–87, 255–56.

53. *Boston Gazette*, May 24, 1804, p. 1; Aug. 1, 1805, p. 2; Aug. 29. 1805, p. 1; *Barbary*, 3:223–224; 4:65, 149.

54. *Barbary*, 4:149, 264–65.

55. *Barbary*, 4:263–64.

56. Ibid., 3:253–54; Lambert, *Barbary Wars*, 142–43.

57. *Barbary*, 3:329–30, 455–56; 4:198–200, 264–65; 5:135–37.

58. Lambert, *Barbary Wars*, 154; Allison, *Crescent Obscured*, 32.

59. *Barbary*, 3:253–54; 4:199–200, 255–56; 5:129–30.

60. Ibid., 6:74, 82.

61. Ibid., 6:88, 156; *Boston Gazette*, Sept. 9, 1805, p. 2; Sept. 23, 1805, p. 2.

62. *Barbary*, 6:95.

63. Zacks, *Pirate Coast*, 302; Irwin, *Diplomatic Relations*, 154; *ASPFR*, 2:18–19.

64. For this section I have relied primarily on reports in the Republican *Philadelphia Aurora* and the Federalist *Boston Gazette*. Both papers printed local reports and also re-printed items from other newspapers, usually those sharing their political persuasion.

65. *Aurora*, Mar. 31, 1804, p. 2; May 19, 1804, p. 2; May 23, 1804, p.2; July 7, 1804, p. 2.

66. *Boston Gazette,* Apr. 26, 1804, p. 2; Oct. 15, 1804, p. 2; Aug. 15, 1805, p. 4.

67. Ibid., Aug. 15, 1805, p. 4.

68. *Aurora,* Mar. 28, 1804, p. 2; *Boston Gazette,* Apr. 5, 1804, p. 2; May 3, 1804, p. 1; July 11, 1805, p. 1.

69. Zacks, *Pirate Coast,* 87.

70. *Aurora,* Mar. 30, 1804, p. 2; Apr. 3, 1804, p. 2.

71. *Aurora,* Apr. 9, 1804, p. 2; Apr. 14, 1804, p. 2.

72. *Aurora,* Nov. 16, 1804, pp. 2–3; *Boston Gazette,* Feb. 25, 1805, p. 1; July 11, 1805, p. 1.

73. *Boston Gazette,* Jan. 21, 1805, p. 2; Mar. 5, 1805, p. 2.

74. See, for example, the complaints of Roger Griswold and Samuel Dana of Connecticut. *Annals,* 8th Cong., 1st sess., 1211, 1219.

75. For similar arguments, see the speeches of Joseph Nicholson of Maryland and John Randolph of Virginia. *Annals,* 8th Cong., 1st sess., 1214–16, 1221–24.

76. *Annals,* 8th Cong., 1st sess., 1225.

Chapter 8. Between Colony and Empire

1. Elizabeth A. Bohls and Ian Duncan, ed., *Travel Writing, 1700–1830, An Anthology* (New York: Oxford University Press, 2005), xxii–xxiii.

2. On the language of expertise, see chap. 2.

3. Bohls and Duncan, *Travel Writing,* xxiii–xxiv.

4. On Britain, see Linda Colley, *Captives: Britain, Empire, and the World, 1600–1850* (New York: Anchor, 2002).

5. Mathew Carey, *A Short Account of Algiers,* 2d ed. (Philadelphia: M. Carey, 1794), 12; John Foss, *Journal of the Captivity and Sufferings of John Foss,* 2d ed. (Newburyport: A. March, 1798), 74; James Wilson Stevens, *An Historical and Geographical Account of Algiers* (Philadelphia: Hogan and McElroy, 1797), 214, 238. In describing the Algerian country people as nomads who lived in tents Foss probably was again using Native Americans as a model (Foss, *Journal,* 78).

6. Karen Odahl Kupperman, *The Jamestown Project* (Cambridge: Belknap Press, 2007), 132.

7. See chap. 5.

8. Carey, *A Short Account of Algiers.* The first edition was published January 8, and the second edition was published October 20, and a third edition, now called *A Short History of Algiers* was published in 1805 in New York City by Evert Duyckinck, probably to capitalize on public interest in the war in Tripoli. The first edition was prominently advertised in the *Pennsylvania Gazette* (Jan. 8, 1794).

9. Carey, *Short History,* 4.

10. For examples of this use of Carey, see Malini J. Schueller, *U.S. Orientalisms: Race, Nation, and Gender in Literature, 1790–1890* (Ann Arbor: University of Michigan Press, 1998), p. 49, and Robert J. Allison, *The Crescent Obscured: The United States and the Muslim World, 1776–1815* (New York: Oxford University Press, 1995), 52.

11. Other sources apparently include Jonathan Carver, *The New Universal Traveller* (Lon-

don: Robinson, 1779), and Philémon de La Motte, *Several Voyages to Barbary* (London: O. Payne, 1736).

12. This passage appears on p. 38 of Carey (1805 edition) and on the fifth page of John Seally's entry on Algiers (which does not have page numbers). As one of the most prominent booksellers and publishers in America, Carey had easy access to Seally's recent publication, *A Complete Geographical Dictionary, or Universal Gazetteer: of Ancient and Modern Geography* (London: Scatcherd and Whitaker, 1787).

13. "A Gentleman Who Resided There Many Years in a Public Character," *A Compleat History of the Piratical States of Barbary* (London, 1750), 36.

14. Thomas Salmon, *Modern History: or, the Present State of All Nations*, 3 vols. (London: Longman, 1744–46), 74–75; Carey, *Short History*, 29–30. On Salmon's life, see *Dictionary of National Biography*, 24 vols. (London: Oxford University Press, 1963–1965), 17:696–99.

15. Carey, *Short History*, 30. The original source for this paragraph is not evident.

16. Seally, unnumbered entry on Algiers (9th page, 1st column); Carey, 51–52. Here Carey also awkwardly interposes a passage from Catherine MacCauley's *The History of England*, 8 vols. (London: I. Dodsley, 1766–83), describing a 1637 Algerian raid on England, perhaps to show the French in a better light relative to the English.

17. Carey, *Short History*, 21, 22–23, 32.

18. Ibid., 76.

19. Stevens, preface to *Account of Algiers*. Brooks was a sailor aboard the ship *President*.

20. For an extended discussion of these and other travails, see Paul A. Gilje, *Liberty on the Waterfront: American Maritime Culture in the Age of Revolution* (Philadelphia: University of Pennsylvania Press, 2004).

21. Foss, *Journal*, 120, 122–23.

22. Ibid., 142–43, 158–59. According to Foss, he was freed in Algiers on July 11, 1796, and arrived in Cape May on July 25, 1797.

23. Stevens, *Account of Algiers*, 86, 250. I've assumed these and certain other passages were influenced by Brooks because of their detailed treatment of the American captives' plight and their distinctiveness from other published accounts of the Algerian captives that would have been available to Stevens.

24. Ibid., 6.

25. Ibid., 32–33. For similar passages, see Carey, *Short History*, p. 30.

26. Foss, *Journal*, 33–35, 38.

27. Ibid., 65–67, 83–85. On "good things" about the Indians, see Father Le Jeune's account in Allan Greer, ed., *The Jesuit Relations* (New York: Bedford/St. Martin's, 2000), 32–35.

28. Stevens, *Account of Algiers*.

29. Stevens, preface to *Account of Algiers*, 161–62; Carey, *Short History*, 30; Foss, *Journal*, 32–33.

30. Stevens, *Account of Algiers*, 77; Foss, *Journal*, 131–32.

31. Stevens, *Account of Algiers*, 77; Foss, *Journal*, 131–32.

32. Stevens, *Account of Algiers*, 259–60; Foss, *Journal*, 35–37.

33. Access to the Orient was an issue for President Jefferson as well as John Jacob As-

tor, who would soon set up the town of Astoria on the Pacific Coast. Clyde A. Milner II, "National Initiatives" in Milner, Carol A. O'Connor, and Martha A. Sandweiss, eds., *The Oxford History of the American West* (New York: Oxford University Press, 1994), 158–59.

34. Merrill D. Peterson, *Thomas Jefferson and the New Nation* (New York: Oxford University Press, 1970), 746.

35. On this policy, see Anthony F. C. Wallace, *Jefferson and the Indians: The Tragic Fate of the First Americans* (Cambridge: Belknap Press, 1999), 206–75.

36. Henry Adams, *History of the United States of America During the Administrations of Thomas Jefferson* (New York: Library of America, 1986), 598; See, too, John B. McMaster, *A History of the People of the United States: From the Revolution to the Civil War*, 5 vols. (New York: D. Appleton and Co., 1892), 3:208–19.

37. Stephen E. Ambrose, *Undaunted Courage: Meriwether Lewis, Thomas Jefferson, and the Opening of the American West* (New York: Simon and Schuster, 1996), 68–107; Wallace, *Jefferson and the Indians*, 75–160; John Logan Allen, *Passage Through the Garden: Lewis and Clark and the Image of the Northwest* (Urbana: University of Illinois Press, 1975); Roger G. Kennedy, *Hidden Cities: The Discovery and Loss of Ancient North American Civilization* (New York: Free Press, 1994).

38. Daniel E. Williams, ed., *Liberty's Captives: Narratives of Confinement in the Print Culture of the Early Republic* (Athens: University of Georgia Press, 2006), 105.

39. *An Affecting History of the Captivity and Sufferings of Mrs. Mary Velnet* (Sag Harbor, NY: Spooner, 1806), 14–15, 55–56.

40. Ibid., 38–42.

41. The 1806 version, *History of the Captivity and Sufferings of Mrs. Maria Martin* (Boston: W. Crary, 1806), copies *Velnet* verbatim on pp. 31, 37–38, 39.

42. Williams, *Liberty's Captives*, 124.

43. *Martin*, 1806 version.

44. *History of the Captivity and Sufferings of Mrs. Maria Martin*. Publishers were: Boston: W. Crary, 1807; Philadelphia: Joseph Rakestraw, 1809; Philadelphia: Jacob Meyer, 1811; Trenton, NJ: James Oram, 1811. *History of the Captivity and Sufferings of Mrs. Lucinda Martin* (Boston: Lemuel Austin, 1810). The later editions would more or less follow the form of the 1807 version, although in one printing the captivity narrative would come before the travel literature and in another Maria's name would be changed to Lucinda.

45. Jonathan Cowdery, *American Captives in Tripoli*, 2d ed. (Boston: Belcher and Armstrong, 1806), preface.

46. Cowdery, *American Captives*, preface and 34–35.

47. Foss, *Journal*, 10.

48. Cowdery, *American Captives*, 5–6.

49. Foss, *Journal*, 73.

50. Stevens, *Account of Algiers*, 205–8.

51. Cowdery, *American Captives*, 7, 13, 24.

52. Ibid., 19, 25.

53. Ibid., 20–21.

54. Ibid., 11.

55. Tobias Lear, Copy of Letter to James Madison, No. 6. Algiers Jan. 1–Feb. 17, 1804,

Including Diary or Journal of Occurrences at Algiers, pp. 20–24, quote from p. 21, William L. Clements Library, University of Michigan, Ann Arbor.

56. Lawrence A. Peskin, *Manufacturing Revolution: The Intellectual Origins of Early American Industry* (Baltimore: Johns Hopkins University Press, 2003); Steven Stoll, *Larding the Lean Earth: Soil and Society in Nineteenth-Century America* (New York: Hill and Wang, 2002).

57. I have found the published letters in the *Philadelphia Aurora* and *Boston Gazette*. I chose these two newspapers because they represent different ends of the political spectrum and were located in two different regions.

58. *Aurora*, Sept. 28, 1804, p. 2; *Boston Gazette*, Mar. 11, 1805, p. 2; *Barbary*, 5:124–25; 3:179–80.

59. *Barbary*, 5:159–60; *Boston Gazette*, Aug. 5, 1805, p. 2.

60. Ray also provided two short chapters on the geography, manners, and customs of Tripoli; portions may have been copied from other sources, but much was based on Ray's own observations. He also inserted nearly one hundred pages of useful primary sources collected from the papers of William Eaton and from government documents.

61. Sean Wilentz, *Chants Democratic: New York City and the Rise of the American Working Class, 1788–1850* (New York: Oxford University Press, 1984).

62. William Ray, *Horrors of Slavery: Or, the American Tars in Tripoli* (Troy: Oliver Lyon, 1808), exordium.

63. Ibid., 46, 49, 24.

64. Ibid., 51, 53, 63, 61.

65. Ibid., 79, 81.

66. Ibid., 82, 104, 97.

67. Ibid., 98, 107.

68. Ray refers to Porter only as "lieut. P____," but anyone familiar with the *Philadelphia* would instantly be able to supply the missing letters (Ray, *Horrors*, 74–75). On Porter's earlier misstep, see Richard Zacks, *The Pirate Coast: Thomas Jefferson, the First Marines and the Secret Mission of 1805* (New York: Hyperion, 2005), 17.

69. Ray, *Horrors*, 64, 83–84.

70. After reading *Horrors*, Captain Bainbridge labeled Ray a "vile calumniator." Responding specifically to the charge of neglecting the crew, Bainbridge provided letters that seemed to indicate that the crew—or at least some of them—had voluntarily given up their meat rations from the United States because they were fed at their work sites. He also refers to a letter written to him by Ray while in Tripoli thanking Bainbridge for his "prompt attention to every communication of our wants." Most likely the ending of the rations was due to a combination of miscommunications and events beyond Bainbridge's control; certainly, it is difficult to say whether he might have done more for the men, just as it is difficult to understand how they would have voluntarily given up food rations. At any rate, Ray admits that at the time he and others believed Bainbridge did "every thing in his power to meliorate our condition," and it was only after returning to America (and, presumably, reading the documents) that Ray came to believe otherwise. Bainbridge speculated that Ray may have been angry with him for ignoring his request for documents to help him with his book. *Barbary*, 5:240–44; Ray, *Horrors*, 87–88.

71. David Canadine, *Ornamentalism: How the British Saw their Empire* (New York: Oxford University Press, 2001). The classic statement on Orientalism is Edward Said, *Orientalism* (New York: Pantheon, 1978). For a recent critical reformulation, see Robert Irwin, *Dangerous Knowledge: Orientalism and its Discontents* (New York: Overlook, 2006).

72. There are two schools of thought about why savagery was such an important issue for British writers before that time. The standard interpretation has followed Edward Said in considering savagery as a means of emphasizing the "otherness" of the "barbarians," thereby making British conquest morally defensible and even necessary. More recently, Linda Colley has argued that captivity narratives emphasizing Barbary savagery also reflected ambivalence and even fear. While certainly intent on conquest, Britons feared that their increasing presence in different quarters of the world heightened their vulnerability to attack by "savage" locals.

73. For a discussion of European classifications of North African races, see Ann Thomson, *Barbary and Enlightenment: European Attitudes Towards the Maghreb in the 18th Century* (New York: E. J. Brill, 1987), 64–93.

74. Lear, Letter to James Madison, 21; Charles Prentiss, *The Life of the Late Gen. William Eaton . . .* (Brookfield, MA: E. Merriam and Co., 1813), 157; Cowdery, *American Captives*, 33.

75. Ray, *Horrors*, 286. For a discussion of Barbary and the issue of free trade, see Frank Lambert, *The Barbary Wars: American Independence in the Atlantic World* (New York: Hill and Wang, 2005).

76. For the classic discussion of the new empire, see Walter LaFeber, *The New Empire: An Interpretation of American Expansion, 1860–1898* (Ithaca: Cornell University Press, 1963). See, too, Bender, *A Nation Among Nations: America's Place in World History* (New York: Hill and Wang, 2006), 182–245.

Chapter 9. Beyond Captivity: The Wars of 1812

1. Henry Steele Commager, ed., *Documents of American History* (New York: Appleton-Century-Crofts, 1968), 207–9.

2. The public was more or less correct, although the larger cause was no doubt American military preparations, which would soon result in the destruction of Indian autonomy in the Old Northwest. See Reginald Horsman, *The Frontier in the Formative Years, 1783–1815* (New York: Holt and Rinehart and Winston, 1970), and Samuel Flagg Bemis, *Jay's Treaty: A Study in Commerce and Diplomacy* (1923; reprint, New Haven: Yale University Press, 1962.).

3. For a detailed discussion of these meetings, see chap. 5.

4. *Columbian Herald*, Apr. 16, 1794, p. 4.

5. Bemis, *Jay's Treaty*, 239–40; Horsman, *Frontier*, 48–49.

6. For a full discussion of the war hysteria, see Bemis, *Jay's Treaty*, 253–78.

7. *Columbian Herald*, June 9, 1794, p. 2; *Maryland Gazette*, Sept. 18, 1794, p. 1.

8. Paul A. Gilje, *Liberty on the Waterfront: American Maritime Culture in the Age of Revolution* (Philadelphia: University of Pennsylvania Press, 2004), 157.

9. *Philadelphia Aurora*, Mar. 30, 1804, p. 2; *Boston Gazette*, Feb. 21, 1805, p. 1; July 11, 1805, p. 1.

10. Gilje, *Liberty*, 160. Emphasis added.

11. *Annals*, 12th Cong., 1st sess., 425, 500; Reginald Horsman, *The Causes of the War of 1812* (New York: A. S. Barnes, 1962), 207–9.

12. *Annals*, 12th Cong., 1st sess., 626, 645. On honor culture, see Bertram Wyatt-Brown, *Southern Honor: Ethics and Behavior in the Old South* (New York: Oxford University Press, 1982); Joanne B. Freeman, *Affairs of Honor: National Parties in the New Republic* (New Haven: Yale University Press, 2001); Norman K. Risjord, "1812: Conservatives, War Hawks, and the Nation's Honor," *William and Mary Quarterly*, 3d ser., 18 (April 1961): 196–210.

13. *Annals*, 12th Cong., 1st sess., 457, 483, 499; Horsman, *Causes*, 218.

14. On the relationship between the Barbary crisis and the naval buildup, see chap. 6.

15. See chap. 4.

16. James Ellison, *The American Captive, or Siege of Tripoli* (Boston: Joshua Belcher, 1812), 22, 37. Original emphasis.

17. Ibid., 20, 34, 46.

18. Ibid., 6, 54.

19. Lawrence A. Peskin, *Manufacturing Revolution: The Intellectual Origins of Early American Industry* (Baltimore: Johns Hopkins University Press, 2003), 162–87.

20. Ellison, *American Captive*, 49, 51–54, 12.

21. George Dangerfield, *The Era of Good Feelings* (New York: Harcourt, Brace, and Co., 1952), 21–24.

22. James Madison, *Message of the President of the United States, Transmitting Copies of a Letter from the Consul General of the United States to Algiers* (Washington, DC: A. and G. Way, 1812), 5–18.

23. Ibid., 16–18; Lear to Consuls of the United States of America in the Mediterranean, July 25, 1812, SDAD; *National Intelligencer*, April 24, 1813, p. 2.

24. Lear to Monroe, Aug. 17, 1812; Smith to John Gavino, Aug. 30, 1812; Smith to Edward Fettyplace, Aug. 30, 1812; Lear to Monroe, Nov. 3, 1812; Smith to Lear, Oct. 2, 1812, SDAD.

25. Smith to John Gavino, Aug. 30, 1812; Smith to Edward Fettyplace, Aug. 30, 1812, SDAD; *National Intelligencer*, Mar. 16, 1813, p. 2.

26. Smith to Lear, Oct. 2, 1812, SDAD; *National Intelligencer*, Mar. 16, 1813, p. 2.

27. *National Intelligencer*, Mar. 26, 1813, p. 2; Lear to Monroe, Nov. 3, 1812, SDAD; Frederick C. Leiner, *The End of Barbary Terror: America's 1815 War Against the Pirates of North Africa* (New York: Oxford University Press, 2006), 23–24.

28. See chap. 1.

29. *National Intelligencer*, May 28, 1813, p. 3; Leiner, *End of Barbary Terror*, 25.

30. *National Intelligencer*, Jan. 6, 1813, p. 2; April 7, 1813, p. 2; Oct. 6, 1813, p. 2; July 25, 1814, p. 2; August 4, 1814, p. 2.

31. Madison, *Message*, 14–15. Copies can also be found in *Niles Weekly Register* 3, appendix (1813): 429–34, and SDAD. *National Intelligencer*, Apr. 24, 1813, p. 2; Leiner, *End of Barbary Terror*, 22.

32. *National Intelligencer*, Jan. 26, 1815, p. 3.

33. Ray W. Irwin, *The Diplomatic Relations of the United States with the Barbary Powers*

(New York: Russell and Russell, 1931), 171; Leiner, *End of Barbary Terror*, 22; Frank Lambert, *The Barbary Wars: American Independence in the Atlantic World* (New York: Hill and Wang, 2005), 183; William Spencer, *Algiers in the Age of the Corsairs* (Norman: University of Oklahoma Press, 1976), 139.

34. Smith to Lear, Mar. 15, 1813; John Norderling to R. S. Hackley, Apr. 19, 1813, SDAD.

35. Raynal Keene to Mordecai M. Noah, May 22, 1814, in Noah, *Correspondence and Documents Relative to the Attempt to Negotiate for the Release of the American Captives at Algiers* (Washington, DC: 1816), 29–30; *Boston Gazette*, Mar. 28, 1814, p. 2; June 9, 1815, p. 2; Lear to Monroe, Dec. 16, 1812, in SDAD.

36. Smith to Lear, Mar. 15, 1813; Norderling to Hackley, Apr. 19, 1813, SDAD.

37. Noah, *Correspondence*, 5–8; Leiner, *End of Barbary Terror*, 28–31.

38. Noah, *Correspondence*, 7. On Jefferson and secrecy, see chap. 3.

39. Noah, *Correspondence*, 21–32; Leiner, *End of Barbary Terror*, 32–35.

40. Noah, *Correspondence*, 35–36. On Keene's alleged indiscretion, see the report of the attorney general in Mordecai M. Noah, *Travels in England, France, Spain, and the Barbary States, in the Years 1813–14 and 15* (New York: Kirk and Mercein, 1819), appendix, xiv–xv.

41. Noah, *Correspondence*, 82.

42. The report was widely published in newspapers with an editorial preface that quoted the dey's incendiary comments without providing a source. See *National Intelligencer*, Mar. 7, 1815, p. 2, and *Boston Gazette*, Mar. 16, 1815, p. 2.

43. *National Intelligencer*, Feb. 22, 1815, p. 3; Mar. 1, 1815, p. 3; *Boston Gazette*, Feb. 23, 1815, p. 2; May 22, 1815, p. 2.

44. *Boston Gazette*, June 19, 1815, p. 2; June 29, 1815, p. 2; *National Intelligencer*, Aug. 31, 1815, p. 3.

45. *Niles' Weekly Register*, Apr. 15, 1815, 105–6; *National Intelligencer*, Feb. 22, 1815, p. 2, p. 3. Both the Republican *National Intelligencer* and the Federalist *Boston Gazette* printed many items in favor of the war.

46. *Niles Weekly Register*, Apr. 15, 1815, p. 106; *National Intelligencer*, May 26, 1815, p. 3; Aug. 8, 1815, p. 3; Nov. 6, 1815, p. 2.

47. *National Intelligencer*, Mar. 23, 1815, p. 2; Aug. 29, 1815, p. 2; May 27, 1815, p. 2; Mar. 2, 1815, p. 4.

48. *National Intelligencer*, July 20, 1815, p. 2. For another republication of Eaton's observations, see "Letters of General Eaton" in *The Polyanthos*, Feb. 1814, pp. 275–80.

49. *National Intelligencer*, May 27, 1815, p. 2.

50. *Boston Gazette*, Aug. 31, 1815, p. 2; *Niles Weekly Register*, Apr. 15, 1815, 105.

51. *Boston Gazette*, Aug. 14, 1815, p. 2. For a similar reaction to the Congress of Vienna, see *National Intelligencer*, Aug. 31, 1815, p. 2.

52. *Boston Gazette*, April 17, 1815, p. 2.

53. On the war, see Lambert, *Barbary Wars*, 188–93; Leiner, *End of Barbary Terror*, 87–122; Robert J. Allison, *Stephen Decatur: American Naval Hero, 1779–1820* (Amherst: University of Massachusetts Press, 2005), 163–68. The treaty is reprinted in Leiner, *End of Barbary Terror*, 189–94.

54. Lambert, *Barbary Wars*, 194; Allison, *Stephen Decatur*, 171; Leiner, *End of Barbary Terror*, 136–37.

55. Lambert, *Barbary Wars*, 194; *National Intelligencer*, Oct. 28, 1815, p. 3; Nov. 6, 1815, p. 2; Nov. 25, 1815, p. 2.

56. *Niles' Weekly Register*, Apr. 15, 1815, p. 105.

57. Leiner, *End of Barbary Terror*, 114–15; *Boston Gazette*, Oct. 9, 1815, p. 1; Oct. 16, 1815, p. 2.

58. Daniel E. Williams, ed., *Liberty's Captives: Narratives of Confinement in the Print Culture of the Early Republic* (Athens: University of Georgia Press, 2006), 164–312; June Namias, *White Captives: Gender and Ethnicity on the American Frontier* (Chapel Hill: University of North Carolina Press, 1993), 277.

59. Joseph Pitts, *Narrative of the Captivity of Joseph Pitts Among the Algerians* (Frederick, MD: Hardt and Cross, 1815); *National Intelligencer*, May 27, 1815, p. 2. On Pitts's account and its publishing history, see Linda Colley, *Captives: Britain, Empire and the World, 1600–1850* (New York: Anchor, 2004), 118, 122–25, 389.

60. *The Captivity and Sufferings of Maria Martin* (St. Clairsville, OH: John Berry, 1815) and *The Captivity and Sufferings of Maria Martin* (Brookfield, MA: F. Merriam, 1818). On earlier publications, see chap. 8.

61. Thomas Nicholson, *An Affecting Narrative of the Captivity and Sufferings of Thomas Nicholson* (Boston: N. Coverly, 1818); *National Intelligencer*, Nov. 25, 1815, p. 3. On Nicholson's publishing history, see Williams, *Liberty's Captives*, 270–71.

62. James Riley, *Sufferings in Africa* (1817; reprint, New York: Clarkson N. Potter, 1965); Charles Hansford Adams, ed., *The Narrative of Robert Adams, A Barbary Captive, a Critical Edition* (New York: Cambridge University Press, 2006); Judah Paddock, *A Narrative of the Shipwreck of the Ship Oswego* (New York: James Riley, 1818); Archibald Robbins, *A Journal, Comprising an Account of the Loss of the Brig Commerce* (New York: Andrus, 1818). On the publishing histories of these books, see Paul Baepler, ed., *White Slaves, African Masters: An Anthology of American Barbary Captivity Narratives* (Chicago: University of Chicago Press, 1999), 306–9.

63. Riley's story was supposedly an early antislavery influence for Abraham Lincoln. R. Gerald McMurtry, "The Influence of Riley's Narrative Upon Abraham Lincoln," *Indiana Magazine of History* 30 (1934): 134.

64. Noah, *Travels*, 58–59, 68–69, and following. The earlier account was Noah, *Correspondence*.

65. Noah, *Travels*, 1, 368, 393.

66. Ibid., 394–95.

67. Ibid., 339, 360.

68. Ibid., 366–67.

69. Horace Kimball, *The Naval Temple* (Boston: Barber Badger, 1816) 10, 20–43, 214–25. Quotes from p. 25, 214, 218.

70. *The Naval Monument* (Boston: A. Bowen, 1816), 298–99.

71. *Analectic Magazine* 4:224–43; 5:231–57; 7:10–17, 111–27. Quote from 7:17. *Port-Folio*, 3:1–23.

72. "The Barbary Captive Released," in *Analectic Magazine* 7:286–287; *The Naval Songster: Being a Collection of Naval Victories and Other Excellent Songs* (Charleston, SC: J. White, 1815), 5–6, 15–16.

73. *Naval Monument*, 15–16; *Analectic Magazine* 7:126.

74. Noah, *Travels*, 359.

75. On "mission," see Frederick Merk, *Manifest Destiny and Mission in American History: A Reinterpretation* (New York: Vintage, 1966). On the role of protecting free trade in Barbary, see Lambert, *Barbary Wars*, 189–202. On "free trade and sailors' rights," see Gilje, *Liberty on the Waterfront*, 163–91.

76. On the Naval Expansion Act, see Kenneth J. Hagan, *This People's Navy: The Making of American Sea Power* (New York: Free Press, 1991); Craig L. Symonds, *Navalists and Antinavalists: The Naval Policy Debate in the United States, 1785–1827* (Newark: University of Delaware Press, 1980), 213–35; K. Jack Bauer, "Naval Shipbuilding Programs, 1794–1860," *Military Affairs* 29 (1965): 33–34; C. Edward Skeen, *1816: America Rising* (Lexington: University Press of Kentucky, 2003), 147–149. Quotes from Symonds, *Navalists*, 214–15, and Hagan, *This People's Navy*, 93–94.

Conclusion. Captivity and Globalization

1. Slavery, of course, would remain important for decades.

2. Thomas Bender, *A Nation among Nations: America's Place in World History* (New York: Hill and Wang, 2006), 231.